MEN OF BLOOD

ALSO BY ELLIOTT LEYTON

Dying Hard
The Myth of Delinquency
Hunting Humans
Sole Survivor

MEN OF BLOOD

Murder in Everyday Life

ELLIOTT LEYTON

Canadian Cataloguing in Publication Data

Leyton, Elliott, 1939 –
    Men of blood : murder in everyday life

Includes bibliographical references.
ISBN 0-7710-5310-x bound   ISBN 0-7710-5306-1 pbk.

1. Murder.   I. Title.

HV6535.E5L4 1996   364.1'5230   C95-932515-8

The publishers acknowledge the support of the Canada Council and the Ontario
Arts Council for their publishing program.

First published in Great Britain by Constable & Company Ltd.

Typesetting by M&S, Toronto

Printed and bound in Canada

McClelland & Stewart Inc.
The Canadian Publishers
481 University Avenue
Toronto, Ontario
M5G 2E9

1 2 3 4 5   01 00 99 98 97

For Mark Sean Bray Leyton

. . . he cursed, Come out, come out, thou bloody man . . .
The Lord hath returned upon thee all the blood . . .
and, behold, thou art taken in thy mischief,
because thou art a bloody man.
(II. Samuel 16:7, 8)

Contents

Preface to the Canadian Edition

"A KILLER WILL KILL YOU" shrieked the headline in a St. John's newspaper. The accompanying article both encapsulated and contributed to the ever-escalating public panic about violence in this country. It continued, with waxing ineloquence:

> There's a killer on the loose right now . . . A stranger. You may pass him on the street and not know it. You may brush gently up against him in the supermarket while reaching for the fresh cut steak . . . You never know . . . In the dark, hollow soul of the killer, you may form the perfect picture of a victim. You may die, screaming in tearful fear as life is torn from you.[1]

The facts that no such murder had ever actually occurred in this city and that murder by psychopathic strangers is an extreme statistical rarity in this *country* were no impediment to the inflamed imagination of the journalist. And why should they be? The Canadian public has long been primed for such hysteria. As sociologists William O'Grady and James Overton noted at the time, the article in question merely "expresses and reinforces the widespread belief that the danger of becoming the victim of a violent criminal act has very much increased in recent years." Indeed, this fear of crime was so intense that 40 per cent of adult residents of every major Canadian city "reported in a 1982 crime victimization survey that they were afraid to venture out at night" – and that anxiety gripped fully half of all senior citizens, whose lives were thus transfigured by the fear of assault.[2]

The terror of crime is thus a major national problem – quite apart from crime itself. The fear is palpable and real, and is to be found in both high and low crime areas, in urbanized and rural provinces, in prosperous and impoverished regions, in provinces with a diversity of ethnic and religious groups, and those with few. Criminologist Ian Taylor observed that Canadians devoutly believe they are in the midst of a long-term increase in crime. "By the early 1980s 'fear of crime' had become so pronounced" that a national survey was commissioned "to measure the extent of this 'fearful attitude.'" The survey found that most people believed both that the incidence of violent crime was increasing and that the *character* of crime was changing. "Many people think that Canada's 'peaceable kingdom' is threatened by a type of violence that was thought to be characteristic of life south of the border."[3]

The president of the Canadian Police Association merely echoed these fears in 1992 when he captivated an audience by making the provocative claim that "times are changing and violence is on the increase everywhere. I've been a police officer for 26 years and I won't get out of my car for a coffee without it [his gun]." The fact that the man was from *Saskatoon*, a city not previously renowned for its doughnut-shop gun fights, was a matter of no concern. The police officer appeared to be sincere; the journalists who reported the comment gave every indication of having believed it; and the majority of the public seemed to swallow the story. Indeed, the public had long before lost its taste for any story that said otherwise.[4]

In the aftermath of the Watergate scandal in the United States, the journalist Allan Fotheringham complained that Canada had no independent tradition of investigative journalism comparable to the one that had unearthed the transgressions of the Nixon administration. He thought that as a rule our journalists were less likely to investigate than merely to pass on to the public the press releases issued by any political party or special interest group that had captured their attention. Most journalists – in lieu of reading anything, or even watching other media – seem to take their lead from their bosses' private and personal prejudices. This was dramatically communicated to me when a prominent journalist working for a national television network telephoned me to discuss 1994's further decrease in homicides. "Hmm," he said. "Homicides are down, there's no story there." "What do you mean?" I shouted. "*That's* the story: homicides have been declining every year since the mid-1970s!" It was lost on him: he continued reading aloud from Statistics Canada's list of disappointingly decreasing crimes. "No story there. . . . Oh, that's down too, no story there." He had never looked at Canadian homicide rates; he did not know that homicide was virtually the only reliably reported violent crime; he did not know that most other violent crime rates (such as those pertaining to assault) were merely a function of changing public (especially women's) attitudes to *reporting* such assaults and varying levels of police activity. He had merely absorbed the prejudices of his peers – especially the unchallenged assumption that violent crime in Canada has been increasing dramatically.[5]

Yet there is nothing uniquely Canadian about such *angst*. Writing primarily of Britain, the historian Geoffrey Pearson observed that every country seems to have its own nostalgic myth of a glorious and crime-free past; every country's citizens seem driven to compare unfavourably their own time with the previous Golden Age. This fantasy admits only that there has been an "historical deterioration in public manners," and it imagines "the novelty of [present-day] crime and violence, [while clinging to assumptions] of harmony and tranquility in the past."

> Among the many questions which impinge upon the question of "modernity," the one most deeply rooted in popular convictions insists that the advance of civilization brings in its wake a deluge of crime and violence. We know only too well the string of accusations, often summed up as the advent of "permissiveness," which are brought against the present tense: the break-up of the family and traditional authority; the erosion of community in the place of "rootless" urban anonymity; the demoralizing effects of "affluence"; the incitements of television and cinema; the surge of irresponsible freedoms among the rising generation . . . things have "gone too far."[6]

Coupled with the notion of a "cultural collapse," of a centre suddenly unable to hold, is the popular connection between *unemployment* and the breakdown of the social fabric – of persons, families and communities. Folk culture interprets this disintegration in a number of ways. "Individual alienation and despair may lead to suicide and mental breakdown," writes William O'Grady. "Vandalism may result as frustrations are turned outward; the family may disintegrate leading to problem children; or community tensions may increase and people may become involved in radical politics."

The essential thing for the public to understand, however, is that this fear of violent crime is not based on any statistical reality, but rather it is *manipulated* by a variety of self-serving special interest groups that stand to benefit from it in significant and material ways – by capturing both media attention and government funding and by expanding their influence. Stanley Cohen was right to observe that "The worse the crime problem becomes, the more professional growth can be justified."[7] Public anxiety is fuelled by cynical governments that routinely dispense meaningless and unexplained crime statistics; by media people whose minds are quite uncluttered by facts but who seem committed to the fantasy that we are in the midst of a crime wave; and by a host of professional, ideological and political groups that have a vested interest – conscious or otherwise – in the public perception of danger.[8]

There is nothing harmless about these matters. The sensationalization of isolated and bizarre violent crimes – for example, the St. Catharines atrocities – has a devastating impact on people far beyond what might be anticipated. It creates an entirely false impression of social danger, turns neighbour against neighbour and adds suspicion and hostility to the bubbling pot of social anxiety. A public already made susceptible to fear by issues that have nothing whatever to do with crime – for example, the natural concerns generated by a troubled economy, disintegrating nuclear families and profound changes in social values – projects its disquiet and its anger on largely imaginary devils.

A Brief Reality Break

The fact of the matter is that the per capita homicide rate in Canada is among the more moderate in the world, and it has consistently remained such at least since the Second World War. Most criminologists agree that America's appalling homicide rate, quadruple Canada's, is "an aberration among industrial nations, not the norm." Despite their geographical proximity, their linguistic and cultural similarity, the two nations simply do not murder at a similar rate. Americans murder more than 20,000 of their own each year, while Canadians murder an average of some 600, a figure that would rise to several thousand each year if our rates were remotely similar.[9]

Quite why this should be so is not well understood. Various theories have been advanced that focus on the (fast-disappearing) Canadian social safety net – universal access to health, education, welfare and generous unemployment insurance – which provides a buffer for Canadians against the potential brutality of an unrestrained class-based industrial system. Yet an equally plausible argument has been made for the dominance in Canada of a Western European *cultural* tradition that emphasizes the community over the individual, group rights and responsibilities over personal rights, and expects civility in the social intercourse of day-to-day life.[10]

In *Men of Blood*, I argue for a third and not entirely contradictory perspective, one in which a civilizing process of socialized repression inhibits the display of violence. Which comes first – the safety net, the collective emphasis or the cultural inhibition – is a matter for further debate and research. Yet there can be no doubt of one thing: if the Canadian murder rate is double that of the English, Canadians are infinitely less likely to murder or be murdered than their neighbours south of the border. Moreover, there is nothing in Canadian society that resembles the plight of those who live in the vast urban slums of America, where homicide is the *leading* cause of death for black males until the age of fifty-five.

What *are* the Canadian figures? Different systems of calculation used by various scholars and international agencies yield apparently conflicting numbers, but a country's *relative* position in the world league table remains much the same, regardless of the classification system. F. Adler and his colleagues, for example, compared homicide rates only for young men in twenty-two industrialized nations. "In that group, Canada ranks sixteenth highest with a rate of 2.9 per 100,000 citizens between the ages of 15 and 24." This puts us in the lowest quarter of industrial nations, with world rates ranging from 0.3 in Austria to 5.0 in Scotland. The country with the highest rate *by an enormous margin* is the United States at 21.9 per 100,000 – "more than four times the next closest rate." Thus, the Canadian authorities Robert Silverman and Leslie Kennedy conclude, "the Canadian homicide rate is not very high."[11]

Between 1926 and 1990, homicide rates in Canada have of course varied, but they have consistently fluctuated around 2 per 100,000. In 1926, they were 1.3, falling gradually in the 1940s and 1950s to just above 1, then rising in the mid-1960s as they did almost everywhere in the western world – once again, for reasons that are not well understood[12] – to an all-time peak in the mid-1970s of 3 per 100,000. After 1974, they began gently to decline, returning towards their 1960s levels. Silverman and Kennedy record the changes in greater detail:

> Homicide rates reach a peak in 1930 (2.1 per 100,000) that is not seen again until 1970. After the 1930 peak there is a steady decline in the rate until 1944 (.89 per 100,000). . . . For a few years immediately following the war homicide rates rose. . . . The lowest rate of homicide between 1926 and 1990 occurs in 1950. Between 1950 and 1965, there is a gradual rise in the rate of criminal homicide (from .82 per 100,000 to 1.41 per 100,000). Then, from 1966 to 1975, the most dramatic rise in Canadian homicide rates took place (from 1.24 per 100,000 to 3.07 per 100,000), a rise of 250 per cent. Since 1975, there has been a rather consistent decline in the homicide rate to 2.4 in 1990 (that is, about the same as the 1970 level) . . . while the Canadian rate has fallen since the mid-1970s, the U.S. rate has continued on a steady rise.[13]

Who are the murderers in Canada? They are much like their English counterparts – young, single, male Caucasians. The majority (87 per cent) of suspects are male, "40 per cent are under 25, 45 per cent are single, and 76 per cent are Caucasian." For those suspects on whom we have social information, 43 per cent "attained a Grade 8 (or less) education, while another 30 per cent achieved a Grade 9 or 10 level." Their low educational attainment was reflected in their occupations: one third were labourers, and they were overwhelmingly working class. Their murders are mundane and unsensational, quarrels between lovers or associates.

In the thirty-year period Silverman and Kennedy examined, "women constitute about 40 per cent of all murder victims," and despite much myth-making, the rate of such offences against women has remained largely unchanged. This overturns the "media-fuelled public perception that violence against women is on the rise." While "male rates rise and fall much more dramatically than female rates," such offences against women have been stable since the mid-1970s. Indeed, Silverman and Kennedy are driven to emphasize:

> . . . contrary to some popular conceptions, femicide has not been increasing. Further, the proportion that is family-related – especially spousal – has declined over the thirty-year period . . . [and the] risk of murder for women is still most likely related to being in a poor domestic situation.

Interestingly, the data reveal that the largest single category (44 per cent) of male victims are killed by friends or acquaintances, while only 12 per cent of males are killed by their spouse or lover; but "love" remains the most problematic relationship for women, and "53 per cent of the female victims meet their demise at the hands of a spouse/lover." What has changed, of course, is women's willingness to *report* sexual and physical assault.[14]

Although the Canadian public has been taught to believe that crime of all kinds is out of control, the redoubtable John Howard Society explains that this is yet another myth: "The results of the recent victimization survey tell us that Canadians were *less* likely to be victims of crime in 1993 than in 1988." Still, the common mythology goes, it is a new and youthful generation that is especially violent: "Young people who commit crimes are the particular targets of public fear and anger," and strong political pressure is unleashed "to 'toughen up' the *Young Offenders Act* – to increase the penalties and to expand the provisions." However, the Society observes, "police-reported data show that police are *more* likely to charge a young person now than they were before the *Young Offenders Act* came into effect in 1984." Moreover, "youth courts are *not* less likely than adult courts to hand out the severest form of punishment – the deprivation of freedom through incarceration." Similarly, 83 per cent of those juvenile cases requiring a custody order were for *non-violent* property offences: and even for the fraction that were violent, "34 per cent were for minor assault involving no weapon and no serious injury." In fact, only a tiny proportion of the people who commit serious personal injury offences in Canada can be classified as "youth"; and they are responsible for only 0.8 per cent of all homicides, 0.15 per cent of sexual assaults involving a weapon or a serious injury, and 3.2 per cent of non-sexual assault involving a weapon or serious injury. Clearly, the Society observes, a punitive political response to youth constitutes a solution to a non-existent problem. And, in any case, an "over-reliance on criminal justice solutions is expensive and ineffective."[15] As in the English case material in this book, it is the under-educated and under-employed who are responsible for the overwhelming majority of serious offences. "A recent study of the factors correlated to crime in 26 of the largest municipalities in Canada tells us that [as in England]: the socio-demographic characteristic that correlates most strongly with all offences under study is *the male unemployment rate*; municipalities with a relatively high proportion of *families living in poverty, in rented dwellings or who are supported by lone parents* tend to have the highest rates of serious assault, robbery, break and enter, theft and the more serious drug offences." Moreover, "the percentage of the population aged 15 and over *without a high school diploma* is the population characteristic most highly correlated with rates of assault and sexual assault." Any system that seeks to control these violent behaviours would focus not on intensifying meaningless punishment, but on educating and employing our most vulnerable citizens.[16]

Oka and Oklahoma City

It is difficult to live in Canada without being awed by national differences: the proximity of our neighbours to the south cannot fail to remind us how similar, yet how distinct we are from them. During the Oka Crisis in the early 1990s, when Mohawk "warriors" and citizens blockaded one of the major highways into Montreal, the army and police were called in to deal with the incendiary confrontation. For a time, especially after one police officer was killed, it looked as if open warfare might break out. As the long days dragged on and the tension mounted, a national television network broadcast an interview with an American tourist who was caught in the snarled traffic. In her country, she explained, this sort of thing would not be tolerated by the authorities: if the Indians would not withdraw peacefully, she thought they should be crushed by force.

She raised an interesting question, not about how the authorities should have handled the Oka stand-off, which was merely one more chapter in the sordid story of the contemptuous treatment of aboriginal peoples in North America – a tale degraded still further by the gunfights between aboriginals and police in 1995. Rather, her question forced us to focus on the level of official and private violence our respective countries are willing to tolerate. She came, after all, from a nation with the highest homicide rate of any western industrial country; a nation that had seen the municipal authorities in Philadelphia respond to a tricky situation with a religious cult by bombing their home (consuming by fire their entire neighbourhood in the ensuing conflagration); a country that had seen a Texas religious cult, the Branch Davidians, charged with various firearms and sexual offences, assaulted SAS-style by members of the Alcohol, Tobacco and Firearms bureau, and then finally obliterated at the end of a crudely orchestrated stand-off. Retaliation seems to have come swiftly from the radical right, with the destruction of the government building in Oklahoma City.

At the time of the Texas massacre, I was with the British police. Experienced hostage negotiators and senior police administrators, they were astonished at the way the Waco fiasco was handled, with heavy-handed violence and utterly without finesse. They speculated freely on what such official action taught its citizens about the use of force. If nothing else, such comparisons with Canadian policing tell us about the two countries' toleration for violence and acceptable strategies for controlling citizens. But they should do far more: they should open the question of what lies behind real national differences in the frequency and intensity of violent assault. These are the issues with which this book deals.

Towards an Explanation

On the surface, the perennial gun control issue is a puzzling feature of the emotionally charged ideological debate about violence, both here and in Britain. The dispute rages despite the facts that homicide rates have been falling for twenty years and that most criminologists admit that with the technology for killing universally available (everything from knives to automobiles to fertilizer bombs) gun control is largely *symbolic* and has little effect on crime. It continues despite the fact that countries with high rates of firearms ownership are found among both high homicide and low homicide nations (see Chapter 1); despite regulations that are already tight for a country with a large rural population, where firearms are a normal part of everyday life; and despite the fact that Canada, the world's second largest handgun market, generates very few homicides each year with legal handguns. The argument is as intense in Canada, where two-thirds of all homicides do not involve firearms at all (and there is no evidence whatever that the firearms-related homicides would not have occurred if firearms had not been available), as in England where more than 90 per cent of homicides do not involve firearms. Clearly, this debate is inspired by middle-class urban ideology, not analysis; so much so that it has prompted criminologist Ted Robert Gurr to remark, "The irony of most gun control proposals is that they would criminalize much of the citizenry but have only marginal effects on professional criminals." In any case, the evidence in this book points in quite another direction for the causation of violence – not to the relative availability of lethal technology, but to cultural conceptions about appropriate behaviour.[17]

The Relevance for Canada of Men of Blood

> The proper study of mankind is murder. (Prison doctor Theodore Dalrymple)

This is emphatically *not* an English book. It uses exclusively English case material, made available to me through various British police services, including New Scotland Yard and the South Yorkshire Police. Yet its aim was always much more than simply to chart the ebb and flow of English homicides. Rather, its aim was to pull together modern criminological theories and contemporary crime data in order to construct a richer explanation of *how modern societies can begin to lower their rates of serious assault*. Thus the book looks at one region with an exceptionally low homicide rate in order to deepen the scientific understanding of the social and cultural mechanisms by which *any* country can lower its rates, and tries to do so not in emotional and ideological terms but through a patient construction of an overall explanation.

How can we work to reduce still further the levels of violent assault? In Canada the solution is especially complex, because people misperceive the problem when they *believe* they live in a relatively violent society. Still, public anxieties arise from a wide and unrelated range of social ills, from the prospect of Quebec separation and continuing high unemployment to the systematic dismantling of the social safety net. These anxieties translate into a morbid fear of violence and a widespread belief that the civilization is crumbling. But like everywhere in the modern world, most homicides are committed by the poor, the uneducated and the disenfranchised. We must turn our ministrations to that class, not abandon them to their fate.

Why does Canada maintain a lower homicide rate than any other major nation in this hemisphere? This appears to be partly a function of the low societal *toleration* for violence at any level, personal or governmental. Although there is no evidence that assaults on women are increasing, the enlightened efforts of the women's movement have made a new generation of women unwilling to tolerate any violence against them and more willing to report it. Money that is currently being squandered on the remorseless expansion of the Justice Industry would be better spent in the proper support of shelters and support networks for abused women and children.

Our low homicide rates are also a function of the *cultural devaluation* of aggressivity. The extirpation of aggression begins in the nursery, says Cambridge criminologist D. P. Farrington. Putting our money into justice enforcement that is often counter-productive, spending hundreds of millions of dollars on attention-distracting tactics such as "getting tough on crime" and gun control, will not calm the relations among our citizens. Where such funding belongs is in the radical expansion of a truly professional day care system for overworked and harassed parents; in the establishment of a sophisticated educational enterprise aimed at inculcating in our youth a distaste for aggressive display; and in meaningful job creation. Without that redirection, this country is set on a self-destructive course; dismantling its safety net under the bogus rubric of insufficient funds and taking the demonstrably unsuccessful American path of "putting government on a sound business footing." Government is not a business: if it were, we would not need a government.

1   St. John's *Metro Advertiser*, June 29, 1986. This quotation is more fun if read aloud, with appropriate dramatic emphasis.

2   Elliott Leyton, William O'Grady and James Overton, 1992, *Violence and Public Anxiety: A Canadian Case*, St. John's, Nfld., ISER Press, p. xv.

3   Ian Taylor, 1983, *Crime, Capitalism, and Community*, Toronto: Butterworths. Leyton, O'Grady and Overton, 1992, p. xiv.

4   In the period 1986-1995, I gave an average of 100 interviews each year to television, radio, newspaper and magazine journalists from around the world – without exception, *all* earnestly believed we lived in a time of unprecedented and increasing violence.

5   *The Evening Telegram*, Dec. 1991.

6   Geoffrey Pearson, 1985, "Lawlessness, Modernity and Social Change: A Historical Appraisal," *Theory, Culture and Society* 2(3): 15.

7   Stanley Cohen, 1985, *Visions of Social Control*, Cambridge: Polity Press, p. 177.

8   See, for e.g., the "violent crime index," a profoundly misleading combination of the one violent crime that *is* reliably reported – homicide – with other violent crimes whose "rates" are a function of levels of police surveillance and ever-changing public willingness to *report* these offences (such as sexual assault).

9   Robert Silverman and Leslie Kennedy, 1993, *Deadly Deeds: Murder in Canada*, Toronto: Nelson, p. 32.

10 See, for e.g., Silverman and Kennedy, ibid. and Neil Boyd, 1988, *The Last Dance: Murder in Canada*, Scarborough: Prentice Hall.

11 F. Adler, G. Mueller and W. Laufer, 1991, *Criminology*. Toronto: McGraw-Hill. Quoted in Silverman and Kennedy, p. 31. Post-Soviet Russian figures are *double* the American rates!

12 For a preliminary attempt to relate this 1960s worldwide increase to the impact of foreign wars, see Dane Archer and Rosemary Gartner, 1984, *Violence and Crime in Cross-National Perspective*, New Haven: Yale U.P. Other scholars have speculated that the unprecedented growth in prosperity in the 1950s and 1960s paradoxically created a new class of alienated and dispossessed – those who had not benefited from the boom. Neither of these general theories have sufficient *cultural* emphasis to be fully satisfactory explanations.

13 This "steady rise" in America halted in 1995, but only time will tell if this represents the inauguration of a new downward trend.

14 Silverman and Kennedy, pp. 11-12, 34, 204-207.

15 John Howard Society of Ontario, *Fact Sheet #4*, Feb. 1995, pp. 1-4.

16 John Howard Society of Ontario, op. cit., p. 4.

17 Quoted in *New York Review of Books*, Nov. 16, 1995, p. 63.

Preface

THE RESEARCH ENTAILED in the writing of this book did nothing to enhance my chronic xenophobia: in fact, it led me on quite the opposite course, evoking in me a respect for a people I had long regarded as an inscrutable curiosity. An extended stay in the United Kingdom was my generation of middle-class Canadians' mandatory Grand Tour; and my own began in 1958 in South Kensington, then shuttled between the Home Counties and the Mountains of Mourne for the remainder of the 1960s. This brush against a rich and complex civilization was often baffling – routinely encountering adults who appeared not to reveal their emotions, men and women with whom friendships grew exceedingly slowly, behaviour that sometimes seemed rigid, constrained, even unfathomable.

It would all have become part of my long-buried past were it not for my staunch friend, Jon Riley, then a senior editor at Penguin Books, who wondered aloud, as our taxi lurched through London's late-night traffic on our way to a London Broadcasting Corporation radio interview in 1989, if I might try my hand at a book on homicide in modern England. The suggestion made little sense that midnight, still less in the grey dawn. What could an untutored colonial have to say of interest, let alone significance, about one of the world's great civilizations? Nevertheless, the challenge was clear: by all the conventional criminological indices – of urbanization, economic disparity, industrial collapse, ethnic and racial tensions – England should have a very *high* homicide rate. Yet it was low, even by the relatively civilized standards of post-war western Europe.

To understand the causes of the "everyday" and often unintended tragedies that form the vast majority of English homicides – rather than the sensational serial and mass killings that have occupied half my career –

forced me to stretch my theoretical imagination and to lose myself for years
in English social, cultural and criminal history. Fortunately I have been
schooled in impertinence, crossing academic borders at will, writing books
about America with hardly a visit: perhaps I could do better with a country
in which I had actually lived? Moreover, the world's response to my two previous volumes on homicide – *Hunting Humans: The Rise of the Modern
Multiple Murderer* and *Sole Survivor: Children Who Murder Their Families* –
had enriched my ideas and tempted me to explore still further the well-
springs of violence. I reached too far when I told Riley that I would try to
write "the definitive" book on the subject – this essay can only be the beginning of a path that will have to be completed by other, more learned, scholars – but it was worth a try.

Many people encouraged me along this route, and did so with a grace
and courtesy that left me gasping – kind critics in the newspapers, maga-
zines and scholarly journals; warm and personal contacts with individuals
in institutions such as the University of Surrey; police from the South
Yorkshire, Surrey, London Metropolitan, Lancashire, Devon and Somerset
forces. Helpful too were Sir Robert Bunyard, Peter Villiers and Sue King at
the Police Staff College, Bramshill; Cambridge University's Institute of
Criminology; and the FBI Academy. Leeds University's Zygmunt and Janina
Bauman, David Canter (now at Liverpool), London's Peter Loizos and
Coventry's Barry Mitchell were especially gracious and provocative; as were
the thousands of inquiring students who have passed through my university course on human aggression. Everywhere I went on this new task,
scholars responded with an altruistic collegiality: there are far too many to
mention, but Professors Linda Colley, David Downes, Douglas Hay, Bruce
P. Smith, Gordon Jones, A. E. Bottoms, John McMullan, Richard Gyug,
Anthony Dube, Volker Meja, Victor Zaslavsky, Judith Adler, Ronald
Schwartz, Terrence Murphy, Peter Baehr and David Farrington must be
singled out for a variety of kindnesses.

The British police have a reputation for what one student of crime
called "ultra-secretiveness," but this was the opposite of my own experience. From the beginning I was treated with extraordinary kindness, not
just by old friends such as Rick Holden of the South Yorkshire Police (who
gave up his office for me), Rupert Heritage of the Surrey Constabulary

(who made me feel that I belonged to this police world) and Roy Hazelwood of the FBI Academy; but also by the London Metropolitan Police's Anne Davies and John Newman, without whom this book could not have been written. At New Scotland Yard, Steve Gwilliam arranged my introduction, Alan O'Gorman shared his office and his gentle wisdom, Steve James and John Ashton baby-minded with finesse and the "war stories" of Eric Bowker and Christopher Flint enriched my experience. Russell Dunlop introduced me both to Metropolitan Police investigations and to real ale; and Lancashire's Stuart Kirby, younger than my own sons, was continuously refreshing. In South Yorkshire, Rick Holden was my friend and guide, my host and my benefactor. That prolonged immersion in all their companionship and their work was illuminating, but my strongest impression of the English police was from the documentary evidence – the typically cogent, professional and humane interviewing contained in the homicide files, matters I describe in great detail in this volume.

At the Home Office, a gracious Christopher Nuttall opened yet more doors, while W. D. Burns and P. H. White guided me through the labyrinth of government expectations and regulations – at the same time providing me with more statistical material than I could have hoped for. In the end, it was also more than I knew what to do with. Indeed, had it not been for the patient advice of my own colleague in sociology, Dr. Lawrence R. Felt, I would still be staring blankly at the Home Office statistical printouts. Unless otherwise noted, all purely statistical data in this volume were provided by the Home Office – data which allowed the selection of a stratified random sample of the major variations of homicide, to which I was given anonymous access by New Scotland Yard and the South Yorkshire Police. All names of victims, witnesses and perpetrators are of course fictitious, and dates and places are disguised: nothing else has been invented. All opinions and interpretations in this book are of course my own, and are endorsed by neither the Home Office nor the police.

Crime statistics typically present Scotland quite separately from England and Wales, and I have continued this distinction in this book. This book deals only with English data, in order to avoid making uncorroborated assumptions that English, Scottish and Welsh cultures have similar reference points. The reader will note that I have made *no* distinctions in the text between the different judicial categories of homicide – murder, manslaughter and infanticide – because I regard these as legal, not socio-logical, matters; as ethical not analytical constructs. Moreover, I have rarely distinguished between the different types of homicides except to show how much they share, since it is apparent from the data that such acts are com-mitted by similar people, with a familiar lack of control over all their behav-iour: that is, someone who kills his wife might, under other circumstances, have killed a friend or stranger.

First at the University of Surrey, and latterly at the University of Liverpool, where I hold an appointment on the advisory board to the "investigative unit" in the Department of Psychology, I was guided by years-long conversations with Professor David Canter: indeed, the ideas on the media contained in Chapter 4 were developed in daily e-mail exchanges with him. Senior Librarians M. A. M. Smallman at The Queen's University of Belfast (where I hold a Research Fellowship) and Mark Ashworth at the University of Surrey, and my teaching assistant at my own university, Carla Jenkins, assisted most ably; as did Professors Michael Staveley, Robin Stuart-Kotze and John Widdowson, *in situ* at Cambridge, Oxford and Sheffield; and Heidi Wells, Jack Lavers and Kim Hammond in Newfoundland. Fellow academic specialists in homicide, especially Philip Jenkins, Robert Silverman, Steve Egger, Candice Skrapec, Janet Warren, Joel Black, Eric Hickey, Dane Archer and Rosemary Gartner, all made the search for meaning intoxicating. Moreover, lectures I delivered at the Dutch Psychiatric and Juridical Society, the University of Liverpool, The University of Utrecht's Pompe Institute and the University of British Columbia in 1995 elicited helpful exchanges.

As I completed this manuscript, my friend – the Vancouver gynaecolo-gist and obstetrician Dr. Gary Romalis – was the victim of an assassination attempt, perpetrated apparently by some anti-abortion ideologue. If this book has no other consequence, it will be sufficient if it launches a sus-tained academic effort to determine how such atrocities might one day be rendered unthinkable in modern nations.

BEAST BOYS

THE MEDIA DEMONIZE HIM, and call him "The Beast Boy" of London. He is one of our nightmares made flesh – a remorseless, violent thug, preying with a savage enthusiasm on the elderly, among the weakest and most vulnerable of our citizens. His brief criminal career seems to encapsulate much that people fear about the new world order, the deterioration of civilization, and the younger generation. The Beast Boy was seventeen when he was convicted in 1994 for murdering an eighty-eight-year-old woman "by stamping on her so savagely that he left the imprint of his training shoes on her face." During his trial at the Old Bailey, it was shown that when he was only twelve he had already begun to assault and rob the old and the infirm – eventually claiming as many as sixty victims, and doing so with extreme brutality. The prosecutor noted that The Beast Boy, illiterate and of low intelligence, "had never shown remorse" – worse still, he "often smirked" when asked about his crimes. The Beast Boy denied killing another elderly woman he had assaulted, "who contracted bronchial pneumonia and died as a result of her injuries." His life sketches for us, many fear, both tone and texture of modern England.[1]

The Beast Boy is at the heart of our conundrum: is he typical of a new breed of Englishman, a generation of vipers? Analytically, by all the conventional criminological criteria of collapsing industries, decaying cities, economic disparities, dysfunctional families and racial tensions, England *should have* a very high homicide rate, and a production of "psychopathic" killers comparable to America's. Yet it has neither. How do we begin to interpret this?

To worry about violence and its ultimate manifestation, murder, is one of the prices exacted by contemporary life; and the public fear is universal, palpable, apparently justified. Everywhere, the conventional wisdom notes that the rotten fabric of civilization is about to disintegrate. In an England terrorized by "soccer hooligans," a dozen corpses are exhumed from a "house of horror" in sleepy Gloucester; and a teenager standing in a queue in Manchester is shot and killed, one of a hundred shootings in Moss Side in six months. In Norway, two toddlers in a playground beat and stone to death a little girl. In Canada, a gunman murders fourteen women at an engineering college. In the United States, a young mother claims her two small children have disappeared in a "carjacking," then spends the ensuing days playing the role of the desperate and loving mother for the media and police. Her performance is flawless, and her celebrity assured, till under relentless police interrogation she confesses she killed them because her new lover did not wish to be a "father." Television allows every sensational killing anywhere in the world to be brought into our sitting rooms, live and in colour; and media personnel, obsessed with violence, yet rarely comprehending what is new and what is not, orchestrate our despair.

This book focuses narrowly on homicide in England, but it pursues several parallel themes: one is to show how public fear of homicide in this country is quite inappropriate, given the mundane, unsensational and unchanging character – and the comparative rarity – of the event. Many scholars have shown how this popular anxiety – a "moral panic" – is created, fanned and manipulated by a variety of self-serving professions, institutions and ideologues, many of whom profit from such fear in significant and material ways such as enhanced visibility, funding and power. Even the "quality" press announces that the "real" crime rate is triple the police estimates (apparently unaware of the fact that it has always been so, that the majority of most crimes have always gone unreported), and that "most people now accept [ever-increasing] crime as part of life." Fears of racial tension translate into unverifiable claims, when in fact there is no evidence whatever of an increase in racist homicidal assaults. Even the most articulate and informed members of the media frequently do not understand that what is changing is victims' *willingness to report* crimes, not the actual incidence of these offences.[2]

This inflammation of public fear is such that the nation's chief constables have been moved to complain of the irresponsible manner in which their statistics are often retailed to the public: indeed, one urged an end to "this sterile performance each quarter," and urged a new system of making facts clear to the public. "Instead of being given alarming global figures," *The Times* paraphrased, the public should understand how police over time turn their attention to different forms of criminality; and their efforts inevitably yield more convictions. But homicide in England is an extremely rare event, statistically insignificant compared to all other causes of death. A population of close to 50 million murders fewer than 600 people each year: fewer than 600 personal catastrophes out of 48 million relatively peaceful lives, a malfunction rate that designers of any mechanical or electronic system might envy. Moreover, that rate is dwarfed by other social toxins: as many as ten times that number are killed every year by *each* of the following: industrial disease, road accidents, suicide or cigarettes.[3]

A second and parallel theme is the historical, social and cultural *origin* of England's comparatively low homicide rate. The rich historical evidence suggests that this relative peaceableness was established in England as early as the thirteenth century; a consequence of the establishment of what was perhaps the first money-based bourgeois democratic nation-state. In a clever calculation to protect both their persons and their estates, the ruling élites began to withdraw from violent encounters by prohibiting the ancient customs of blood feud and its associated notions of "honour"; while at the same time the emerging centralized state offered both legal and personal *alternatives* to violence for an ever-increasing proportion of its population. Thus England appears to have begun long ago what Elias has called the "civilizing process," *the culturally programmed internalization of shame and fear*, of learned inhibitions about violence. These "conditioned" inhibitions were transmitted from generation to generation through a variety of socialization techniques, including the provision of increasingly non-violent culture heroes (or "role models") upon whom Englishmen and -women were expected to model their behaviour. This ideal personality was so clearly defined by the end of the nineteenth century that Robert Baden-Powell could describe it as "a stolid, pipe-sucking manhood, unmoved by panic or excitement, and reliable in the tightest of places."[4]

If violence was once the primary dominion of the noble and the knight, making war upon one another to enlarge their estates, it has for centuries everywhere been at the other end of the social spectrum – the bottom of the working class – in which "insults to honour were taken seriously, and violence was the accepted means of settling disputes." What is especially interesting about England is how few of even this "underclass" actually kill. There are no precise figures on the social origins of killers, but it is clear that nine out of ten homicides, perhaps more, are now committed by members of this underclass – persons with little education and no professional qualifications, chronically unemployed and on welfare, living in council housing, with chronic drug and alcohol problems, often mentally ill. These are most often disordered and uncontrolled people for whom the "major benefit of many crimes is [mere] relief from momentary irritation"; people who "tend to have minimal tolerance for frustration and little ability to respond to conflict through verbal rather than physical means." Perhaps the collapse of the traditional family, however vile it may allegedly have been, assured the easier production of the undersocialized, the uncontrolled, the disinhibited, the "uncivilized."[5]

Still, it can be misleading to dwell upon homicide at all. To do so is inevitably to distort our perspective, frightening us by obscuring what an infrequent act it actually is. Until the mid-1970s, England's homicide rate was among the very lowest ever achieved in the industrial world. But today, even with the troubling increase that has since occurred, the rates still remain at the bottom of the least violent stratum in the world. England's homicide rate is forever dwarfed by the average American city – the 1993 New York City rate was, for example, *twenty-five times* the English rate. Nevertheless, the English rates continue slightly to rise, and an understanding of the phenomenon is vital if society is to reassert its control over its most dangerous members, and begin the construction of an even more pacific civilization. Table 1 shows how many are killed each year in contemporary England.

In fact, of course, even in the most murderous nations for which we have records, homicide – which typically everywhere occurs not in a brutal assault by a stranger, but in a mundane quarrel between lovers, friends or acquaintances – pales into insignificance when compared with the murder-

TABLE 1 Number of homicides in England, 1982–1990.

Year	Number of homicides
1982	521
1984	518
1986	546
1988	516
1990	579

Source: Adapted from statistics supplied by the Home Office. Precise annual numbers vary according to the many different means of counting, and whether the offences are categorized according to the dates they occurred or the dates they were reported to the Home Office.

ousness of governments in warfare, or in the official suppression of political dissent, or in the terrorizing of populations by both the state and its enemies. The 60 million victims of Stalin's Great Terror are matched by no constellation of individual killers. Moreover, it takes a profoundly bankrupt political and cultural tradition to produce an apparatchik such as Stalin's NKVD killer, Pavel Sudoplatov, who can calmly recall his orchestration of assassinations with the cheap pseudo-philosophical sentiment – "One does not choose the time to live, die or kill."[6]

Why then the popular fascination with murders, the overwhelming majority of which are mundane and unsensational; and with murderers, dull and limited men, lacking in the most elementary social skills, and often victims of mental illness or incapacity? One ancient chord that is sounded here is the role of the killer in our folk traditions – cultural presentations in which those who commit the most terrible deeds are held up to intense public scrutiny, not in order to validate their acts, but as lurid examples of evil and wrongdoing. But there is another, less wholesome, motivation, one that turns in admiration to these defectives for a kind of inspiration, one that can warp the limited imaginations of our most vulnerable citizens. We must choose with great caution the folk heroes we present to one another, and the qualities they embody, for they shall surely return to haunt us.

If the public presentation of The Beast Boy may be garlanded with a fearful mythology, it is our task to show that few cases better encapsulate the primary qualities of the *reality* of a "typical" English homicide than the prosaic milkman's that follows. Customarily, killer and victim are friends, acquaintances or relations. Perhaps there has been a long-simmering feud; and the future killer is a difficult and troubled young man, often with an extensive criminal record, and a history of alcohol abuse. Chronically unemployed, he lives on state benefits in council housing, separated from his wife and child. At a moment of extreme tension for him, there is an insult or a misunderstanding, and he "loses" control. We shall never know all the details of any human event, but there is enough here for us to begin to understand the manner of person who kills; the confused, the ineffectual and the uncontrolled.

"HE LOST HIS TEMPER": THE MILKMAN REPELS HIS COUSIN'S HOMOSEXUAL ADVANCES

Mark Dutton was the child of a divorced couple. He lived in a council flat with his mother and his younger brothers and sisters; at twenty-one, he had already separated from his wife and son. He had an alcohol "problem," and had left school at sixteen without any qualifications. His father had been a milkman, and Mark was offered several chances for a career at the dairies, but each time he seized an opportunity to fail. Thus he flitted from work in one dairy to another, then back to the first till he was dismissed for "bad timekeeping." He attended, but failed to complete, a college course in man-agement. He left his next job as a warehouseman because he thought he wanted "outdoor work," but quit and was rehired as a dairies milkman, only to resign from that within weeks. At the time of his arrest he was a van driver: his salary as of 1981 was £70 per week, from which he paid £15 in rent to his mother and £15 to his wife and child (who were also in temporary accommodation in a council flat). Unlike the majority of our killers, he had no previous criminal convictions. Neither had the victim, Mark's cousin, Stephen Potter, twenty-four, a London-born bisexual who had briefly dated Dutton's wife before her marriage.

The Killing

Later, after the trial, the police summarized the case: Dutton had been charged with murder after repeatedly striking his victim with a knife. The motive was thought to be his response to an unwanted "homosexual advance," and "provocation" was the basis of his defence. Dutton had been drinking with his cousin, Stephen Potter, and other members of the family, in several public houses in Kentish Town. Dutton drove everyone home except his victim, Potter, and police concluded that the pair had bought a takeaway meal and then gone to Dutton's old matrimonial flat.

"Whilst at the flat," the police continued, "Dutton alleges that the deceased made unwelcome homosexual advances towards him, coupled with insulting and scathing remarks about his wife from whom he is separated." This provoked Dutton into "temporarily losing control of his good sense." Dutton left the building and ran several hundred yards to his van, where he found his sheath knife. When he returned to his flat, he claimed Potter was undressed; and in panic, Dutton began to stab him, before driving off in his van. Meanwhile, the victim somehow left the flat and climbed down a flight of stairs before he collapsed and died from what the pathologist later described as fifteen stab wounds to the body.

Moments later, two police constables saw Dutton erratically piloting his van along the road, and pulled him over. "Dutton had blood on both hands and was holding his left arm as though it had been injured." His attempt to explain this to the constables was unsatisfactory, and they insisted he come with them to Kentish Town police station. In the station, Dutton offered many fanciful stories, but eventually told police "that he had stabbed an unknown man in his flat after this man had made homosexual advances towards him."

Witnesses to His Life

Few who knew Mark spoke ill of him. Mark's mother told police the brief history of her son's troubled marriage: "To me they seemed a happily married couple: when they came over at Christmas you couldn't have seen a happier couple, they were there with the baby, everything seemed fine. Then just before the New Year, Mark came over to me and told me that Tracy wanted a trial separation. She had told him that she had no more feeling for him. We talked about it that night. He stayed at my place on the settee. I didn't interfere with the two of them. I asked Mark if he wanted me to speak to Tracy, but he said no. He said that she was all flash, and 'going out with the girls,' and that she probably wouldn't even listen to me. Mark went back to the flat on New Year's Eve: he took Tracy to work and brought the baby over to me. That evening, Mark went to try and sort it out with Tracy, but he told me she hadn't listened. He came over to me with the baby and she went out with the girls, she said. Since then Mark has been going over to see his son at Tracy's mother's house about three times a week and has paid maintenance for the boy. I don't think Mark has tried to get back with Tracy since then."

Mark's estranged twenty-one-year-old wife told police, "I married Mark on 8 December 1979. We lived continuously at the same address until New Year's Eve 1981, when I left him, taking the baby with me. We separated because he did not like me to go out when I wanted to – and he also has hit me a few times. When I left Mark I went to stay at my mother's house. Early in January, the council gave me a flat. The baby has not stayed with me because the accommodation is unsuitable. He has stayed with my mother. I collect him early in the morning and take him to a nursery for the day and then collect him in the evening and take him back to my mother's and stay with him until he goes to bed. Mark has the baby every Sunday, and sees the baby Wednesdays and Fridays.

"About three years ago I used to go out with Steve Potter. We broke up in May 1979 and then I started going out with Mark in June. Steve and Mark are cousins. Mark hated Steve, I don't know whether Steve hated Mark. It wasn't only because of me: Mark hated him because he thought he was a homosexual. It didn't help that I had been going out with Steve prior to going out with Mark. Whenever Steve's name was mentioned in public or in conversation with me, he would make some offensive comment or call him a 'poof' or something. In the four months that I went out with Steve, we slept together three or four nights a week. We did have sexual intercourse on one occasion, but after that he refused, saying that he did not want me to become pregnant. I told him that I was on the pill, but he still wouldn't have sex with me. He never told me that he was homosexual, but I got that impression because he was very effeminate in his ways. My sexual relation-ship with Mark was a normal one and was not a part of the reason for the breakup. To my knowledge Mark is not a homosexual.

"When I went to Italy I brought Mark a knife back as a present. Mark never said he would stab me, but he did say if I ever went with another bloke he would kill me and them. There was one occasion when he held a kitchen knife to my throat. This was just before Christmas 1981, and I was going shopping with my little sister. Mark didn't want me to go and he just lost his temper and held the knife to my throat and said I wasn't to go. My little sister shouted at him not to, and he then seemed to come to his senses. He wasn't a violent person, but when he lost his temper he didn't know what he was doing."

Revisionist History

The first tale

Mark lied to police until skilful interrogation broke his story, although he never told the full truth about how he and his cousin came to be together in his empty flat. When first pulled over by the police, he claimed he had been stabbed by a stranger. "I've been attacked," he told them. "A man came up to me and knifed me. I was stopped at some white lines in Caledonian Road. I can't really remember [what he looked like], just that he was big, a white bloke. When he opened the door and went for me I just grabbed it [the knife] and drove off."

The second tale

In the cells, he embellished his story. This time, the stranger who assaulted him also made homosexual advances: "I don't really want to say [what happened]. When the man opened the door he put his hand on my leg. He was queer. He just smiled at me. That's when I got the knife and stabbed him. He just touched my leg, so I stabbed him and kept on stabbing him."

The third tale

Within hours he changed his story once more and admitted to suspicious police, who still did not know there had been a murder, that "it didn't happen in the van. I did go to the house to pick up any mail, I went in and bent over to pick up this letter. There was this queer in the place, he came up and touched me between the legs. I turned round and he was naked from the waist down. He just smiled at me. I ran out of the flat down to my van, I got the knife out. I ran back up and showed him the knife and said, 'What are you going to do now?' He just smiled at me and stood there and laughed. I stabbed him, I just kept stabbing him. I turned to go and he tried to throttle me, he must have leant against me. I ran down to the van and drove off. I don't know [if I killed him], he just slumped against the wall."

The Police Interrogations

The police soon understood that there had been a murder, and the formal interviews began in the police station. As always, the first task of the interviewing detective was to force a shattered, undisciplined and incoherent mind to construct a narrative version of what had occurred; and then search for the internal inconsistencies that might point to innocence or guilt.

Mark initially insisted he had no idea whom he had stabbed. After cautioning him, the detective asked, "Tell us about it, please?" "What, *all* of it?" "Yes, please." "I went out last night for a drink with my brother Gary and my cousins Stewart and Steve and my Uncle Jim. Then Jim suggested we go to another pub, so I said I'd get my van and we could all go in that. We all drove down to The Angel and had one drink each. Then we all got back in the van and returned to The Falcon. We stopped in there till half-past two this morning."

"What happened then?" "Gary said, 'Do you think you're all right to drive the van?' I said yes, so we all got in. First of all we went to Royal College Street and Jim and Stewart got out: Stewart lives there. Jim was staying there as well. Then I drove to Lady Margaret Road and dropped off Gary. That left me and Steve. I said, 'I'm going to go home.' He said, 'You're going a different way to me, so I'll walk and try and get a cab.' Then he started walking and I went up to the flat where I used to live. I parked the van and walked up to the flat and opened the door. I've still got a key to the flat.

"I opened the door, looked behind it and there was some letters, as I bent down to pick them up, this guy grabbed me from behind. He got me on the shoulders with both hands. I turned round and said, 'What the hell are you doing?' or 'What do you want?' Then I stood up and pushed him away and ran downstairs. I went to the van and got the knife out of the van and went back up to the flat. The door was already open and I pushed it. He was standing just behind the door. I said to him, 'Don't do that again' or 'Don't try that again.' He just smiled and laughed.

"I just went for him. I hit him with the knife a few times, and then as I turned to get out he got hold of me again. So I swung round and pushed him against the wall." "How many times did you hit him?" "Four or five. After I hit him with the knife, I turned to go and got to the front door, and he come and got me and tried to hold me back. I've never seen him before. He got me and I pushed him away against the wall and just run down the stairs. I run all the way down out of the flats, got into the van and drove off. I got to a road just off Kentish Town. and two policemen stopped me because I was driving a bit funny. I got out of the van and they asked me what was wrong. So I told them what happened. Well, first I told them that a man had stopped me in the street as I was driving the van, and then they radioed for one of their vans to come; then they took me to the police station. We went upstairs and [I] told the policeman that someone stopped me in the street. Then they put me into a cell."

When the detective told Mark he knew the identity of his victim, Mark's absurd ruse – that his victim was a stranger – crumbled. "Most of what I've told you is the truth. *All* of it's the truth; apart from the man in the flat. It was Steve. I did drop him off, and I said to him, 'I'm going to my old flat, you can get a cab home.' I went to pick up some letters. When I got to the flat Steve was standing outside. So I said to him, 'What are you doing here?' and he said, 'I just come to see where you used to live.' I said, 'I'm only going up to see if there's any letters.' I started walking up the stairs and when I got to my flat, he was coming up the stairs behind me. So I opened the door to get the letters and he walked in."

At this point, police noted, Mark "broke down" and began to cry. The detective tried to soothe him, but Mark continued to sob: "He started touching me. I told him to piss off. He started saying things like 'I like you' and things like that. I hit him. He went down. That's when I ran down to the van to get the knife. I come back up and he was getting undressed. Then I hit him with the knife." "Why didn't you leave when you went down to your

van?" "I don't know. He made me feel sick. I just wanted to get back at him."
"When you say you just wanted to get back at him: was this because you had
committed a homosexual act with him?" "No. I told you. We went up to the
flat and he just started, so I punched him. Perhaps he thought it was a game
or something. Everybody knew he was queer. It repulsed me."

The detective pursued the many anomalies in Dutton's story, trying
first to establish if they had shared a meal at the flat: "There's one or two
points I'm not clear on. I can't work out how it was that Steve got to the flat
before you?" "I don't know, but he was there when I got there." "In the flat
there was the remains of a Kentucky Fried Chicken meal. Where did that
come from?" "Unless he had one of those meals, I don't know. I didn't see
him with it." "There's no question that the pair of you bought a Kentucky
Fried Chicken each and took it to the flat?" "No."

"Was there anything in particular that made you dislike Steve?" "He
was queer." "Didn't he used to go out with your wife before you were
married?" "Yes. Just lately I disliked him more because I knew he used to go
out with her, and I married her. I only used to see him about twice a year. He
moved away to Nottingham and that was probably for the better because I
never saw him." "Did you ever have a relationship with him?" "No. He was
my cousin and that was that. I didn't use to see him much anyhow."

The following day, Mark gave more details: "Steve said he'd like to see
me come all over his face. Then he said something about my wife. He said
she was no good when he was with her. It was probably best that we split up
because she was a slut. That was all he said." "I understand that you don't
like queers?" "Yes, that's true, but he's my cousin as well. I couldn't just
ignore him if we were all out together. I was probably talking to him more
than the others. We were all in the same group together standing by the bar.
We were talking about how I left my wife, that I'd got a driving job now. He
was saying that he was out of work." "Isn't it true that you intended to take
him to the flat?" "No." "How did he get to your flat?" "I don't know." "You
said yesterday that he was there before you." "Yes." "How could that be so?"
To counter this difficulty, Mark now introduced a new incident: "When I
was going towards his flat, I hit a parked car with the van. So I stopped and
sat there for a while cause I was shaken up."

With inconclusive responses to his suspicions, the detective explored the presence of the weapon: "When did you take to carrying the knife?" "When the firm gave me the van just before Christmas. A couple of times I picked up sacks and I used to keep string and labels in the van. A couple of times the sacks have had the wrong label on." Turning from the weapon to the killing, the detective remarked, "You told me yesterday that you stabbed Steve in the chest. Where else did you stab him?" "Just in the chest. But he put his hands up so I could have caught him in the hands as well. He said, 'No, don't do it,' so I pushed him away to run out. He caught hold of me so I just pushed him again against the wall and run." "Steve's body has been medically examined today and several stab wounds were found in his back. How did that happen?" "I don't know. I just kept hitting him with the knife. He was just holding on to me. I was just swearing at him. Just telling him to fuck off and leave me alone and things like that. I just wanted to hurt him for what he'd done to me. He touched my leg and put his arm around me; he tried to kiss me, and said things about my wife – he said she was no good. I just wanted to hurt him badly. To get him. It's probably the drink more than anything. Just wanted to make sure that he knew I couldn't stand him."

"Did you realize he was seriously hurt when you left?" "I knew he was bleeding. He was just standing there holding his chest." "Why didn't you stop to help him?" "I just wanted to get out of there and get home. I was scared." When the detective warned him that he would be charged with murder, Mark made no reply, and merely nodded. During his trial, he was found guilty of manslaughter, and sentenced to four years' imprisonment.

ISSUES IN THE STUDY OF HOMICIDE

If English killers are very much alike, so are modern societies. In most western industrial nations the social indicators are all similar – the proportion of marriages that end in divorce, the types of disease and the average age at death, the approximate standard of living, the size of families and the literacy rate. This is emphatically *not* the case with homicide, virtually the only index which varies enormously between countries. "In some societies, homicide is an hourly, highly visible, and therefore somewhat unexceptional cause of death," write Dane Archer and Rosemary Gartner, while "in other nations, homicides are so infrequent that, when they do occur, they receive national attention and lasting notoriety." Expressed in terms proportionate to population, rates of homicide per 100,000 population vary from as low as 0.5 per 100,000 in England during the 1950s, to *twenty times that rate* in America in the 1990s (and twice that again in post-Soviet Russia). Thus an individual living in a high-violence country such as modern America has from ten to twenty times the chance of being murdered as someone living in low-homicide regions, such as Switzerland, Japan or England.[7]

A nation's homicide rate is also remarkably consistent over the years, changing only gradually up or down (except in the chaos that sometimes accompanies a war). Moreover, the relationship between different nations' homicide rates is usually also consistent – thus, whether the world rates rise or fall, for example, Canada's homicide rate is usually double or triple that of England's, and one quarter that of the United States', and the three rates tend to rise and fall together over the years. One phenomenon that captured the world's attention was the increase in homicide that occurred almost everywhere in the world (including England) in the late 1960s and early 1970s: in most countries, however, that increase had stopped by the mid-1970s and even, as in Canada, begun to decline. That increase has been provisionally explained by Archer and Gartner, who argued that during a war a culture reorients itself so that violence and killing are now rewarded, and these messages have a profound impact on the larger society, acting to desensitize people to violence. Still, there are other plausible explanations especially the notion that the unprecedented prosperity of the 1960s created a new class of embittered losers who sought vengeance upon all around them.

Table 2 sketches the extensive differences between countries. It also illustrates some of the problems inherent in international comparisons – not only in the different criteria often used to categorize homicide, but also how some killings do not pass into the official record. An especially flagrant example here might be modern Germany, which has a relatively low homicide rate because the interpersonal homicides we study are relatively rare in that country – except in periods of social chaos. But to leave out of the equation the *millions* of German gypsies, Jews, homosexuals, retarded and mentally ill persons and political dissidents murdered by both German

TABLE 2 Homicide rates among the world's major industrial nations, victims, by frequency strata, *circa* 1992 (adapted from *World Health Statistics Annual 1993*).

Frequency stratum	Country	Victimization rate, males	Victimization rate, females
Very high	Mexico**	31.5	3.5
	Russian Federation	24.9	5.4
	United States**	15.9	4.2
	Lithuania	11.2	4.4
	Argentina	8.5	1.5
High	Italy	4.8	0.6
	Scotland	4.7	0.9
	Finland**	4.6	2.4
	Poland	4.5	1.4
Moderate	China (urban areas)	3.1	1.6
	Canada**	2.9	1.6
	Norway	2.2	0.9
	Greece	2.0	0.9
	Australia**	1.9	1.3
Low	Sweden	1.7	0.9
	Switzerland**	1.6	1.3
	Netherlands	1.6	0.8
	France	1.5	0.7
	Denmark	1.4	1.3
	Germany	1.4	0.9
	Spain	1.4	0.5
Very low	Ireland	0.8	0.4
	Japan	0.7	0.5
	England & Wales	0.6	0.5***

**Denotes countries with exceptionally high rates of private firearms ownership. *CAVEAT:* International comparisons of homicide rates are highly problematic since, Robert Silverman rightly warns, "for statistical purposes each country defines homicide slightly differently." Moreover, countries that inherited Roman law often include *attempted* homicides in their homicide figures. This necessitates *extreme* caution in any attempt at precision (e.g., is Switzerland's rate really higher than France's, or did they use slightly different criteria in their definition of homicide?) – a dilemma that has unfortunately kept many criminologists from using them at all. Nevertheless, the rates tend to be *relatively* consistent; and their location in broad frequency strata appears to be both useful and real. In any case, England and Wales are at the very bottom of the lowest stratum. Conclusive figures permitting proper comparisons between countries must, however, await further research.[8]

***Note the international phenomenon that the lower a nation's overall homicide rate, the closer the rates of male and female victimization. This appears to be because in low homicide nations, there are proportionately fewer stranger killings, and more provoked by the most intimate relationships such as spouses and lovers.

private persons and the state is to give an entirely false picture of the culture's homicidal capacity. One needs to be reminded that no comparable atrocities have ever been undertaken in England. Such anomalies are among many in the system of recording homicides, and they must be understood, and the crude data approached with caution.

The sheer scale of these differences between nations demands an attempt to explain them. Nevertheless, only a few national studies exist – for Canada, Switzerland and the United States. Scholars have largely ignored the subject, perhaps considering it too vulgar for the Senior Common Room, perhaps concerned that studying it will detract from their efforts to rehabilitate its perpetrators. Perhaps it is simply unfashionable. In any case, this book is an attempt to intensify this comparative scrutiny, using sampled data on all English homicides in 1982, 1984, 1986, 1988 and 1990, and anecdotally comparing them with ethnographic data from similar homicides in the United States.[9]

The fundamental question is *why* should homicide rates vary so much from country to country? Modern urban intellectuals are as subject to fashion as anyone, and their assumptions and values jostle everywhere in the ideological marketplace. Archer and Gartner venture that "nations with the lowest rate of *inequality* also tend to have the lowest rates of violent crime." Certainly it is true that there is a worldwide relationship between low homicide rates and compassionate social systems that buffer their citizens from misfortune and deprivation (as in most of western Europe). But the *causal* relationships are inconsistent, since some low homicide nations, such as England, have profound social and economic disparities; and some impoverished regions, such as Newfoundland, have much lower homicide rates than more prosperous areas of Canada. Indeed, it may well be that inequality does not cause violence, but rather that any truly civilized and non-violent country naturally struggles to minimize inequality and injustice.

Perhaps there is insufficient punishment for evil-doers? This argument traditionally centres around the use of capital punishment as a deterrent; but recent major work examining an international sample of countries that abolished the death penalty has found no consistent impact of any kind (in some countries, homicide increased after abolition, in others it decreased, while in still others it remained unchanged). In any case, the vast majority of homicides in all countries are spur-of-the-moment affairs, unplanned "acts of passion," in which the possible penalties are rarely considered by the perpetrator. Punishment seems hardly the issue, and nations with the most severe penalties such as the U.S.A. and Russia have the highest homicide rates.

Perhaps it is all part of a misogynistic "worldwide conspiracy for the mass extermination of women," as one radical feminist recently expressed it. The position is challenging till one notes that males are everywhere in the world both the perpetrators and primary victims of homicidal assault. Perhaps what is required is even more intensive control of firearms? This case is plausible too till one observes that homicide rates in Europe were *much higher* before the invention of firearms – when the ordinary agricultural tools of scythe and knife were the only available weapons; that only a small and unchanging 9 per cent of English homicides are committed with firearms; and that the modern nations with the highest levels of private ownership of firearms (especially Switzerland and Canada) often have low rates of homicide. The facts insist that we search elsewhere for an explanation.[10]

TENTATIVE HYPOTHESES

The theses of this study are that a truly low homicide rate – operating even in times of social dislocation – is only likely in a country where the social order provides reasonable legal alternatives to physical confrontation. More importantly, its culture must inculcate in its members a repertoire of valued personality traits which inhibit aggressivity – devaluing violence through a variety of means, including the display of models of non-violent culture heroes. Thus this book is a tentative exploration of some of the *cultural differences* that keep the English homicide rate one of the world's lowest, and a comparison of the cultural codes (wherever possible) with those of its close relative, the United States (which for decades has maintained the highest homicide rates in the western industrial world).

The lowest homicide rate that urbanized human beings anywhere seem able to manage is about 0.5 per 100,000, the approximate English rate from the late nineteenth century until the 1960s. In any society which maintains rates in the lowest international stratum – near or about 1 per 100,000 (the current English rate) – these rare homicides are committed only by the occasional mentally disturbed person, or in a drunken or drugged stupor, or by a tiny number of undersocialized and socially incompetent individuals from the bottom of the social hierarchy, often as an accidental consequence of their uncontrolled behaviour. The level rises beyond that lowest stratum – to three, five, even ten or more – when the notion of private vengeance is still embedded in the culture. Such civilizations continue to provide emotionally charged instructions and cues validating violence as an appropriate and manly response to the frustration and humiliation that are a normal part of every person's life. The exploration of these propositions constitutes the remainder of this book.

1   *Guardian Weekly*, Sept. 25, 1994, p. 8.

2   *The Times*, May 18, 1991, p. 1; *Guardian Weekly*, Nov. 8, 1992, p. 4.

3   It is not our place here to give chapter and verse of the manipulation of public hysteria and fears of violence in a nation with such a low rate as England. Other, more able, scholars have already done this, as in Stanley Cohen's classic 1972 volume, *Folk Devils and Moral Panics: The Creation of the Mods and Rockers*, or in Philip Jenkins' 1992 work, *Intimate Enemies: Moral Panics in Contemporary Great Britain*. See also Elliott Leyton, William O'Grady and James Overton, 1992, *Violence and Public Anxiety: A Canadian Case*, St. John's, Nfld.: ISER Press. See also P.E.H. Hair, "Deaths from Violence in Britain: A Tentative Secular Survey," in *Population Studies* 25 (1, 1971): 5–24.

4   Some other nations have also experienced similar declining levels over the centuries: Pieter Spierenburg reports, e.g., that the homicide rate in Amsterdam dropped from 47 per 100,000 in the mid-fifteenth century to between 1 and 1.5 in the early nineteenth century. See *New York Times*, Oct. 23, 1994, p. 16. R. Baden-Powell, 1908, *Scouting For Boys*, quoted in Bill Buford, 1992, *Among The Thugs*, London: Mandarin, p. 12.

5   See Stuart Palmer, 1972, *The Violent Society*, New Haven: College & University Press, p. 40. Michael R. Gottfredson and Travis Hirschi, 1990, *A General Theory of Crime*, Stanford: Stanford U.P., p. 90.

6   See Pavel Sudoplatov, 1994, *Special Tasks: The Memoirs of an Unwanted Witness – A Soviet Spymaster*, New York: Little, Brown & Co., p. 81.

7   Dane Archer and Rosemary Gartner, 1984, *Violence and Crime in Cross-National Perspective*, New Haven: Yale U.P., p. 4, and p. 171ff.

8   Robert A. Silverman, 1992, "Crime Rates," in E. Borgatta and M. Borgatta (eds), *The*

Encyclopedia of Sociology, vol. 1, New York: Macmillan, pp. 347–353. WHO rates for England and Wales are based on vital registration data in this country, and are consistently rather lower than recorded Home Office rates. For 1994, for example, the Home Office's recorded rate for *all* homicide was 1.3 per 100,000.

9   See H. C. Brearley, 1932, *Homicide in the United States*, reprinted 1969, Montclair: Patterson Smith; Robert A. Silverman and Leslie Kennedy, 1993, *Deadly Deeds: Murder in Canada*, Toronto: Nelson; M. E. Wolfgang, 1958, *Patterns in Criminal Homicide*, Philadelphia: Pennsylvania U.P.; Barry Mitchell, 1990, *Murder and Penal Policy*, London: Macmillan; and Philip Jenkins, 1994, *Using Murder: The Social Construction of Serial Homicide*, New York: Aldine de Gruyter. There are, of course, many specialized studies: cf., for e.g., Frans Koenraadt's work on patricide, or Rick Holden's "The Facets of Stranger Homicide: A Feasibility Study," M. Phil. Thesis, University of Surrey, 1995.

10   Personal communication; Archer and Gartner, 1984: 159.

A CIVILIZATION GONE MAD?

AN EXPLICATION OF THE UNTHINKABLE

"MAN FOUND GUILTY of attempted murder for pushing woman into path of speeding fire engine in London," begins one year's litany of personal and social catastrophe from the annual index of *The Times*. "Police release photos of clay model of dead teenage girl," it continues;

police attempt to identify body of infant found abandoned on rubbish tip; 11-year-old charged with murder of father; London man alleged to have committed murder while subject to electronic curfew; Cheshire police hunt killer of elderly women; four accused of murder following raid on Soho amusement arcade which led to death of two guards; police attempt to identify body found in burned-out car in Essex; mother pleads guilty to manslaughter of son and daughter; body of man found in Regent's Canal; man accused of murder in England detained in Tenerife on rape charge; police hunt murderer of 75-year-old woman found drowned in bath; man who killed baby and stabbed 13-month-old brother dies after deliberately crashing van; man stabs wife then himself to death; man jailed for life for second time after murdering fiancée; customer stabbed to death in fight at Brixton minicab office; gunman kills two then gives himself up at Bury St. Edmunds; man who poisoned two workmates dies from heart attack while serving life sentence; elderly disabled man found stabbed to death in burned-out flat in Croydon; 13-year-old girl sent for trial accused of murder of twin babies and attempted murder of mother; two gunmen flee on motor cycle after shooting man dead in London pub; pair who spiked employer's pie with LSD are cleared of causing his death by heart attack;

20

man whose wife and child were found battered to death killed by train; husband denies trying to kill wife by feeding her rat poison; merchant seaman accused of trying to murder two boys aged five and seven by imprisoning them in car boot; woman, husband and lover stabbed to death after love triangle is exposed; couple accused of murdering six-week-old daughter; man who killed mother and grandmother ordered to be detained at secure psychiatric unit.[1]

Inscribed testimony, surely, to the widely entertained proposition that the nation has gone mad. The public's fear is fanned by an alarmed press: "BIRCH THESE THUGS WHO PREY ON OUR OLD FOLK," the *Sun* headline demands, its text accompanied by lurid photographs of beaten elderly people. Violence, it claims, is "the big issue facing Britain today." Blood runs so freely in the streets that in modern Britain "there cannot be a single elderly man or woman who does not live in some fear. Fear of being *robbed*. Fear of being *attacked*, perhaps *murdered*, in the street or even their home." An accompanying folk history of the nation proposes that while "this was once a country where women and children, the old, the weak and vulnerable, went wherever they wished by day and night . . . now they are afraid to venture into the streets at any time." Indeed, "the appalling indictment of our society is that there is NO peace, NO safety for our old folk" because at any moment "a killer can *pounce*." The *Sun* offered statistics to bolster its case, noting that the total number of "violent crimes" committed in Britain in 1980 had been 97,200, while in 1991 that total had risen to 190,300 "and rising."[2]

It is a pity that so few understand the problems in the compilation of "violent crime" statistics, let alone the manner in which they are retailed to the public. In fact, violent crime statistics, seemingly so scientific and precise, are (as every criminologist knows) nothing of the kind; they are merely indications of increased willingness of the public to report offences, of decreased levels of public tolerance of violence, and increased levels of police surveillance. Similarly escaping public understanding is the fact that the *only* reliably reported violent crime is the exceedingly rare offence of homicide – it is difficult to hide a person or a body forever; while it seems simple for a woman to be convinced that an assault upon her person was somehow her fault, and should not be reported. Still, the whole people seem demoralized: an essay in the *Los Angeles Times* notes "a pervasive sense of social and political malaise" in Britain, a loss of pride, a common desire to escape through emigration.

THE ABYSS OPENS

> I believe human nature spurts out freaks. These two were freaks who just found each other. They were evil. (Sergeant Phil Roberts, interviewing officer, Bulger case[3])

The videotape from the shopping precinct as James Bulger is dragged past the camera is beamed around the world: everyone on the planet watches, transfixed. In Hong Kong and New York, London and Moscow, we watch the boy being escorted to his doom. The images are endlessly replayed. Each time we see them we are surprised we are not desensitized to what is to come: and the panic returns. With each repetition, we cannot help ourselves from hoping "this time someone will see what is happening, this time someone will intervene." But no one does. Each time, the Bulger boy walks again trustingly to his brutal death.

No one can say what reservoir of feeling James Bulger's murder touched. The videotape of the boy's last moments will haunt our memories for years because it testifies for the unthinkable: a child is to be murdered by two other children. "Among the images," *The Times* records, "was a freeze frame of the toddler and his mother making their way to the butcher's shop the last time they were to walk together. A minute later, at 3:38 P.M. on February 12, James is picked out by the camera standing on his own. A little over a minute elapses and Denise Bulger, his mother, is seen searching for him." Then we see James leaving the shopping centre in the company of the two young assassins. Just five minutes have elapsed. When children are both victim *and* perpetrator, the world is challenged. The images appear to announce the collapse of civilization, the murder of all understanding. People speak of "guilt," of "responsibility," of an inability to comprehend; but they feel they have witnessed a turning point, as brutal and obvious as an invasion.[4]

Yet there was nothing particularly new in this atrocity, and this was not the first time one child had murdered another. A brief article in *The Times* summarized the most notorious cases: in 1968, in Newcastle upon Tyne, in the company of a thirteen-year-old friend, eleven-year-old Mary Bell strangled four-year-old Martin Brown and three-year-old Brian Howe. They seem to have murdered "solely for the pleasure and excitement afforded by killing," as the prosecution charged. Five years later in Liverpool, two eleven-year-old boys murdered a two-year-old. The court was told that "one of the boys had accidentally hit the youngster on the head with a brick, panicked and drowned him." In 1988, in Hertfordshire, a thirteen-year-old boy suffocated two-year-old Sharona Joseph and "dumped her abused body by a railway line," near where he lived in a "den." The boy, "described in court as a 'sharp, streetwise teenager with a background of social problems,' had absconded from care when aged 12." But this time it seemed especially savage and meaningless, symptomatic of some deep sickness in the nation. The problem was even worse in America: the FBI Academy told *The Times* that in 1992, American children nine and younger committed four murders while children aged between ten and twelve committed thirty. Those under ten were also responsible for 1,104 aggravated assaults, 291 robberies and 123 rapes.[5]

In England, however, the Home Office notes "very little" change in the number of juveniles convicted of murder and manslaughter: few seem able to believe it. Perhaps they do not wish to do so?[6]

On the last day of James Bulger's life, he had accompanied his mother and aunt to the Strand shopping precinct in Bootle. According to *The Times*, James had been "in high spirits": "in one shop, a baby suit fell on his head and he started throwing it around; in Tesco he helped himself to some Smarties." In the meantime, his assassins pursued their own form of lightheartedness: according to *The Times* their destructive activities had first attracted attention at 9:45 A.M., but it was not till midday that "they tried to abduct another little boy," an attempt that "was thwarted when the child's mother saw one of the boys beckoning to her two-year-old son." They left the precinct for an hour, and when they returned "they were seen shouting, laughing and acting stupidly," the prosecution said. Their antics so annoyed a woman stall-holder that "she swung at them" with her bag.[7]

TABLE 3 Juveniles convicted of homicide in England and Wales, 1982–1990.

	Aged 10–13			Aged 14–16			Total		
	Male	Fem	Total	Male	Fem	Total	Male	Fem	Total
1982	0	0	0	25	2	27	25	2	27
1983	1	0	1	21	3	24	22	3	25
1984	0	0	0	19	2	21	19	2	21
1985	2	0	2	12	1	20	21	1	22
1986	2	0	2	25	2	27	27	2	29
1987	0	0	0	18	3	21	18	3	21
1988	2	0	2	17	1	18	19	1	20
1989	1	0	1	22	1	23	23	1	24
1990	1	0	1	22	0	22	23	0	23

Source: Home Office. Based on offences first recorded during each year rather than on court proceedings.

At 3:40 P.M., James Bulger went missing. During his two-and-a-half-mile Calvary to Walton village, he was sighted by twenty-seven different people who saw him being abused, struck, kicked or apparently enjoying himself. But each witness, the prosecution told the jury, "appeared to have taken the same view: the little child must have been with an older brother." One woman, The Times recorded, saw bumps on James' head and demanded to know why he was crying. One of the kidnappers told her "they had just found him at the bottom of the embankment," and would take him to the police.[8]

Speaking for the prosecution, Mr. Henriques outlined James' final torment on the infamous railway line, some time around 6 P.M. Heavy stone and metal objects were thrown at him, "and death resulted, in the pathologist's words, from multiple (at least 30) blunt force injuries to the head." His attackers placed his body on the railway track, where it was later mutilated by a train: it lay there undiscovered for two days. A thorough police investigation and forensic evidence linked Jon Venables and Robert Thompson to the murder: the blood on one of the assassin's shoes was matched with James', and "a pattern of bruising on the two-year-old boy's face closely matched features on the bloodstained shoe of the other boy."[9]

The police conducted nineteen separate interviews with the assassins.

At first they were evasive, *The Times* reported, but they soon began to implicate each other. After five police interviews, Venables confessed that he had killed James; and Thompson capitulated during his sixth police interview, after "his mother told him, 'It will all be over in a few minutes if you just tell them the truth.'" At this, Thompson said, "Venables threw a brick in his face. I don't know [why]. And then he just fell on the floor. He was on the floor crying." Thompson blamed Venables for the abduction, and claimed that it had been Venables who threw the bricks at James and struck him with a metal bar: "'I asked him [Venables] why he did it, and he said because he felt like it.'" Asked why he had not at least pushed James' body away from the railway tracks, he replied with the remark that would become internationally infamous: "*Blood stains, don't it*, and then my mother would have to pay."

For his part, Venables implicated Thompson: "We took him [James] to the railway and started throwing bricks at him. A big steel pole knocked him out. We left him lying on the track on the rails. Thompson threw paint in his face, blue modelling paint, then a brick into his face. He said, 'Pick it up and throw it,' and I just threw it on the floor. I picked up little stones, because I would not throw a brick at him, but Thompson did. He [James] fell over and kept getting back up again. He would not stay down. I took some stones but I missed, not by mistake but deliberately." When asked if either of them had kicked James, Venables exonerated himself once more: "Yeah, me. But only light. And I punched him light." After Venables made his admission, the court was later told, his mother spoke harshly to him for lying to the police, then embraced him. As he sobbed, he asked, "What about his Mum? Will you tell her I am sorry?" Later, he claimed to be haunted by his memories: "Terrible. I'm always thinking about it. All the time. I didn't really want to kill him. I didn't want to hurt him. I thought Thompson was doing it for fun or something because he was laughing his head off. He was grinning."[10]

Who were these infant assassins? Their behaviour in court seemed astonishingly unremorseful. When they first appeared in the magistrate's court in Bootle, with a baying crowd outside, the *Guardian* noted that "each boy spoke only to confirm his name and age. Neither showed any sign of nervousness. One yawned and stretched and kept turning his head to look at his co-defendant. The other leaned forward, chin on hand, looking intently at his solicitor." The parents of Jon Venables were in court for the trial, sitting beside the dock containing their son. *The Times* noticed that "they did not even look at him, nor he at them," and as the trial progressed, Venables and Thompson "began occasionally to fidget, squirm and stare at the ceiling." Psychiatrists who had examined them told the court "that both boys knew right from wrong"; and this judgement was confirmed by the head teacher at their school, who said, "They would have known that it was wrong to take a child from its mother and to strike a young child with a brick."[11]

Thompson's mother did not appear in court till the trial was well under way, and at first she maintained her son was innocent. "They are all saying he told lies from beginning to end. Yes, he did tell some lies, but he also told the truth about one thing from beginning to end. He did not kill that baby. I honestly do believe him." As for the Bulgers, she told *The Times*, "I couldn't even begin to say I'm sorry for what's happened. There's nothing you can say to that family." Asked why her son had refused to discuss the killing, she said, "Well, if you had just seen somebody slit somebody's head in, what kind of state would you be in?" She said she had not explored how her son was now feeling: "I will take it step by step and we'll get to the truth." When asked what might happen to her son, she replied bitterly, "It's obvious. He's a little liar, he's devious, he's a scally, he robs, he plays truant . . . [but] he's not a murderer." But when she was asked how she thought her son's night-mare might end, she said, "In a coffin."[12]

Demonstrating both a flair for deflecting responsibility and a quite remarkable self-absorption, Mrs. Thompson complained, "They always blame the parents. It's a difficult situation, when you face the world alone, the same as I'm doing now. We look over our shoulders. I have got one son left. He can't go to school. I am not sending my kids to school for another one to end up in prison." When it was suggested her son might have been sexually abused, she replied, "I was waiting for that to come out. I have asked for a doctor to get my son examined, because I know I have not sex-ually abused him in any way. I want help. If they don't give me help, I'll show my face on TV and cry for help. They don't understand how I feel." She said her son had begun playing truant the previous year "when Jon Venables came on to the scene. He played truant because he didn't like the head-mistress. There was victimization. My cry is, 'Why didn't the headmistress get on the phone and phone social services or the police? She failed to do her job properly.'"

Artlessly, she then told us how she had unconsciously *taught* her son to behave. His cheekiness after the murder, she thought, was admirable: "I think that's part of me coming out in him. *I liked the way he talked to the police*, but they were putting a thing to him that he definitely saw something, then they'd say, 'But we think . . .' and he'd reply, 'What, you only *think*?'" Mrs. Thompson said her family was always reviled by their neighbours. "Name one family in the area who would have a good word for us. If things went missing from washing lines, people would say, 'It's the Thompsons.' I am not saying they are innocent, but they got blamed for things they did not do." Asked why her son had been involved at all in the abduction, she said, "I don't know why he was with that baby from the beginning. I want to find out. What I really think is, he's frightened of Jon Venables. And he won't admit it, because he actually said downstairs [in court] the other day, 'I feel like crying when I'm upstairs.' I said, 'Well, why don't you?' He said, 'Because all those people are looking and they would call me a baby.' The attitude when you live around Walton is, you have to be tough or else you don't survive."[13]

The Bulger family had insulated James' mother from the most painful evidence, but she chose to attend the last day of the trial. The judge reminded the jury that psychiatric examinations of the boys had revealed no sign of mental abnormality: upon hearing the jury's guilty verdict, he ordered that Thompson and Venables be institutionalized for "very, very many years until the Home Secretary is satisfied you have matured and are fully rehabilitated, and until you are no longer a danger to others." Detective Superintendent Albert Kirby, who had led the investigation, reminded us that the convicted killers were not only "wicked beyond anyone's expectations," but "had a high degree of cunning and evil" and seemed trained to the task of manipulating the police during their interrogations: "They could foresee the questions to be put to them and could counter the evidence which was to be put to them."[14]

How do we begin to understand such a crime? An insightful profile on the assassins in *The Times* noted that Thompson, whose father had abandoned the family when Robert was six, was the fifth son, and "was often bullied by his older brothers." Mrs. Thompson, an unemployed office cleaner, had "a reputation as a troublemaker." "Robert began to pass on to other children the family habit of bullying and some mothers began trying to keep their youngsters away from him," and Mrs. Thompson frequently asked police officers to give her children "a good telling off." Ultimately, all of her children were put in the care of the Liverpool Social Services department. More often than not, Robert played truant at school. A source told the newspaper that Robert "has convinced himself that he played no part in the killing. He will talk quite easily about it all. Sometimes he does cry but there is no remorse because he doesn't accept he has done anything he has to be sorry for." The source added that the two boys had earlier bragged to classmates that "we're going to kill someone."

Jon Venables' parents had been divorced, but the father had not abandoned the family, and regularly spent weekends with his son. Mrs. Venables described her son as "one of those children who if you told him to put his hand in the fire he would. He didn't want to hurt him [James Bulger] but he was weak and he was provoked." "Provoked?" In any case, the court and public constructed Venables' personality as the weaker of the two, led into his crime. Nevertheless, his history suggests an independent development of aggressive behaviour, and "he is remembered at junior school as unruly and disruptive," with bizarre and violent outbursts: once he "grabbed another boy from behind and held a ruler against his throat. It took two women to break his grip." When he moved to Thompson's school in 1992, the pair became instant friends, and often played truant together. His solicitor told *The Times* that Jon "does express remorse to his mother. He has told me he wishes he could put the clock back. He has nightmares and flashbacks to the incident. When we get to the stage of who did what, he clams up. When we started he had a mental block, with uncontrollable tears every time something was mentioned. We still haven't got a full story of what happened on the railway line, and will never get from him the truth of who did what." Mrs. Venables rejected suggestions that she and her husband had been poor parents: "He has had a lot more love and attention than a lot of children I know. He has been educated."[15]

At the funeral of James Bulger, the biblical text selected to be read by Detective Superintendent Albert Kirby was from the Book of Revelations:

> And God shall wipe away all tears from their eyes; and there shall be no more death, neither sorrow, nor crying, neither shall there be any more pain: for the former things are passed away.

Alas, it is not true. The only real consolation can come from ensuring that there will be no more such abominations.

How can this madness have come to pass? Many offer explanations and cures. In the *Guardian*, a column summarized the leftist view: "There are three million people out of work," and:

> you cannot divorce these events from their social context. A society which offers no more than a future of unredeemed aimlessness; a society which is taught to venerate greed, as this society was during the Thatcher years; a society where violence is glamorized (see any local cinema or video shop); a society, above all, where people come to believe "that there's no such thing as society" – here, surely, is a machine designed to deliver exactly what we are getting.

The home secretary retailed the conservative view, vowing to deal with "nasty, persistent juvenile little offenders" and accusing social workers of failing children. He accepted that young people had suffered a "loss of purpose and a loss of values." The prime minister called for "a crusade against crime, and change from being forgiving of crime to being considerate to the victim. Society needs to condemn a little more and," he added curiously, "understand a little less." While political left and right assaulted each other with characteristic disregard for accuracy, the reality appears to be that both sides understood a portion of the truth, and shared in the responsibility.[16]

Yet we should not comfort ourselves with the delusion that this is an entirely foreign experience. In a shattering reminder of our shared humanity, Andrew O'Hagan described the violence in his own British childhood,

of how things might "get out of hand," how what might begin "as a game of
rounders or crazy golf would end up as a game of clubbing the neighbour's
cat to death," how "now and again people would get into things that you
sensed were about to go over the edge, or were already over it." He recalled
one boy he and his friends had bullied unmercifully, beating him "whenever we thought he'd 'been bad,'" till one day things got out of hand and
they beat him savagely, "practically skinning the screaming boy's legs." The
only reactions that mattered were those of his friends, and "there were
times when I'm sure we could've led each other into just about anything."
Still, he notes, "*Some of us knew how to stop it*, though, while others just kept
it up. A couple of my boyhood friends assiduously built bridges between
their mindless, childish venom – their bad-boyish misdemeanours – and
adult crime." Why did "some of us" know how to stop it, and others not?[17]

Some of us neither know how to stop nor appear to care. Does this
mean the nation has gone mad? Are there more insane and murderous
people on the streets than ever before? For some, the arrests of Frederick
and Rosemary West of Gloucester, implicated in the death and burial of at
least a dozen women, seemed to confirm this judgement. But if we return
our attention to statistical reality, only a tiny and unchanging percentage of
homicides can be understood as the result of actual madness. Truly
"insane" murderers are relatively rare everywhere, in terms either of hallu-
cinatory derangement and dissociation from the conventional world or of
legal or psychiatric technicalities. English police categorize as "mental" only
an average of 6 per cent of killers; and these cases have special qualities.[18]

BECAUSE OF INCEST AND ALL THAT

In a bizarre explosion of deranged sexuality and rage, Anthony Anderson
murdered his grandfather, his grandfather's common-law wife and two
male neighbours. Anderson's subsequent babbling to the police is that of a
lunatic, but the insane have no copyright on foolish ideas and incoherent
means of expression. The police, not inexperienced in these matters,
thought he was merely a consummate liar, one who finally presented his
half-baked theories about "incest" and black magic first to mask, and then
to justify, his robberies and killings. Certainly he seemed like any vicious

and inadequate person who derived his sense of pleasure, identity and self-worth from frightening little girls or other defenceless persons, comforting himself with bogus delusions of revenge upon his imagined enemies. Insane or not, the important issue remains how relatively few insane English persons – in contrast, say, to their American counterparts – choose to kill, and how relatively personalized are their homicidal encounters – killing relatives and neighbours, rather than strangers.

During most of the extended police interrogations Anderson denied all charges, claiming that two other men (whom he named) were responsible for the killings. As he was led from the magistrate's court after a preliminary hearing, he shouted to the enraged crowd the single word, "Innocent!" It was necessary for him to do so, for in the behavioural lexicon of his society, what he had done could garner him nothing but public contempt. English culture accords no prestige to the perpetrators of such carnage, refuses them "permission" to paint themselves as righteous rebels against the establishment. Later, Anderson admitted his crimes, although he claimed no understanding of them, and he fumbled for an explanation in his idiot monologues to police, with ideas plucked from popular folklore – "because of the incest" that had occurred, years before his birth, between his mother and his grandfather.

The Offences

He was born in 1967 in a grimy northern industrial town, the son of Zoe Velt and Richard Anderson. In time, he would be the middle child, with two brothers and two sisters. In 1971, his mother left the matrimonial home, leaving her five children to be cared for by their father; but soon after, his father became depressed and was admitted to hospital, while all the children were taken into the care of the local authority. Anderson was described as disruptive, and he remained in care until he reached the age of sixteen. Official records show that he was employed by the National Association for the Care and Rehabilitation of Offenders from 1984 to 1985, and periodically by the local district council voluntary services agency. He also worked on a casual basis at a local scrap yard.

He first came to the notice of the police when he was seventeen: by the time he was twenty-one, he had many convictions for burglary, theft, deception, damage and arson, and he was renowned in his community for his compulsive lying. In July 1985, he was sentenced to thirty months in youth custody for aggravated burglary. When released in September 1986, he first went to live with his mother, who could tolerate him for only a few weeks. After that, he lived with his father in Granville Road, in a neighbourhood of council flats and bungalows housing young families and disabled pensioners. He was sentenced to a further six months in August 1987, and returned after that to his father's flat. His neighbours were Raymond Faversham and Marcus Lamont, whom he would soon murder. It was then that Anderson learned that his grandfather, Stasys Petrov (who had served a three-year prison term for committing incest with his daughter, Anderson's mother), lived nearby in Ruskin Avenue. A relationship began between them, but within a short time, Anderson (who frequently asserted that his grandfather was his father) was no longer welcome at his grandfather's house. Petrov warned his friends to be wary of him, and asked him to cease visiting the house, as Petrov's common-law wife, Elsa Konrad, was frightened of him.

After Anderson's most recent release from prison, when he was in his early twenties, police thought he earned a living from theft and casual employment. In any case, he did not claim state benefits for several months. It was entirely in keeping with his character that he might precede his homicidal explosion with a series of offences against property. In the early hours of Thursday, 25 August, he opened the unlocked door of one sleeping neighbour, forty-five-year-old alcoholic former schoolteacher, Raymond Faversham, who lived alone in a clutter of empty bottles in a council flat in Granville Road. Once inside the flat, Anderson seized the opportunity to steal a microwave oven and a clock. A few hours later, he approached a secondhand goods dealer and offered to sell the clock and oven. Late the following night, Friday, 26 August, he threw a dustbin through Mr. Faversham's front window.

At 8:50 A.M. on Saturday, 27 August, four police constables went to Anderson's address to speak to him about the thefts, but he refused to come to the door, forcing the police to break through a window to arrest him. Anderson admitted to them that the goods in question had once belonged to Mr. Faversham, but insisted that he had purchased the items and there-fore had every right to sell them. But in a second interview he admitted the theft: "Yes, I did it in the middle of the night," he told police. "Door were wide open so I went in for a look round. Just looked round. He were asleep on settee or bed, so I took this clock and microwave." Anderson was charged with burglary, theft and criminal damage, and released on bail. By this time he had already begun to kill, murdering four people in as many days: but he would have several days of freedom before the bodies were discovered.

In retrospect, police thought Anderson had "been building himself up to commit some major offence," first stealing property, then making wild accusations and frightening people, boasting of what he had done and would do. He took to donning a plastic devil mask – first welcoming a visitor to his flat, then retiring into the bedroom and jumping into the sitting room wearing the mask. Drinking at the Bull's Head, he boasted to a fellow drinker that he had killed two men at a night-club in Sheffield three weeks before. He told one acquaintance that his neighbours in Granville Road should be "shot like in Belfast," and promised another that he planned to blow up a petrol station. A week before the murders, local children had overheard Anderson threatening to kill Lamont. Lamont himself had an extensive criminal record, which ended abruptly in 1987 when a motorcycle accident fractured his skull and left him confined to a wheelchair.

After the first killings, as he left yet another pub, he shouted, "See you next Friday at two o'clock, if I don't get twenty-five years on Wednesday." In the Towers Hotel, Anderson spoke to acquaintances of killing two people and getting twenty-five years for murder, telling one woman, "I'll see you in twenty-five years' time as I've murdered two people." In a less than roman-tic overture, he told a woman friend, "I'll only stop here if I can go to bed with you, because I'm going to get twenty-five years for murder." After his preliminary arrest and questioning by police in the early hours of Saturday, 27 August, he drank all day at the Brown Bear public house with three male friends. As they made their way home that evening, he tried unsuccessfully to get them to throw a cast-iron gutter cover into Marcus Lamont's bunga-low. Obviously revelling in the fear his behaviour provoked, he asked one of his friends, "Have you heard about mad axeman in town? He's supposed to be coming this way!"

Police Crime Complaint: Monday, 29 August

Raymond FAVERSHAM: Deceased found in bedroom under pile of clothing naked apart from underpants which had been pulled down, repeatedly
stabbed by the use of two knives still inside. Bungalow heavily bloodstained. Body cool.

Marcus LAMONT: Deceased found bound in living room of bungalow
with multiple stab wounds and his crutch rammed into his body. Unlit cigarettes found in orifices and around body. Watch found thrown on roof,
keys from house found at rear of bungalow. Furniture and carpet heavily
bloodstained. Body extensively stabbed around head and upper body.

Many witnesses told police of the "bad blood" that had existed for some
time between Lamont and Anderson. Lamont's body was discovered by his
mother, who had unlocked the front door to find her savagely mutilated
son. He had been bound with his own clothing and had suffered seventy
stabbing and cutting wounds. His crutch had been rammed through the
flesh of his stomach, and his body had unlit cigarettes in its orifices. Part of
his internal organs were outside the body. The presence of condoms suggested the possibility of an additional, sexual, assault. A post-mortem
determined that Lamont died of shock and haemorrhage caused by multiple stab wounds.[19]

The second victim to be discovered, Raymond Faversham, had worked
as a schoolteacher in Africa until 1975, when it was found that he was
suffering from both epilepsy and malaria. Because of his illnesses, he was
unable to obtain a position in England, and by then he had developed a
severe alcohol dependence. After the deaths of his father and stepmother,
Faversham moved to the flat at Granville Road where he would meet his
death. During this period, he continued to drink heavily, and a crippling
arthritis in his hands, feet and hips left him with a pronounced limp.
Among his few habits were the daily reading of the *Guardian* and the com-
pletion of its crossword puzzle. In the last few weeks of his life, according to
witnesses, Faversham was to be "terrorized" by Anderson.

Faversham's council flat was renowned for its squalor, and he preferred
to spend his money on drink rather than other necessities. Police complained they "could hardly get into the lounge for bottles and newspapers."

When they entered the flat and passed through its bloodstained hallway, they could not even see the body, which was eventually found under a pile of old clothes. Faversham's body had been horribly mutilated. His body had suffered some 500 stab wounds, his intestines had been pulled out from his abdomen and spread over the bed, and as with Lamont's corpse, there was a suggestion of sexual assault. There was a knife in his back, and the post-mortem found yet another knife (the property of Anderson) buried in his body.[20]

The third victim, Elsa Konrad, had lived in Lithuania until the Second World War made her a refugee. She settled in West Yorkshire, and worked in the local mills; remaining there until 1966, when she met Stasys Petrov (Anderson's grandfather) and began to live with him as his common-law wife. Neighbours described her as a quiet and pleasant person who was dominated by her husband. Konrad's body was not discovered by detectives until Friday, 2 September, when they made a routine visit to ask Petrov for details about Anderson's behaviour. A police sergeant entered the house through an insecure bedroom window and found Konrad lying dead in the kitchen. The post-mortem examination determined that death had been caused by massive head wounds. The assault had taken place in the kitchen where Konrad had been ironing. A sheet had been spread over the upper body, partly hiding the murder weapon, an axe, the handle of which could be seen protruding from beneath the sheet. The bedrooms had been thoroughly ransacked, and Anderson's tie was found in the toilet bowl. A subsequent search of the house by Anderson's mother revealed that jewellery, watches and a flick knife were missing. Anderson's mother added that her father kept large sums of money in the house but none was found on a subsequent police search.[21]

The last victim to be discovered, Stasys Petrov, Anderson's grandfather, was born in Lithuania and lived there until the outbreak of the war. He arrived in Denmark in 1945, where he and his common-law wife had a daughter, Zoe (eventually to become the natural mother of the killer, Anthony Anderson). Shortly after Zoe's birth, Petrov left Denmark and settled in Yorkshire, where he was joined by his wife and child in 1949. His wife divorced him in 1961, when he was given a prison term for committing incest with his daughter, Zoe. He worked at a local coal mine until 1966, before moving to the local authority until his retirement in 1985. Neighbours described him as an active man who spent much of his time at his modest allotment, where he would meet his death. Police quickly found Petrov's body after they discovered the body of his wife. The door of the allotment shed was locked and had to be broken down, and there they found Petrov. He had been tightly gagged, and beaten to death with a sledgehammer. Death had been caused by massive head injuries: Anderson had earlier made comments to a number of people about how he had opened his grandfather's skull to find that brains looked like "baked beans."

The case against Anderson was obvious, linked by physical evidence and the fact that only he was connected to all the victims. But Anderson's performance was a masterpiece of orchestrated evasion, psychic fabrication and nonsense; and his interviews with the police dragged on for days.

The Interviews

On Monday, 29 August, before all the murders had been discovered, he poked his head through the inspection hatch of his cell and began a conversation that would be widely reported. He asked the supervisor, "How do you know there's only one [body], there may have been two or three? I'm psychic, when they find the other body in that area they'll know it wasn't me because I'm here." When asked for details of his movements on Sunday, 28 August, he placed a deck of cards on the table and, pointing to one card, said, "This is the master card." When asked what he meant by that remark, he replied, "This means you have four bodies and a madman on the loose." When the interrogating officer asked, "Is that four bodies altogether?" Anderson said, "You've found one, but there are three others." "Where are they?" "I can't see that. I can see Marcus [Lamont] but the others are indescribable. They are just too horrible to describe." Detectives broke into thirteen houses before they found the remaining bodies.

During the interviews that followed, his answers rarely bore any relationship to the question asked. When the officer said, "I propose to question you regarding your friendship with Marcus Lamont," Anderson replied, apropos of nothing, "Yes, I want something to eat." When asked if he knew a witness named Gary, he first denied knowing him, then said, "I saw this woman. I've forgot her name but she lives opposite Gary further down the path. I said to the woman, have you heard the news about Marcus? She said she had already heard. I was swearing a bit and her mother told me off about my language." He then insisted that "a little girl between four and five years old" had told him about Marcus' death – "She said, 'Marcus has done himself in.' I knocked on Angie's door on Granville Road. She was in. This woman popped her head round the corner and told us that Marcus had been found strung up, she said he had been tied up in his house, 'suspicious circumstances.'" There followed hard upon this hours of lies, denials and evasions until he was returned to his cell. Now he began to refuse all food, as some form of protest, against what it was not clear.

Later, the detective asked how he knew there were three more bodies. Anderson insisted his special psychic powers had enabled him to determine this. "I come in the door, I had some supreme adrenalin and I picked up the cards and without looking at the cards whilst the officers were present I dealt them out. I put both of my hands on the table first before I dealt the cards. I took a card from the middle, I mean I split the pack, I opened them up to the dark side. The officer Humphries took the card, and it was the '4.' I told him that there was four bodies, including Marcus, and there is three others already out there because it says it in the cards. People say when you die you see your past shoot in front of you: when I tamper into the unknown I go forward and meet up with the beginning of the black purple. If these officers would come in and write in their own signatures underneath what I have said, it is the truth."

"Why don't you think about the people you have killed?" the frustrated detective asked. "Prove it," shouted an enraged Anderson. "Prove it! I deny it were me. Because you know fuck all about black magic! It says it in the cards. You're supposed to be the best police officers. Find them. Would I help you find them? Help me find my own destiny!"

Then he blamed his victims: "Mark and Sid Lamont come to my flat Friday night, and Mark shoved me against the boiler in the passage, got me down on floor. Sid says, 'I know you know 'bout it 'cos we've seen you go back in.' Mark says, 'No matter what you fink, you'll get dragged in down with us if you grass us up.' I says, 'I'm going to grass you up as soon as you get off me.' Sid said that if I grassed 'em up, then I'd get the same as what my family got. Mark put his hands behind his back and whipped out some kind of an army knife. I tried going for knife, and he cut me finger. Mark was saying, 'Shall we do him?' and Sid said, 'No.' They were just telling me what they were going to do, and they said that 'if you reported it, the police would think it was you.' They just convinced me that I was in with 'em. I knew what I was going to do to Sid and Mark. I was going to kill them because I was going to get dragged down to nick for something I never did. All they told me was they'd done me family. They showed me some items, and they must have pinned them on me when I was drinking. I thought, 'It's not *every* day that you get a nice watch, a gold ring, a nice pocket watch.'"

At this point the interview was broken off. It resumed again that same evening this time with Anderson's mother, Zoe, in attendance. "I can't really remember much," he told the detective. "Mind keeps switching off and on, I reckon it's got summat to do with seeing a body. The first body in my life. All I saw was a great big lump. The feet were up in the air and I just shot out faster than I've ever done in my life. And I ran straight into Sid, in front of me. As I run he shoved me shoulder up against the wall. The officers present, and my mother, everything I say is the truth, and if my mother believes me or not, or some of you officers do, so I say to you, prove it, any evidence you have got if you think that I killed them. Myself personally, I am sane. Any other questions, officer?" Anderson then refused to reply to a long list of personal questions, finally bursting out with, "There's a lot of personal questions in these forms what mean so much to me. It's not every day that my brother shags Margaret Thatcher. If you want to know why I aren't talking now, I'm talking about a personal matter what I keep between my family. No more questions." Despite this newfound sense of delicacy, he bragged endlessly to his jailers about his sexual prowess.

Later he tried a new approach, casting his grandfather in the role of Cause and his mother as Executioner. "Me Grandad told me he was my father. He raped me mother. She's only after that £3,000 [of grandfather's money]. I'm gonna tell the truth, I witnessed her do two murders, and I did the other two. Me Mam killed Marcus. She stabbed him in neck: it didn't go right through, it went down. I said to him, 'Feel your neck, you daft cunt, you're not bleeding, you're not going to die.' I want to tell you my lifetime story first, and I'll have sommat to eat. Remember me to tell you about jumping through Faversham's window in a crash helmet. Have you been to the scene? You'd probably faint, a sledgehammer through your skull. I've killed a man who shagged my mother and is my father. I suppose I do love me Grandad. It's not every day that you find out he's your third generation. My Grandad is my third generation and my Grandma isn't because there was a documentary on TV about it. That's why I love my Grandad, for trying so hard – in keeping the generation going. Reasons why I answer some questions, there's somewhere in my heart when somebody talks about my family. It makes me start to concern and sometimes I like to talk about them. It makes you feel a lot better I think. That's all I have to say. No further questions."

Not long afterwards, Anderson began an explication of his own insanity: "It's a word for somebody like me is not too sure about one's self, and I know it's personality disorderment or summat. I have [had it] for a long time through my life and I smile for no reason, and I've had that whilst I have been in prison. I never had it before. With the supreme knowledge of Anthony Paul Anderson, the reason is telepathic, it whizzes through my head, through all the doubts, through all the bad things and I might not have no memory, it goes the speed of light, half of me is all done in, and somewhere it still allows me to get through the worstest things I've gone through and I know it could switch off any time and leave myself like a cabbage. I never went to school, I never could read or write, I never had no knowledge, always on the wrong side of the law; and this knowledge has come telepathic fast. My mother said to me, 'You nearly were off your head' and I said, 'it would be wonderful that I ant.' There were one time when I was living with me mother I was scared of me own shadow. They had to keep giving me drugs to keep me going."

The detective interrupted Anderson with the sceptical comment, "You can talk as much rubbish as you like. I know how clever you have been in planning what you've done, but are pretending to be stupid." This annoyed Anderson, who demanded, "Why don't you show me your identification in being psychiatrist or a doctor?" "You don't need medical qualifications to recognize a liar," the officer answered. "That's what you are. I can prove and have proved you're telling lies. Not only that, your reputation where you live is one of persistently telling lies. That's what you're famous for, isn't it?

That's your only claim to fame. As soon as you are faced with the truth, you haven't the courage to face it, have you?"

This launched Anderson into an extended monologue. "This is reality and my nickname comes and goes like day and night. You follow your destiny and I'll follow mine, all the way to the light, and we'll see who creases up the first. You will never know from me if I'm guilty or not guilty because the only judge in the world is God. Why should I kill somebody when I can kill myself like I am now, I'm going into my fourth day without no food. We're not talking about ten years or forty years or seventy years or a hundred. We're talking about eternity for something I never did. And innocent people also have died through prison, on the streets, and they're dying every day and there's nothing you can do about it. Personally, people go to prison for something they never did and they get life and you get a big laugh out of it and when somebody has dealings in it they get to find out they're innocent and that's why the home department, the Home Office, have always got something in common. Where's the money coming from? It's going to come from your pocket, one way or the other. Who knows who's done it, but if I take the rap I'm going to die and they're going to live and when you talk about fantasies you never become a judge.

"Inspector, I am on a death-bed. The reasons why, it is to prove to anybody or to the world or to God, even the devil himself, to show the truth and the understanding through the truth and the truth through the under-standing that's why I am innocent. And there is a lot of things been done and said regards the forms and other people's innocence who have got life for something they haven't done and because I'm innocent and through my death and while I'm going through it I want them to bring back the hanging. People want it and I want it and this is a protest with the help of the people and politics in the House of Commons and I know certain police officers would like to see them hang. I should say there is nothing else you could use to give them a slowing dying death because imagine three days or three hours or three minutes and then walk in down with the hood on your head. That's the biggest death, horriblest way a murderer can die, then they'd be far less murders and I know I am the first person in history to go through and to do so and to talk about this way and if they fetch back the hanging and I know she won't because it is like this. When you want a police officer he's never there when you're poor, or when you're poor and you don't want one you get one. The rich person always gets a police officer because they're always sat outside your door. I fink it's about time you had a little chat with somebody new like myself because putting people in prison you are losing out and when poor people haven't got it or the rich people have got it they won't give you nowt, so I think isn't it about time you opened your eyes to the bright light like myself.

"I heil Hitler. Hitler was a Catholic and so am I and it'll be two against one and I will look for you throughout history and when I get you, me and Hitler will go through you like fifty million billion hells and balls and it will be a wet stormy night so if you're not going to do it for the people who're innocent, what about the people who murder people and who get their own colour TV set, carpet, bed and the luxury, and why should they help to donate funds to people whom they've done away with, and I think it is said in the Bible you are not a woman and you are not a man, you are a black falling empty unfamous star. Yes, I have been famous because I have been on Concord when I was sixteen with an intermediate treatment called Dr. Barnardo's Intermediate Treatment and the judge sentenced me to something where I could have the biggest wide laugh of all just for burglaries.

"Why live to see your kids grow up in a world of rebels? There's no way that I could live under the authority of the government any longer, because I have been under the authority since I was four to twenty-one in different mediums, and the rest in and out of prison, and what's left out of them words an been wi' me family. I suppose somebody does love yer, who is it, the government or you family? The bit of freedom I got I'd rather die for. I was born like writing a blank cheque what bounces from every doorstep, and I think whatever controls me to live on like I do, I should have been dead a long time ago."

Late in the evening of Wednesday, 7 September, after an entire day of babbling in which he first claimed he had killed not four, but six people, Anderson finally told the truth. He then led police to where he had hidden the knives, claiming, "I'm going to get it all sorted out today. You see that bungalow, number two, the two knives are in the roof gutter at the back, there's a big one and small one." Seated in the police vehicle once more, revelling in his power, he suddenly shouted, "Faversham fucking shit himself, you knows. When I jumped through the fucking window with that mask. Devil's mask, ain't you fucking found that either."

In Court

From the moment he was imprisoned, the local newspaper chronicled his increasingly bizarre behaviour. The story in one edition, accompanied by a photograph of Anderson shouting at surrounding police and onlookers, showed the reporter's fascination with Anderson's performance: "Asked if he understood the new charges he replied, 'I might do.'" As Anderson was driven off in a white police van, there were only a few shouts of "Murderer" and "string him up." Anderson responded in kind, shouting, "Bastards, bastards, bastards."

One month later, the newspaper reported, Anderson informed the court that he was losing his mind: "I am going off my head bit by bit now. Five days in a strip cell, four days on a concrete floor without a blanket. I am coming up here and forgetting who I am. I keep talking to myself and hearing voices. If I go off my head and don't know who I am you can't get any more information out of me." The reporter added that Anderson "asked if he could appear at his next court hearing because then he would know who he was."

After the trial, given fifteen minutes to speak before he would be sentenced, Anderson said, "I liked sweets. I started taking things from a young age. I was born into a world a dream that was to be free and well in a world of love. I've killed a man who shagged my mother, who is my father." Anderson concluded with a comment on the murder of Mr. Faversham: "I've not killed him because I wanted to kill him. I just did it. I don't know what came over me. Maybe my Grandad, because of incest and all that. I know what I'm expecting. I'm not saying it to make it any better. I'm just explaining. I've had something out of life. I do a bit of poetry. If you put me away in prison or hospital I'll put that out and see if anybody reads my book. I want to write a book about my life and how I've been tret."

Resolution

It is impossible for us ever to perceive true cause in this case, to state with any certainty whether his killings were merely a consequence of the very practical greed of a disordered, unintelligent and resourceless young man (with adolescent fantasies of illusory power through black magic), indifferent to himself and to the well-being of all those around him – to claim the rumoured £3,000 in cash in his grandfather's home, and the jewellery and cash he took from his other victims, while wreaking vengeance for real or imagined slights. Clearly this is what the police believed. They may well have been correct. Perhaps the killings really were the result of his morbid brooding over the possibility that his grandfather was also his father, and the desire for revenge that might have generated. Perhaps – as three psychiatrists plausibly thought – he was merely acting out a mental disorder.

In any case, Anderson was found guilty at Sheffield Crown Court on three charges of murder and sentenced to three terms of life imprisonment, with the stipulation that he serve a minimum of twenty-five years. Soon after, he was transferred to a mental hospital, where he will almost certainly spend the remainder of his life.

---

1   *Times Annual Index*, 1990, p. 722.
2   Jan. 5, 1993.
3   Quoted in *Time* magazine, Dec. 6, 1993, p. 14.
4   *The Times*, Nov. 4, 1993, p. 3.
5   Alice Miller's 1990 book, *For Your Own Good: Hidden Cruelty in Child-rearing and the Roots of Violence*, third edition, New York: Farrar, Straus & Giroux, pp. 229–231, refers to an article by Paul Moor in a 1979 issue of *Die Zeit* which described the relationship between Bell and her mother, a prostitute specializing in sadomasochistic practices, who took pride in the delicacy that she always kept her whips "hidden from the children": "On May 26, 1957, seventeen-year-old Betty McC. gave birth to Mary at Gateshead. 'Get that thing away from me,' Betty is said to have cried, and she recoiled when the baby was put in her arms a few minutes after birth. . . . In school Mary was a troublemaker. For years she hit, kicked, and scratched other children. She would wring the necks of pigeons, and once she pushed her little cousin from the top of an air-raid shelter onto the concrete eight feet below. The following day she tried to choke three little girls on a playground. At the age of nine she started at a new school; two of her teachers there later stated:

'It's better not to delve too deeply into her life and circumstances.' Later a police-woman who got to know Mary during her pretrial custody gave the following account of finding Mary choking a cat: 'I realized that she was holding the cat so tightly that the animal couldn't breathe and its tongue was hanging out. I ran over and pulled her hands away. I said, "You mustn't do that, you're hurting it." She answered, "Oh, it doesn't feel anything, and anyway I like to hurt little things that can't defend themselves."' Mary told another policewoman that she would like to be a nurse – 'because then I could stick needles into people. I like to hurt people.'" See *The Times*, Nov. 25, 1993, p. 3; and Nov. 26, 1993, p. 18.

6   P. H. White, Home Office statistician, personal communication, March 8, 1993.

7   *The Times*, Nov. 2, 1993, pp. 1, 3.

8   *The Times*, Nov. 29, 1993, p. 3.

9   *The Times*, Nov. 2, 1993, p. 1; Nov. 10, 1993, p. 3; Nov. 11, 1993, p. 5.

10 *The Times*, Nov. 3, 1993, p. 3; Nov. 13, 1993, p. 3; Nov. 17, 1993, p. 4; Nov. 28, 1993, p. 10.

11 *Guardian Weekly*, Feb. 28, 1994, p. 3; *The Times*, Nov. 3, 1993, p. 3; Nov. 12, 1993, p. 3.

12 *The Times*, Nov. 25, 1993, p. 2.

13 *The Times*, Nov. 25, 1993, p. 3. Later that same year I was reminded of Mrs. Thompson's parental style: in St. John's, a woman brought her unaccountably vicious Labrador to an obedience school for dogs. The instructor was puzzled at first, since Labradors are not usually a troublesome breed, but then he watched the woman sneak treats to the dog each time it growled savagely at her. When he asked why she was rewarding the dog for its misbehaviour instead of disciplining it, she replied, "Oh, I couldn't punish the dog: it would bite me if I tried."

14 *The Times*, Nov. 24, 1993, p. 3; Nov. 25, 1993, p. 1.

15 *The Times*, Nov. 25, 1993, p. 3.

16 *Guardian Weekly*, Feb. 28, 1993, pp. 7, 3.

17 *London Review of Books*, March 11, 1993, p. 21.

18 As opposed to claims, concocted largely by defence lawyers in America, that their clients suffer from a wide range of alleged mental disorders – sparked, for example, by eating too much sugar, watching too much television, or being temporarily taken over by their "dinosaur brains." In fact, psychosis is rare in homicides every-where: Kenneth J. Levi, "Icemen: Detroit Killers in a Conflict Model," PhD disser-tation, University of Michigan: Ann Arbor, 1975, p. 4, quotes a 4 per cent psychosis rate for U.S. homicides in 1973.

19 As the forensic pathologist wrote: "I am habitually extremely cautious about deducing the state of mind of an assailant from the wounds he has inflicted on his victim, but in this case the ferocity of the attack upon a disabled person ... strongly indicate that Lamont's assailant was at any rate temporarily mentally deranged."

20 The forensic pathologist wrote: "In almost 30 years of murder investigation, I cannot ever recall seeing more wounds inflicted on one person by another."

21 The forensic pathologist concluded: "... this woman had been battered to death with the hand axe in the kitchen."

FEARS AND ALARUMS

TWO TYPES OF HOMICIDE seem especially to frighten the public – spouse killings and sexual murder. The fear is orchestrated both by legitimate concerns and by a variety of professional, political and ideological groups. Yet it is only the former, spousal homicide, that is anything other than a bizarre and infrequent tragedy: killings in the course of sexual assaults are only a small fraction of homicides. In reality, as everywhere, the only *common* violence in England is family violence, that physical assault which is endured behind closed doors, too often protected by the secrecy of the family: as demeaning and unacceptable as such assaults may be, they rarely result in death. An average of 127 spouses and lovers are murdered each year in England, most of them women. These constitute perhaps half of all homicides against women – who are rarely killed by strangers, since homicide remains "a crime involving the passions and mental disorders of offenders who are closely connected to their victims by family or other similar ties."[1]

ABUSIVE HUSBANDS – "I COULDN'T STAND IT FOR HER TO BE HAPPY": ALAN NORMAN MURDERS HIS WIFE IN THE WOMEN'S REFUGE

In the illusory sanctuary of a women's refuge in a northern industrial city, Patricia Norman began to catalogue her suffering during her twenty-year marriage. The thirty-eight-year-old grandmother had finally found the strength to break away from her abusive husband and their degrading union. Seated at the refuge's kitchen table, she took the staff's suggestion and inscribed in her uncertain hand the assaults upon her soul.

Mental cruelty

Sexual arrisment

Dident have any privacy. Couldnt take a bath without being interrupted.

Couldn't have any mony for my self.

Worked 10–12 hour a day 7 days a week.

Shown up all the time in front of his friends.

I couldent have any friends.

Wouldent let me visit my sister or mother.

Wouldent let me go out, only could go out with him (dident go out drinkin', just visiting his friends).

If he did go out for any reason, such as fishing haveing a hour with is friend when he came home he accused me of having men in the house and going to bed withe them.

Didn't dare bye any new underwear. If I did he would say who you bought them for

He checked my underwear for any stains. I had to keep checked my underwear myself for stain, If there was any I had to try and clean it of with toilet paper before he seen it, dident dare change them because he checked to see what I put on in a morning.

As her Biro traced each word on the cheap lined notebook, she could not have known that her sister (who was having an affair with her husband) would betray the refuge's telephone number, that her husband's friend with connections in the telephone company would then trace the address of the refuge, and that her forty-two-year-old husband, Alan, would find the refuge and crash through a window wielding a knife. As she composed her autobiography, she could not have known that she had only a few days to live.

Yet if the husband's frenzied attack was vicious, he still followed the violence-denigrating script of his culture, and seemed overwhelmed with incomprehension, grief, surprise and remorse for what he had done. As if to prove this, in the distinctively English manner of so many killers who commit suicide after their murders, he made a fumbled attempt to do away with himself, slashing his wrist in what the examining physician called a "serious" but "not fatal" injury – a deep wound that split one of the tendons but failed to find an artery. He was disappointed in the hospital's swift response: "I didn't want 'em to save me life. I wanted to die. I still want to die."

The Murder

The Normans were the joint owners of the Pennines Fish Bar, a shop with a good trade that was nevertheless in severe financial difficulties. They lived in a council house which they were in the process of buying, and they had borrowed additional money to purchase the fish and chip shop. Financially pressured by the two loans, the Normans considered moving into the flat above the Fish Bar, but the cost of refurbishing it made such a loan unacceptable to the bank. Problems began to accumulate by that autumn, the bank manager noted: "some cheques were returned unpaid and difficulties emerged in particular in connection with meeting the VAT bills due." Norman, able neither to read nor to write, tried to cope with this pressure on his account by asking for further financing, which the bank refused. In fact, the bank suggested the business be sold, advice which the Normans – who were confident that the business could survive – refused. Ultimately the business was forced on the market in the summer of 1991; but no one offered to purchase it. At the time that Patricia Norman left her home in October, the couple owed £114,575.81.

Alan Norman, who like most of our killers had several previous convictions for various offences, had made his marriage so unpleasant that Patricia had told her family she was "up to her limit" with him. Ultimately, she abruptly left her home and sought safe haven in the women's refuge. A worker at the refuge remembered her first glimpse of Patricia: "Patricia came to the refuge seeking help. She arrived at approximately 7 that evening in a very wet, dishevelled and distressed state. She stated that she had left home at approximately 3:30 P.M. that day. The next day I sat down and talked with her about her problems and the reasons she had left home, which basically were her husband's totally unreasonable behaviour towards her and violence towards her. I made arrangements to relocate her and we decided that the refuge was the right place as her husband never went there and he didn't know anybody there. I made the arrangements and went with

Patricia to my car. When Patricia got in the car she got on the front passenger floor and I couldn't get her to sit on the seat. All she would tell me is that she was terrified her husband might see her and start trouble. No matter how much I tried to reassure her, she would not get off the floor on to the seat until we were well out of town."

Meanwhile, Alan Norman had reported his wife was missing, and he began to deluge the police station with telephone calls. Suspicious of what they called "his manner and his obsession with his wife," the police acted with extreme caution. When they found her a week later, one officer recorded, "I spoke to her in the refuge and she appeared safe and well. She did, however, express an intense desire that her whereabouts should not be disclosed to her husband, or for that matter *any* members of her family." Patricia made no formal complaint and told the policeman that she had left her home because of marital problems: she wanted her daughter to be informed that she was safe, but she did not want anyone to know where she was staying. A few days later, Norman appeared at the police station and demanded to know his wife's address. The police officer said, "I repeatedly told him that she was safe and well and that I could not disclose where she was. He went on asking if I could tell him the area where she was and the type of accommodation she was staying in. Once again this request was refused. Norman appeared very annoyed and upset that his wife's whereabouts were not divulged."

He then enlisted the local newspaper in his campaign. Under the headline, "PLEASE LET US KNOW," the story ran: "A heartbroken husband yesterday pleaded for his missing wife to contact him. Said desperate Alan, who runs the Pennines Fish Bar, 'I just want her to contact someone, even if she just writes a letter to let us know she is alright. But really we want her home.' He said their two daughters, Diedre (19) and Jeanette (17), who each have a child, are missing her very much and are so upset they cannot sleep. Mrs. Norman went missing after receiving VAT bills totalling around £10,000, which the couple could not afford to pay. 'She has never done anything like this before,' said a distraught Mr. Norman." Demonstrating his customary lack of insight, he told the paper that "'there was no argument or problems at home, the pressure must have just built up, and she did a runner, taking just £80 with her.' Patricia Norman is described as 5 ft 4 ins tall, of medium build, with dark brown hair and brown eyes, and when she left home she was wearing black leather trousers and a three-quarter length green nylon coat."[2]

Several days later, under the headline, "COME HOME PLEA TO RUNAWAY WIFE," Norman portrayed himself again as a devoted husband: "A chip shop owner whose wife ran off after their business was hit by a huge VAT bill pleaded: 'Come home, we'll sort it out.' Trish Norman vanished last Thursday after being handed the second instalment of a crippling £10,000 VAT demand. Husband Alan has spent three days walking around Blackpool after a suggestion she may be in hiding in a guest house. He is also terrified she may harm herself after a bizarre warning from seafront fortune teller, Gipsy Rose Lee. 'She told me to go home because somebody old needed to see me before he died. She was right – last night my father Barney passed away,' said Alan. 'She also said that she feared the worst for my wife – and the thought of that cuts me up.' Trish, 38, a grandmother of two, left after being overwhelmed by financial worries about the Pennines Fish Bar they bought three years ago. With the bank's help, she and Alan, 42, had paid off a £7,000 VAT bill – but they were floored the next day by another for £3,000. 'That was the final straw for her. She let the whole thing get on top of her. I went out to the shops for 10 minutes and when I came back she had gone. If she is reading this, I just want her to come home, or at least telephone me. If she never wants to set foot in the fish shop again, she won't have to,' said Alan."

Norman's efforts were unsuccessful until Patricia made the fatal error of contacting her sister, Olga, with whom Alan, unbeknownst to Patricia, had had a long-term sexual relationship in return for cash payments. Patricia had telephoned her sister at her place of work, but her sister could not be reached immediately. Patricia could not call again because she had only one 10p piece for the pay telephone, so she took a chance in violating refuge policy and left the refuge's telephone number, asking her sister to return the call. Her sister passed the number to Alan, ostensibly so that he could inform the police of her whereabouts. Instead of alerting police, however, Alan began to make frequent harassing telephone calls to the refuge. One refuge resident remembered: "Everyone got on with Patricia well [and] she often spoke openly concerning her problems. She had left because Alan had been a possessive person, had not allowed her any money and she was allowed few friends. She was never very happy, had never been herself, and I did see her on occasions, daydreaming, speaking to herself and saying, 'That bastard should know better. After all I've been through, going back, and going through that again.' She seemed always to be saying that. The caller would ask, 'Is Tricia Norman there?' I would say in a negative voice, 'Who is Tricia Norman? I don't know who she is.' He would say, 'Please tell her I love her' and 'Look duck, have you got a heart?' I would say, 'Yes,' he would say, 'Would you stop [a man] from trying to kill himself, trying to commit suicide?' I would say, 'No, I don't know who you are, why would I try and stop you?' This conversation would be repeated over and over again on different days."

More ominously, Norman passed the number to a friend who had connections within British Telecom. After the murder, devastated by the consequences of what he had done, the friend, Philip Arkwright, told police that Alan Norman had been a friend and business associate for a decade. "I never met his wife, [but] he bought quite a lot of supplies from my firm. Alan appeared to be distraught by her leaving and he lost a couple of stones in weight. An article was put in the local newspaper about how upset he was, and that he wanted her back. Alan came to see me. He looked ill and very upset. He told me that he knew Patricia was living somewhere in the area as he had managed to get a telephone [number] of where she was. Whilst Alan was in the shop he started to cry and I genuinely believed he wanted to trace Patricia because he cared for her. I asked him to give me the telephone number he had and I told him I would try to help him locate her. I checked the number against her friend's mother and it wasn't the same. I checked the number with all the usual places – Citizens Advice Bureau, Yellow Pages for hospitals, nursing homes, etc. I even rang Directory Enquiries but I was told that addresses cannot be disclosed. Alan telephoned me that same day, asking if I'd got anywhere with the number but I hadn't. He sounded very distraught and was talking about committing suicide. He sounded so desperate I told him to leave it with me and I would see what I could do."

Arkwright then approached his friend in British Telecom. "I telephoned David at work and asked him if as a favour to me could he get the address to the telephone number. Dave agreed to do this, purely as a favour to me." The following day, David entered Arkwright's shop "and handed to me a map. Dave had highlighted the matching address on the map and written 'Women's refuge, No. 6.' I thanked him for the favour. I left work and went round to Alan's shop. I handed him the map with the address. I asked him when he was going to go and he said that night. I told him not to go on his own and the daughter said she would go with him, as it was obvious to anyone that Alan was too upset to drive on his own. I left them both in an upset state, the daughter crying. As far as I am aware I had done a favour for a man distraught to have his wife back. Had I known what the next chain of events were to be I would never have provided Alan with the address, or indeed asked Dave to provide me with it."

Unaware of these developments, Patricia continued to hang up whenever Norman rang the refuge. On the afternoon of the day of her death, on the same lined notepaper on which she had previously catalogued his abuse, Patricia composed her eloquent final testament.

Alan

I shall not be coming back. I hate you for what you have done to me, made me leave my home, my family my grankids, the village I lived in. Why did you drive me away

Why did you make my life like hell

Why was you so hateful to me.

I did love you.

Was it my fault you became like this. Tried to tell you what you was doing to me but you wouldent lisen would you always tried to make a big thing about everything dident you. Twisted everything even twisted my mind. you even mangage it for me to be taking in to hospital dident you. Couldent take any more pressure from you, oh dont worry Im out know.

What joke have you telled your mates. I bett you havent telled them that I had to *run* away from you. you will never do this to me again, for the simple reason is that I shall not see you again. Hope you are suffering like I have. Whats it like not having knowone to moune at.

Oh by the way dont think I have gone away with someone eles. anyway who would have me the state you have put me in. Why did you do it to me. Now I'm all alone dont know anyone don't know what to do. Keep haven blackouts. dont know what I am doing you really did a good job dident you.

Why should I be crying like this Ive done nothing wronge. if I have I don't know about it. You couldent even be a husband or a father could you. over 20 year we have been together what for all them years just gone waisted.

I can remember when I really really loved you. Couldent get enough of you, but now I want to forget try and make a new life for myself. When I get well enough. Woke up last night thinking you was shouting me. you see you are just playing on my mind. haved to try a forget what it is you have done to me. hope you find yourself alone. the way you are, probly you will. never had a kind word for me did you. dont know how I lasted so long these past few years living with you, it was horrible for me, it seamed as if everything was closing in it seamed as if you were trying to get into my mind.

I just couldent escape you – I was thinking all the time what will he be mouning about next. Should I do this before he starts should I do that thinking about what you would say next. I am just like a nervous wreck. Thats it have a good laugh. You could show all your mates this letter then you can all laugh. don't try and find me. I am in no Fit State to be able to cope with you. If it wasent for the staff in this place I don't know what I would have done. So stop looking because no one will tell you were I am I am even having my name changed. I did keep telling you that you was going to far with me dident I.

It better this way me laving. If I'd had stayed I would have properly have killed myself. Can you remeber when I got those sleeping table[ts] from the doctor I did take all the table but I dident exseed did I in dying. Think back what life did I have with you not very good was it wasent alound a money to spend on my self. not being able to go out. well dident hae any friends to go out with did I dident have any privacy had to work all hours accused of going to bed with everybody had to have sex everytime you felt like it. If you worked as many hour as I did you wouldent have had the strength to do it – next thing is becoming a alcoholic all because of you.

Norman drove to the refuge and stared unobserved through the window. He returned to his home but a few hours later, accompanied by his son-in-law, he was back at the refuge, trying to force his way through the rear door. The door was sturdy and resisted his attempts, forcing him to run around to the front of the house. Here he smashed a large window and entered the house through the gaping hole. The noise of his forced entry frightened the four women and five children inside the refuge, and they locked themselves in the second-floor bathroom. Norman went through the house room by room until he found the locked bathroom door. One refuge resident later described her ordeal: "Kelly was shouting, 'Someone's trying to kick the back door in. Phone the police, phone the police.' I didn't react at first and asked her what she was going on about. I understood there was something wrong as they were half frantic, pushing each other all over the place. I was then standing in the doorway of the room and I said, 'Someone has left the inner door open,' meaning the one on the inside of the front door. At the time I said it I could see the handle on the front door turning down and then a load of banging coming from the front door. The door is solid. I had no idea who was behind it. I do know that the door was locked, and I ran to the inner door and locked that. One of the front windows was smashed. I was becoming very frightened by now. The children were screaming. The next thing I knew, everyone had run upstairs and left me and my boys on our own. I heard Kelly shout, 'Everybody get into my bathroom.' That bathroom was on the second floor, the attic area. I shouted up the stairs, 'Don't lock the door, I'm coming up.'

"As I got in everybody was piled against the inside of the door. The door has a lock on but I doubt whether it was that secure. I could see that every member, including children of the house, were in the bathroom. There was still a panic but efforts were being made to keep the children quiet so as not to give away our presence in that room. I had no idea who was trying to get in. We could hear doors opening, banging closed. There was no other sound apart from footsteps, no voices or anything. No one made any comment on who it could be. Then whoever it was began to hit the bathroom door, with what I do not know. The bottom half of the door went in. I actually stood with my body against the door. As soon as I felt the broken wood hit my leg I moved away from the door. Everyone seemed to follow me. The bathroom is not large and there was no room to move. The whole door and its hinges then came off and immediately a man wearing blue jeans ran in wielding a knife in his right hand. He pushed everyone out of the way and grabbed Patricia by the hair or collar with his left hand. She had stood in the middle of us. Everyone except myself and my two children ran out. We seemed trapped in a corner of the bathroom."

Norman stabbed Patricia fifteen times. As another resident remembered: "A man came bursting into the bathroom. As soon as he did so I threw the fire extinguisher at him but missed him. I then just bent down holding my two children protecting them. I was at the side of the bath and I saw the man grab hold of Patricia by the hair, pulling her downwards. It was then that I saw him leaning over Patricia, who was curled up on her side, her face facing away from me. The man was knelt on her with his left knee pressed into her side. He was holding her hair with his left hand and to my astonishment I saw he was holding a knife in his right hand. Everyone just ran out of the room leaving just myself and my children crouched at the side of the bath. The next thing I saw was the man lunging the blade of the knife towards the side of Patricia's body. I clearly saw him stab Patricia at least twice. I was powerless to do anything and I believed he was going to cause injury to myself and my children. I was terrified and just pulled myself and my children out of the bathroom."

A third resident of the refuge had similar memories: "There was no names mentioned, no voices, just this man dragging Patricia down on to the floor and began plunging the knife into her body whilst holding her down on to the floor. He was laughing as he was doing it. Patricia did not shout out anything except I heard her choking as she grabbed my legs. She was kicking her feet. I began shouting at him and tried my hardest to push this man off her; but he did not move except just kept sticking the knife into Patricia's body. The children were screaming. I was screaming at him, noticing that Patricia was covered in blood. Then Patricia's feet stopped moving. He then stopped. I ran out of the door with my children more or less with me. I ran downstairs. The other women and children had run out of the fire exit. I got out through the smashed window. Patricia had said that afternoon, 'I think I'm going to write a letter to my husband. I feel sorry for him and I'll be glad when I can get my own house with a garden so I can live again.' That was something she just wanted to say."

Norman then fled through the fire escape at the rear of the building, and cutting at his wrist, ran into an alley where his son-in-law was waiting for him in a car. Here, Norman continued slashing at his left wrist with his knife. The police officer who arrived minutes later at the refuge wrote that he "could see a woman I now know to be Patricia Norman lying on the floor in a pool of blood, and I could see her clothing was heavily bloodstained. She was lying face up and was trying to move her legs. I knelt down beside her and could see she was conscious. She looked at me and said, 'I feel faint, I can't breathe.' I lifted her top where most of the blood appeared to be coming from. I could see a deep puncture under her chest and several other wounds on the top of her chest. I grabbed a towel and placed it over the larger wound to try and stop the flow of blood. Again she said, 'I can't breathe, I can't breathe.' I tried to comfort her."

Norman was arrested and taken to the hospital. At first he claimed that he had attacked his wife because she had been having an affair with another man, whom he named. These charges were found to be without foundation, but it was confirmed that Norman had a long-standing sex-for-money relationship with Patricia's debt-ridden younger sister, Olga.

The Family

Astonishingly, the couple's daughter, nineteen-year-old Diedre, thought her parents' marriage had been a tranquil one, and told police, "From as far back as I can remember they appeared happy. I cannot remember any real domestic argument between them, although they did have the usual disagreements to do with family matters. Up until the end of July everything appeared to be running smooth in the shop, my mother and I were serving behind the counter and doing the frying, whilst my father did all the work in the rear of the shop, preparing the fish for frying. Shortly after the end of July my mother started to get depressed and lose all interest in the running of the shop. She started to only work two nights a week instead of the seven dinner-times and seven night-times. She would just leave us in the shop and go and sit upstairs in the living quarters. She never went out on her own, but occasionally would go out with my father to friends or to the local pub. Both my parents started arguing then, always about the finances of the shop, my mother wanted to get out but my father didn't. They constantly argued about this but there was never any violence used from either side. In fact I am not aware of any violence from either side. My father would damage some property in the house rather than use violence on my mother. The arguments continued up until my mother disappeared. Since my mother disappeared, I have seen my father every day and he has been in a very depressed condition, not sleeping or eating at all." After the assault, "my Dad told me that he had stabbed my mother and that I would be able to go and see her in hospital, he didn't want anyone else to have her, and he loved her."

Patricia's mother had quite different memories of the relationship. "I was opposed to the marriage from the start because I was aware that he had come from a children's home and had been in trouble with the police for petty thieving. I got the impression throughout the marriage that he got on at her all the time, picking faults with whatever she was doing and even ridiculing her in front of his mates. Tricia was the type of girl who bottled all her problems up and did not discuss it with me at all. Alan continued over the years with his mental torture of my daughter, always wanting to know where she was and what she was doing to the extent that she was almost being followed around constantly by him."

This negative view was reaffirmed by Patricia's eldest sister. "I would say that around two or three years ago Patricia became increasingly depressed with the marriage. The marriage had been unhappy prior to that time, but had become increasingly so once they had purchased the shop. During all the marriage, Patricia regularly complained to me that Alan was very jealous of her. Alan became even more possessive with her as the years went on. He was frightened to let her out of his sight. Patricia often complained of being a prisoner in her own house. I often thought that Alan had assaulted Patricia, but she would never admit nor deny it. I never saw any facial injuries but I saw numerous bruises to her ribs, arms and legs: it was obvious to me that Alan was responsible for causing the bruises."

Interviews with the Police

As soon as Norman was arrested, a police sergeant noted that his clothing and shoes were heavily bloodstained. "I saw a deep open wound across his wrist. At this point Norman said, 'Don't bother about me, I want to die, I've done something stupid.' Norman said to his daughter, 'I only wanted her back. I loved her so much I didn't want anyone else to have her.' He was quiet, staring into the distance. After a time he said, 'I only stuck her once. Stabbed her with that knife. I know what I've done. I just want to die.'"

The following afternoon, this time in the presence of his solicitor, Alan Norman tried to "explain" his actions. "Just that I've been under a lot of pressure, a hell of a lot of pressure. Me wife run away 'cos of the business pressure on us. They put a ninety thousand pound mortgage on us and then they, we come off of unemployed, we didn't have no money at all, the bank's just banged us a ninety thousand mortgage, we didn't put nowt up in front. Still again we'd no more, we couldn't carry on; me and me wife falling out all time.

"Me wife decides to do a runner, she can't take no more. Off she goes. Takes me four week, I put it in every paper, it were on television, it were on wirelesses, nobody could find her nowhere. Eventually she made contact with one of her sisters and said that she was at a certain phone number, that's all she gave her, and I phoned up and they said she doesn't live here, nobody lives here, it's just a private house. Finally, I just went all over Blackpool, three days, couldn't find her nowhere. All over. She sent a letter to me daughter, it stated in the letter the post office box number and the post code. I traced it up." Mistaking the post office for "one of their society homes," Norman admitted he "stood outside and I watched people pulling up in vehicles, just picking the girls up and taking them all over, Pakistanis and everything. It ate me all up, ate me up, ate me up. I come home, couldn't sleep again. Went back down there the next day. Sat outside all day. Couldn't find her nowhere. Then I came back home, studied a little bit, I thought, Well, I'll try this number again, so I rung the number up and pretended I was a CID officer, and she said I'll ring you back. I said, 'You've no need to ring me back. I sent two officers down to check if Patricia was there,' and she said, 'just a minute, I'll fetch Patricia for you.' She fetched Patricia to phone and she just said, 'hello,' just like that, and I thought, 'Oh, they've got her there now.' I couldn't find the address nowhere of the home where it was.

"A chap came along, this Arkwright, he said, 'tha' keeps it under the hat, tha' don't say nothing. I can get the address for ya,' and he come back with that address I've gid ya. Have you seen it, the one with the map? And he said, 'That's where your wife is,' so off I went and had a look, see me wife. She was as happy as owt, laughing and giggling through window like and everything, and I thought me and me daughters at that end, pressurized. I can't read or write, can't fill the books in, can't do cheques, can't write a cheque book out or nothing, which got top side o' me, and then another VAT bill come in. After that come in I rung up to the bank manager and he says we can't pay it. I didn't know which way to turn. I rung up to the girl again asked to please, to beg for Patricia to come home. Me daughters crying on steps every morning non-stop. Child's roaring, four-year-old child's saying, 'Mama's dead, Mama's in the hole.' I went and told the woman on the phone and she said she doesn't live here. I said please tell her, duck. So I decided to commit suicide, I said at twelve o'clock tonight, duck, I'm gonna commit suicide. She turned round and said, 'fucking commit suicide then, my husband did and Tricia says you get it done now' and put phone down on me.

"Next morning I phoned Social Services up, Samaritans, everybody, nobody'd come out to me, I was hysterical. I then popped back to the house. I sat under the window listening to 'em. They were laughing and giggling and I heard me wife say to one of the girls, 'Where we going tomorrow night?' So I just banged on the door and banged on the door, I couldn't get in, so I went round the front. Yes, kicked that [front] door. It wouldn't open. I smashed the window. Then when that smashed I put me hand in and opened the window and climbed in. I run into the kitchen where they wa' there, and I don't know if I picked the knife up there or where it wa', then I run upstairs, trying all bedrooms and then, I could see this door was shut like, they were holding back at it. I didn't want to hurt any people what was in there, I just wanted to talk to me wife. I just says, 'Are you coming home, are you coming home?' We got struggling and fighting then that, that's what happened. She got it [the knife], got hold of me hands and as we went down to the floor, the knife hit me in me leg."

He then volunteered the absurd suggestion that Patricia had struck the first blow. "She says she wanted to come home and she got hold of me hand and stuck the knife into me leg and then that's when it all started. We were on the floor and I think I stuck the knife in me wife twice or three times, I don't know. I was sorry I did it, but . . . I then walked straight to bottom of the stairs and just slashed me wrist, slashed it till the blade snapped. It snapped and then went on the floor, I picked it up, went outside and chucked it in one of the yards at the side, the corner of a building. An' that's all, that's all, that's all what it's about really. Just pressure. I didn't expect her to die or owt like that. I just wanted to injure her so she'd come to her senses and know that what she was doing were wrong to us.

"Excessive force? No, I didn't want to hurt her, I laid down kissing her after I'd done it. I kissed her twice, put me arms round her and said, 'I'm sorry, love, I'm sorry, duck, I'm ever so sorry,' and she just kept saying to me, 'You don't realize I loved ya, you don't realize I loved ya, give over please,' and then I ran out, ran down to bottom of stairs and slashed me wrist. I didn't know what I was doing, I was in a bad state. I didn't mean to do any harm to me wife at all with the knife, I thought, Well, if she sees the knife she's gonna come home. I were gonna put her over me shoulder and come back through the window, get in me van, then take her home.

"I couldn't take no more pressure. It build up, over the debt and everything. That morning, that's what did it, the morning just before I went to see her, the bank sent me a statement saying I owe 'em seventeen thousand pound and to ring the bank up straight away. I asked the bank what situation was and I says, 'What about me wife, din't she no responsible for it?' He says, 'it's all on your shoulders now, nowt to do with your wife. It's all on your shoulders.' I says, 'I can't do this all on me own, it's impossible.' "

Norman was uncharacteristically honest when the detective asked if the debts were the only reason Patricia left home. "No, I were getting on to her all time, saying stupid things like, you know, she were talking to somebody, I'd turn round and say what's he been knocking you off, or if peas boiled over, that's your fault. If summat went wrong wi' gases and that, that's your fault. Mainly Tricia said it weren't the fish shop like, but it was, it were, she were sat up roaring some nights when I used to go to her. [One night] me wife just hit the pillow, roaring, roaring, roaring, saying to me what we gonna do, what we gonna do."

The detective asked if Patricia was seeing another man. "No, she's not seeing another woman, I mean another man. To my knowledge, no." "What about you, have you been seeing anybody else?" "Yes. Her sister, Olga. She were taking money off me. She's got money problems, borrowing money off me wife, fifty pound and wouldn't give it us back and everything, then she were charging me twenty, thirty pound a go, just taking her out in a van, doing it in back of a van about three times a week." "Your wife, was she aware of this relationship at all?" "No, I don't think. She caught us once, about five year ago, well more about ten year ago. I went out once, came back in, me and me wife and she caught us on the settee together."

"You decided it wasn't right that she should be happy and you should be so unhappy?" the detective asked. In his habitual confusion, Norman replied, "No, I didn't think that at all. I just thought, Why is she laughing, why is she giggling? Me daughter's there working all hours under sun, we're all under pressure and everything and she's making it out as though she were badly and she was just laughing and giggling."

"Why did you cut your wrists when you got to the bottom of the stairs?" "I wanted to die with me wife. I just didn't want to live no more. I knew I'd done injuries to her and I thought, Well, look, do injuries, do yourself now. I didn't want 'em to save me life. I wanted to die, I still want to die. I think there's something up, up in me head, there's something wrong. I just can't understand it, it's like you say she was happy and I couldn't stand it for her to be happy. I wanted her with me. It kept ticking over in me brain, you know. I know there's something up, but I've tried three appointments at the doctors, freeze every time I got there, I just said, 'It's chest pains, I think I'm going to have a heart attack.' They just checked me and said there were nothing wrong with me."

The man who was raised "in care," the illiterate businessman murdering his wife in the presence of screaming women and children – themselves in the care of a protective institution – made no attempt to deny his guilt in court, and was sentenced to indefinite detention under the Mental Health Act.

SEXUAL MURDER

The palpable public fear of sexual murder is based in part on a misapprehension that such crimes are rampant – although this is not the case. Quite the contrary: for the closely studied period of 1967 to 1971, sexual motive for homicide averaged only 6.7 per cent of the total number, and there is no evidence of any disproportionate increase in these tragedies.[3]

By the 1980s, the traditional British literary fascination for its killers changed: heightening fears, especially about "psychopathic" or "insane" sex killers, became the basis for a moral panic which focused on "sexual predators." Philip Jenkins has demonstrated that one of the chief qualities of the 1980s was "the sheer scale of media coverage concerning the alleged events, and the extent to which the offences were believed to represent a very widespread threat that could affect almost any family." Who are these sexual predators? Most of them are like all our killers, malformed and defective males, often mentally ill, with criminal records, and living on the edge of society.[4]

"I HEARD A VOICE SAY 'COME IN'": MARLON SAUNDERS MURDERS A YOUNG WOMAN

The case shocked the country, not only because of the brutal and unprovoked assault upon an innocent twenty-year-old woman, but because two of her neighbours in her block of bed-sitters heard her cries throughout the hour-long attack, yet refused to come to her aid. The neighbours' indifference was so appalling, one of the investigating officers noted, that their conduct made "the Pharisee of the Good Samaritan story seem like an angel." English common law assigns only a civic, not a legal, duty to assist someone in distress, and those who ignored her cries escaped any form of punishment.

The courts decided the killer, twenty-three-year-old Marlon Saunders, was "mentally unstable," and undoubtedly he was; although the police, often wiser in these matters than they are credited, merely thought him a clever liar. Certainly there is plenty of evidence that he was simply a disordered young man who took whatever he wanted from whomever he wanted, the personal script for so many criminal offenders. Certainly he did not appear to *care* who he was harming or what he was doing when he murdered and raped Susan Getty. Moreover, his subsequent attempt to escape from police custody suggests less a deranged person than someone who has a rather clear idea of the events that are transpiring.

History of the Killer

Marlon Saunders was born in the West Indies, and had lived in England since he was twelve. He was clearly an impulsive and uncontrolled young man long before he stole the life of Susan Getty. Before the murder, he had already accumulated numerous previous convictions for dishonesty and theft; his police record includes five convictions for theft, and three for evading taxi and rail fares – for which he was invariably fined, or given a suspended sentence. He left school at sixteen, and was first employed as an apprentice engineer with Leyland Motors. In August 1979, he left Leyland and found work in the catering trade in Torquay. After a short time he moved to London where he worked in various hotels, periodically visiting his family in Lancashire. At the time of his arrest he was employed as a hall porter at a hotel in London, earning an estimated £157 each month in addition to his meals.

His erratic behaviour was obvious to some, but not all. He "dated" sixteen-year-old Kathy, who remembered him fondly: "During this time I had sexual intercourse with him. He was the first man I had ever been with in that way. When we had sex it was in the normal way, there were no deviations." Still, she remembered a certain oddness to him: "He often talked about a false Utopia and religion and time ruling our lives."

Twenty-two-year-old Patricia had a much more harrowing encounter with him, one in which Saunders rehearsed his rape and murder of Susan Getty. Patricia said Saunders "used to dress up sometimes in clothing like a man's leotard and wear lots of body paint, also plenty of facial make-up. Marlon even went through one stage when he would wear facial make-up when he was out walking around Torquay . . . [a friend] mentioned something about Marlon going very strange and religious."

Patricia lived alone, and began to grow apprehensive of Saunders after an evening in which he had invited himself into her flat and then overstayed his welcome. Several days later, Patricia's doorbell rang: "I got up, I was dressed in my nightie, it was about 10:30 A.M. As I opened the door he threw his arms around me. I just said, 'Hello,' told him to sit in the lounge and went to make him some coffee. I got dressed and sat with him and we talked – just casual conversation – about what he had been doing.

Eventually I had to ask him to leave because I was going to have dinner with my parents. He must have been there about two hours. He said he would come back in the evening but it was his suggestion, not mine. At about 7 P.M. that same day I returned home, and about five minutes after, the front downstairs doorbell sounded. It was Marlon. I made him a coffee and he sat down and watched the television. I would not describe him as welcome but it would have been rude to have asked him to leave. We talked and he was asking questions about my relationship with [a previous boyfriend]. He knew we had split up. We were both sitting on the only thing in the room that could be sat on, that was the sofa. We were sitting at each end and I was keeping a healthy distance between us. He came towards me and started to put his arms around me. He kept trying to kiss me and in doing so he would force my face round towards him by holding my chin between his thumb and index finger. I would manage physically to resist him [and] he would calm down and start again. At no time did I give him the impression that I was prepared to give in, even telling him he would have to leave if he continued.

"He kept asking if I had got any 'hot oils' so he could release my tension by giving me a massage. I just laughed off his request. He then started to get really forceful. I had started to cry by this time and was at one end of the sofa. I was crying because he would not stop, but I had not yet become too frightened. Although he was physically very strong his voice was very soft and gentle. He would not give up although I was crying and he came over to my end of the sofa. At one point I was even sitting on the arm of the sofa but could not go any further because the wall was in the way. Somehow he physically managed to [force] me back down on the sofa with me facing upwards and him kneeling on my chest and stomach across my body. We were both still fully clothed. He must have had me pinned down for about two minutes. Whilst he did this he said things to me in a soft voice in a creepy manner. The exact words I cannot remember but he told me that he could rape me and nobody would be able to do anything about it, that it would be my word against his. He said that he could go in the kitchen and get a knife – I can't remember him actually threatening to kill me but he said that I would be dead, he could walk out and no one would find me for days. I was telling him not to be silly; I had a job and parents and they would know. Everything was happening really fast and I was trying to fight him off by pushing him.

"It is not easy for me now to remember the exact sequence of events, but at one stage he did say that he thought all women had a secret desire to be raped. I argued against him in a strong manner on this point. During the struggle I said phrases like 'Marlon, I'm not like that,' meaning I did not sleep around. Anyway, eventually I managed to stand and fight him off. I threatened to go to the public house next door and call someone to have him thrown out. I even suggested getting a fireman who I knew lived next door. At this he started to apologize, told me to calm down and that he would leave. I remember him trying to kiss me as he was leaving but I wouldn't even let him do that. He left and I think it was about midnight. I had got really very frightened and after he had gone I was really shaken.

"I was still frightened in the morning. The following day we drove up the road outside my accommodation to see if he was waiting. [Since Marlon was] black I could not see him but when I got to my doorway he was standing there. I said, 'I am not opening this front door, you know.' He said, 'Oh, come on, Patricia,' and I said, 'No, you can't come in. I'm not going in until you have gone. I will get someone out of the pub.' I walked towards the pub and he said, 'Okay,' and walked off up the road. That was the last time I saw him."

We cannot know how many women he maltreated in this way, but police records make it clear that he made at least one other aggressive move. While visiting his family in Lancashire at the end of December, he approached a sixty-four-year-old friend of his mother. As she recalled the incident: "Marlon came round to my house. As soon as he came in he embraced me and kissed me. He had never done that to me before. He came into the living room and sat down and started talking very strange about the Garden of Eden and about Noah and his Ark. He then asked me why I hadn't got married. He was generally talking very odd, he mentioned about there being evil in the house and that he had come to get rid of it. He kept trying to give me a Bible which he had brought with him. I asked him to leave the house, but he started shouting and getting very excited. I eventually managed to contact my next-door neighbours who sent for the police. Marlon left the house before the police came. About 10 the next morning

Marlon again visited my home. As soon as he came into the house he took hold of me and shouted, 'There is evil in this house and I have come to kill you.' He kept repeating this and shouting at the top of his voice. I have known Marlon since he was at school, but I have never known him behave like this before."

Saunders' "unusual" behaviour continued. The following day he entered a Preston discotheque and, as the manager remembered: "Marlon came up to me and he took hold of my jacket on the sleeve and tugged it, saying, 'I want a word with you.' He was saying things like 'You're scared of us blacks and you always will be' and 'We are the chosen few.' He rambled on about religion and the blacks before I could get away from him. Each time I went to go he stood in front of me and blocked my way or took hold of my jacket. Marlon had a vacant expression and all his words were in one tone. About 8:30 P.M., all of a sudden everything [in the discotheque] went quiet. This was very strange because to get over one thousand people to be quiet was quite something. Then I heard the same monotonous tone of Marlon over the PA system. All the crowd were wolf-whistling and shouting to get him off." The murder was only weeks away.

The Murder

One neighbour who overheard the entire assault and did nothing to help was Patrick, a twenty-six-year-old "friend" of the victim, who later told police, "I heard the sound of a female screaming coming from the direction of the landing. It was similar in every respect to that of Sue's voice. I heard the female voice scream, 'Leave me alone, why are you doing this to me, Marlon, leave me alone.' Then I heard a male voice say words and phrases like 'I want to save your soul, love me, I've saved half of it. I've come back especially for you. Don't struggle. Be calm. Don't fight me.' There was more shouting from the male voice about God and souls, the Divine and Satan. It all sounded very weird. The female voice kept screaming and shouting words like 'Help, I'm not joking, come out.' This continued for about five to ten minutes then it went calm for a short time. Then it started again with words similar to that previously described and continued for almost an hour during which the voices still remained loud. The female voice sounded very scared. Eventually the male voice said, 'Put it in your mouth. Suck it, all of it. Put it all in,' and words like that. The female voice replied, 'I have never done this before' and 'Let me breathe.' The male voice replied, 'Don't worry about breathing, I'll let you breathe.' It then went calm until the male voice gave a yell similar to that of someone in pain. It continued saying, 'Don't move. Don't fight me,' and then it went quiet. Prior to that I had heard sounds of struggling but at this point it stopped. The male voice continued as if talking to himself with words like 'No heart beat, no pulse, brain dead.' It then started shouting, 'Come on out and have a look at a perfect body.' I then heard a stereo player coming from the direction of Sue's room and a mouth organ being played as before. Shortly after I heard the sound of radio transmitters on the landing and I went out and saw two policemen in uniform."

Patrick expressed some remorse for his amazing cowardice and inhumanity: "I knew it was Sue from the beginning and she was terrified. I know now I should have done something but I was scared – it is pathetic, really, because no matter what she wanted, he was going to have his way with her. When I went outside and saw her body I knew I should have intervened. I went downstairs and burst into tears, I couldn't sleep that night."

Another neighbour, a hotel porter named Peter who also overheard the assault yet did nothing, lost no sleep that night: "As I was walking up the stairs I saw a girl lying on the floor on the landing and a coloured man kneeling beside her. I saw them as I opened the fire door on the landing. I stopped and stared in amazement as I had not expected to see anyone in such a position. They stared back at me but said nothing. As they said nothing I thought it was a lover's quarrel and so I did nothing, but continued upstairs. I heard shouting from the corridor. I heard the man shout, 'Last week you ignored me. I love you, I love you, I love you' over and over again. I heard her saying, 'It's untrue.' He continued to shout 'I love you' and she said, 'Go away, you're hurting my leg.' I thought that he must be sitting on her leg. He shouted, 'My father and myself are the lights of the world.' He then shouted loudly as if wanting everyone to hear, 'All my pupils, come outside and look at a pure young lady.' He then shouted, 'Don't hit me, Sue, I don't want to fight you. Wars are crazy, they don't solve a thing.' At 10:30 P.M. I left the room to go to work and on the same landing that I had seen the couple, the girl was lying naked on the floor motionless. I said, 'Get up, he's gone,' but she remained motionless. I thought that the man might still be about and might attack me, so I left the building and went down to Bayswater where I saw two policemen. I told them what had happened and brought them back and showed them the body."

When police first arrived, they saw "a record sleeve being pushed out under the door of flat 7 into the hallway where the police are standing. It is pushed out obviously by Saunders as he is the only person in the room when the police enter. The importance of this record sleeve is its title, which is 'Scientist Rids the World of the Evil Curse of the Vampire.' " When police kicked open the door, they found "Saunders lying crossed-legged, naked on the bed. He is alone." As the police constable noted, "I immediately approached him and held his arms behind his back and handcuffed him. I said, 'Is this your room?' He said, 'No, me live next door.' I said, 'What are you doing in here then?' He said, 'Me heard a voice invite me in and me come on in.' I said, 'Who invited you in?' He said, 'Me don't know, nobody here.' I said, 'How long have you been here?' He said, 'Ten minutes.' I said, 'Do you know that girl lying over there?,' and I indicated the girl's body. He said, 'No.' I said, 'Did you hurt her?' He said, 'The body is a beautiful thing and me would not want to harm it.' I said, 'Was the girl in this room when you came in?' He said, 'She was not in room when me went in. The room was empty.' I said, 'Why have you taken all your clothes off?' He said, 'The music is beautiful, the body is beautiful, me feel free.' Throughout this interview I noticed that his speech was slow, but lucid and not slurred. His eyes were glazed." Saunders was arrested and taken to the police station. During his initial interrogation, he jumped up and said, "Me want to take a shower to cleanse me body." When the detective asked, "Why do you want to cleanse your body?" Marlon replied, "Me not pure any more." After examining Susan's body, the forensic scientist concluded that she had been sexually assaulted after her death.

The Interviews

Saunders at first insisted that he had murdered a man, not Susan Getty. The interview was conducted in the presence of a social worker, and Saunders "became very awkward and refused to speak." "An officer tells me you want to confess to a murder?" the detective asked. "Yes, sir, a man," Saunders replied. "A man?" "Yes, sir." "You killed a man?" "Yes, sir." "What's his name?" "Don't know, sir." "When did you kill him?" "I don't know, sir." "How did you kill him?" "I don't remember, sir." "Do you remember killing a young girl?" "No, sir, a man, sir."

"What were your movements yesterday afternoon?" "Well, sir, I don't know what time but I went past the hotel to say Happy New Year." "What did you do then?" "Back home. To put my records away. I had borrowed some records, and I also had some books with me. I borrowed them from a friend and as they were my responsibility I kept them with me all the time." "Where are the records now?" "I don't know, sir." Included in these records was the one he had shoved underneath the door of flat 7.

"Did you then go straight to your flat?" "No, sir, I heard a voice say, 'Come in.'" "A voice, a voice from where?" "In my head, sir." "Was it male or female, this voice?" "I don't remember, sir. Just a voice saying, 'Come in.' The door was open so I went in and took all my clothes off – it's better to relax like that – and played some records." "Was this in your room?" "No, sir, next door." "What did you do then?" "I had a cup of tea, sir." "What happened then?" "A policeman knocks at the door and they took me to my room." "When they took you to your room, do you remember seeing a girl on the landing floor?" "No, sir." "Have you heard voices in your head before?" "No, sir." "Have you ever been to a psychiatrist?" "No, sir."

With a clear idea of what had happened, the detective told Saunders, "I have listened to you for some time now, about you hearing voices, and I will tell you what I think happened. When you got home last night you went to Julie's room. Susan answered the door and somehow you got her out of the flat and on to the landing where you made her have oral sex with you. At some stage you were made to cry out or shout out, and I think she bit you, or did something to annoy you and you hit her across the head with your hand. She fell backwards on to the floor and you then strangled her. After she was dead you took all her clothes off and had sexual intercourse with her. You then went back into her room and were heard playing your mouth organ again. I have witnesses who will verify this and the forensic evidence will prove it."

Marlon tried to divert attention from the issue: "No, sir," he said. "I never saw the doctor put anything in the bottle, there was a policeman with him. I didn't see him put anything on the labels. The policeman could have changed the labels or put anything in them." "Are you saying the doctor is going to lie about the samples taken from you?" "Yes, sir. Because you all lie in court: you will no doubt lie about this." "We have a written record of this interview: do you now wish to read and sign it?" "No, sir." "Why not?" "I don't think I should, sir."

In a second interview the following day, the officer asked, "Is your mother your only living relative?" and Marlon once again shook his head. He nodded when asked if he had any brothers or sisters. "I have three brothers beside myself, my father and mother and two half-brothers makes five altogether. Sisters I have four. Do I get to make phone call?" "You saw your mother Christmas Day?" "Yes, sir." "Are you close to your mother?" "Yes, sir, as all the family are." "Is your mother religious?" "In what way do you mean religious? Do you mean does she go to church? Yes, sir." "What church?" "United Reform Church: it was Methodist but changed to United Reform, the exact day of the transaction I cannot remember. I am just a Christian, sir." "Do you go to church?" "Not any more, sir. I did until I was sixteen years at regular intervals. When my father died I stopped going to church on a Sunday at 10 A.M., this is because on Sunday morning I took up football and took up martial arts. I just went with a friend for training. The style he used to do was called Wadaroo, but I have never considered using any of the things I was taught: people have assured me in past and tried and tried to sway me but I have never ever used anything I have learned or was taught. I am a passive person by nature and never argue. I always discuss problems and situations with people."

"Have you ever behaved violently in the past?" "When I first came to this country people they abused me, calling me 'little black nigger' and such names. My first reaction was of defence not knowing really what I was up against, so in retaliation to their attacks I fought back, the only way I knew how. The first person I met with different skin colour to my own we formed a friendship which has lasted all these years." "What's his name?" "John." "What's his other name?" "It eludes me." "Where does he live?" "Chorley." "Whereabouts does he live in Chorley?" "John lives in Chorley, period." "Are

you refusing to tell me John's address?" "Yes, because I do not know for sure."
"You don't know where he lives?" Marlon shook his head to indicate "no."

Saunders refused to answer any further questions. "Would you like a
cup of tea?" the detective finally asked, which received no reply. "You're not
helping by not answering." "You're saying it all for me, aren't you?"
Saunders replied, before ceasing once more to speak. Then, apropos of
nothing, he asked, "Can I make that phone call now, please?" "No, not until
you give me your mother's telephone number." "Why?" Marlon asked, and
then refused once more to respond.

A few moments later, the detective remarked, "I believe you are not
insane." Marlon responded to this with, "I never said I was." "Not only are
you not insane, but you are perfectly capable of knowing the consequences
of your actions." This piqued Marlon's interest once again: "Which are?
Please write that down as I said it."

"Is there anything you want to tell me or your social worker about your
treatment since you have been in police custody? Feel free, but go slowly."
Saunders nodded yes, and said: "It has been very good, gentlemen, very
kind, considerate, pleasant, apart from the abuses which haven't swayed
me, have you got that Mr. Social Worker? No, he is writing down what I say,
you are writing down what I am supposed to say. Has the interview
finished, sir, what is there to add, sir? May I ask for my chain and medallion,
that's all I want, you have my blanket back, that's all I ask. I will go quietly
back to my cell and sit and wait. Thank you for being present as you said you
would be."

Turning to the social worker, Saunders asked, "Are you a social worker
or a psychiatrist or what?" The man admitted, "I am a local authority social
worker." "So, you are not part of the police?" "No." "Are you here on my
behalf? Did I ask for you? Did I send for you? Strange." Marlon expressed no
interest in a private conversation with the social worker, and the interview
was terminated: on his way out of the office, he tried to escape and had to
be forcibly restrained before he could be returned to his cell.

In court, Saunders pleaded guilty to manslaughter on the grounds of
diminished responsibility, and he was sentenced to be detained in
Broadmoor hospital for the criminally insane for an indefinite period. He
will probably remain there for the rest of his life.

1   In the five sampled years between 1982 and 1990, 1,130 women were killed; an average of 226 per year; Morris and Blom-Cooper, 1979, op. cit., p. 6.

2   For the purposes of anonymity, many newspaper quotations are unattributed, but special thanks to Rona Biggens.

3   Evelyn Gibson, 1975, *Homicide in England and Wales, 1961–1971*, Home Office Research Study No. 31, p. 21.

4   Philip Jenkins, *Intimate Enemies*, p. 9.

CULTURE HEROES

... it apparently takes social scientists much longer than poets or critics to realize that every mind is a primitive mind, whatever the varieties of social conditioning. (Northrop Frye[1])

HUMAN BEINGS LIVE in simple emotional and intellectual worlds; and they draw much of their inspiration for appropriate behaviour from cues – myths and values – embedded in their culture. Children absorb these beliefs through the customary socialization mechanisms of worthy example ("role models"), of reward and punishment; and they internalize them as their own, as absolute truths, as behaviour and thought that have become "only natural." Human learning is such that by the time the child is ten or twelve the child is a product of that civilization; and the adult and parent will transmit that culture to the next generation. In any person's instant of personal crisis, only these culturally coded inhibitions will stop him from exploding in violence. Therefore it follows that the less attention a civilization pays to encoding such inhibitions, the more it offers illustrations of "noble" violence, the greater the likelihood that the least "educated" will act out their tension in bloody explosion.

We only understand in principle how people model themselves after officially sanctioned behaviour; but we know that mass culture – films, books, television, wireless, newspapers, education – has a considerable impact, especially on our most vulnerable citizens. For example, studies of television's effect on adolescent London males have suggested that "high exposure to television violence increases the degree to which boys engage in serious violence"; and the introduction of television to an isolated Canadian community shaped "a significant increase" in aggression among both boys and girls. American mass culture has made the advertising and promotion of violence a specialty in all its cultural forms; but we cannot suggest that the effects of viewing U.S. media violence are immediate – no one becomes a serial killer after watching one film. Rather, violent messages express and reinforce a nation's aggressivity as well as create it, and the public affirmation of violence appears to function over extended periods as an "important but incremental change agent." This explains why Americans and English can view the same violent media yet still maintain very different homicide rates. Such massive change in values and behaviour usually take a very long time to reach the central core of a culture.[2]

The civilizing process through which non-violent ideals and behaviours are transmitted through a culture seems everywhere the same – "the modern state spread its power over the populace," warring knights became well-mannered courtiers, and "official justice administered by courts replaced private vengeance conducted by feuds, fights and duels." Much of this process is almost subliminal, one in which the system provides cultural markers which delineate the desired values and behaviours, in this case self-control. The intensity with which they demand such refinements determines their success in teaching people to respond to insult and challenge with non-violent means – through conflict avoidance, verbal retaliation or the judicial process. These "dominant themes" in a culture's common narrative are definitive of civilizations, but vary utterly between them.[3]

> There can be no coincidence that Japan has a high incidence of suicide and also enshrines within its classic dramas of *Kabuki* and *Bunraku* the resolution of the hero's central conflict by him committing *seppuku*. The differences in the way violence is handled on the screen, its causes and consequences, between the few films made in Britain and those made in the U.S.A. appear to reflect the differences in the degree and nature of violence in those countries. (David Canter[4])

If so much of American culture can be described as a romance with murder, half-consciously extolling its virtues in every mass cultural pulpit, English culture has only tolerated such violence when it was part of a larger moral purpose – to correct injustice or to advance the empire. One of the primary mechanisms for the inculcation of these sensibilities in a population is the use of the "culture hero," which represents the valued qualities, an object for admiration and imitation. In this fundamental cultural sense, life *does* imitate art, as the developing child struggles to mould his or her personality in accord with the dominant cultural atmosphere. Half-consciously, these notions affect perception, decision and response, on aggressivity as on any other dimension of behaviour; and each personality incorporates these cues in the construction of his identity.

MYTHOLOGICAL ORIGINS: ROBIN HOOD

English mass culture's heroes tell us a great deal about the construction of English character. The traditional hero is Robin Hood, whose virtues have been widely promulgated since the fourteenth century. Scholars tend to dismiss the legend as a romantic "escape," but it was much more than that: it reflected and reinforced both the rhythm and pace of changes in English society and character. For Maurice Keen, the story of Robin Hood demonstrates "the glamour that so easily attaches, in any age, to the activities of the 'gentleman bandit' whose misdoings are redeemed by the courage and generosity of his nature and of the manner of his robbing." Still, it was not Robin Hood's career as a "glamorous" criminal that influenced the common imagination, but the fact that the "legend displays many of the characteristics traditionally associated with fictional knightly heroes – courage, courtesy, loyalty, generosity, a free and open bearing."[5]

J. C. Holt attributed the legend's longevity to its flexibility, its ability to acquire in each generation "new twists from shifts in the composition, outlook and interests of the audience." Thus as the nation's social requirements evolved, as new personal qualities came to be valued, fresh tales and characters were introduced. Robin began as a yeoman, "then turned into a nobleman unjustly deprived of his inheritance, later into an Englishman protecting his native countrymen from the domination of the Normans, and finally into a social rebel who, in the peasant's struggle against the grasping landlord, retaliates against the person and property of the oppressor." To make the story worth retelling to a largely illiterate audience, it was presented in terms of "simple adventure stories, tales of combat, contest, disguise and stratagem." Robin Hood was always about justice, "an embodiment of honour and an agent of retribution" who in the name of his beloved king corrects "the greed of rich clerics and the corruption of royal officials."

If his success is due in part to the fact that he is "a superlative archer [and] a consummate swordsman," it is also because he is "a master of disguise and stratagem," emerging alternatives to physical aggression. If Robin Hood "was at first a glorification of violence," reflecting and reinforcing the violence endemic in medieval society, even then he embodied gentler values of "chivalry towards women, devotion to the Virgin, generosity, courtesy, loyalty, obedience, in all matters except his deer, to the king." If Robin "kills bloodily and with zest," he does so only to correct imbalances in the system and to redress wrongs: it is never "rebellion against authority, for the outlaws are at one in the veneration of the king," but against the abuse of that authority by evil men.

How was the legend transmitted? The audience was larger than one might think, and even in illiterate medieval times it percolated throughout the society. It was originally

> spread by minstrels who were themselves employed in the households of the aristocracy. Through them it was broadcast from the hall to the market-place, the tavern and the inn, wherever a worthwhile audience might collect. In this fashion it traversed class boundaries. It was played before knights and was sung by peasants.

Its task, and its greatest achievement, was to provide a "moral fibre," a set of increasingly stringent instructions for virtuous behaviour.[6]

THE IRON PATH OF IMPERIAL DUTY

At the peak of empire in the nineteenth century, Charles Kingsley could write that "the age of chivalry is never past, so long as there is a wrong left unredressed on earth." These were the heroic qualities summoned from the English, and the heroes were selected to live and die in the service of the nation. Writing on the idolized missionary Sir Wilfred Grenfell, Ronald

Rompkey describes the rhetoric of English honour, quite different from its Mediterranean equivalents (with their cultural assumption that honour was inextricably linked to blood vengeance). Propagandists for empire drew "upon the writings of Charles Kingsley, the reforming ideas of Carlyle, and the cult of mediaevalism" to make "a personal appeal to the youth of England, incorporating images that fitted Grenfell's personal style: religion was 'chivalry' and life was a 'field of honour' calling for service." In at least thirty books written about Grenfell, their subject was retailed to the public "as a model of manly behaviour." In these and similar books, each hero of this time emerged "as the aggregate of certain traits of *homo imperiosus*: characteristics dominated by an acute sense of duty, application to task, strenuous sustained effort, and bursts of energetic action."[7]

The nineteenth-century English schoolchild did well to attend to these lessons, which charted all the superlatives relevant to the culture. The idealizing rhetoric ran deep: Grenfell, for example, was "a gifted surgeon, a fearless navigator, who runs within a hair's breadth of his life every week, a knight-errant enthused with the passion for his fellow kind throbbing in the greatest souls." After the end of the Great War, empire propagandists attributed stirring British personal qualities to "the spirit of an ancestry of fighters by land and sea." Such heroes exercised a wide influence, Rompkey noted, and literally "play a part, model themselves on the function to be performed, thus losing something of their own identity while at the same time acquiring identifiable mannerisms, turns of phrase, and habits of mind."[8]

Like Sir Thomas Stamford Raffles, Frederick Selous, Capt. C. H. Stigand and many others, the culture heroes spent their lives advancing the cause of empire, and died while struggling against the enemies of civilization. The personal qualities that were continuously emphasized were courage, an indifference to danger and a reluctance to display emotion. Selous applauded one English gentleman friend as "a very cool and courageous man, one whose pulse beat as calmly when face to face with a wounded elephant and snarling lion, as it did when quietly eating his breakfast." Selous' adventures were extraordinary, exemplary and widely read, reprinted in five editions through 1907, and many after that. His triumphs included escaping from "cannibals" by slipping away through the tall grasses and swimming across a crocodile-infested river, ever aware of his stature as representative of the empire.

> I had had time to realize the full horror of my position. A solitary Englishman, alone in Central Africa, in the middle of a hostile country, without blankets or anything else but what he stood in and a rifle with four cartridges . . .

Selous died appropriately in the Great War, while serving with the "Legion of Frontiersmen." There was some debate between *The Field* and *The Times* about the dramatic correctness of his heroic death, but his biographer J. G. Millais concluded he was killed instantly by a bullet in the head while "using his glasses to ascertain the position of the enemy's advance guard." In his final eulogy, Millais wrote: "Thus died Frederick Selous of the Great Heart, a splendid Englishman, who in spite of age and love of life, gave up all pleasant things to follow the iron path of duty. To him his country's needs were ever before his private interests."[9]

COLONEL JAMES CORBETT

Corbett was perhaps the ultimate expression of English imperial values. Although his international reputation was based on his hunting of man-eating tigers and leopards in India, he was photographed only once in his life with a firearm, and his expressed thoughts are singularly gentle, even noble. He consistently preferred nature photography over hunting, and he killed only when asked to do so by his country – whether dealing with rogue animals, or commanding soldiers during both World Wars. Corbett died full of years, just days after recounting his reverent shepherding of Princess Elizabeth on the night that she became Queen.

Corbett was born in 1875 in British India; but it was not until 1944 that he sat down to write about his life. He quickly became a hero of the empire with the first of his international bestsellers, *Man-eaters of Kumaon*, which documented his life in India, his extraordinary knowledge of the jungle, his despatching of man-killing cats and his love for the common people of India – but most of all displayed in their fullness the central core of imperial values. As Lord Hailey commented in an appreciation of Corbett that must have enraptured schoolboys,

> From boyhood he set himself to gain that intimacy with the jungle and its life that he would need if he was to enjoy such sport as his modest means allowed. He never forgot in after life the habit which he then taught himself of noiseless movement in the jungle nor his rare understanding of its sights and sounds, and it was then that he began to acquire that unique combination of speed and accuracy in the use of the rifle to which he was later to owe so much. One who knew him at that period has said, however, that even in his youth he took no special pride in this achievement. Good shooting was to him an obligation rather than an accomplishment. If things were to be killed, then this should be done instantly, and without pain to them.

Corbett's understanding of natural history is incomparable, as is his ability to communicate it; but from the perspective of our narrow inquiry, the *values* he dispensed were most significant. What were those values? One was a reluctance to legitimate any form of aggression against human beings or animals; another was a veneration for authority combined with a rejection of all such pretentious claims for himself. Ever "the most modest, companionable, and unassuming of men," R. E. Hawkin wrote of him, "he was equally at home with a viceroy or a poacher." Given the Freedom of the Forests of India, Corbett was made a Companion of the Order of the Star of India, and an Officer of the Order of the British Empire.

And yet it was "my friends, the poor of India" who forever seemed more important to him, as when he encountered a severely wounded Indian veteran who twenty years before had seen him despatch the killer of 124 human beings: "And now, sahib, I will go back to my home with great joy in my heart, for I shall be able to tell my father that with my own eyes I have seen you and, maybe, if I can get anyone to carry me to the fair that is held every year at Rudraprayag to commemorate the death of the man-eater, I shall tell the people I meet there that I have seen and had speech with you." Such values and myths sustained the empire and shaped an entire social ethic.

If he was the ultimate Great White Hunter, he was also a pioneer con-
servationist with a reverence for life. It was through his hunting, however,
that he displayed his controlled emotional qualities, as "when, at the age of
8 or 9, he learned to control his fear." Not yet an adolescent, armed with a
single-shot .450 rifle, he gave generations their approved emotional repertoire. Corbett epitomized, communicated and promoted the central core of
positive imperial values, and did so with a literary talent that gave him millions of readers. His influence was incalculable.[10]

ENGLISH AND AMERICAN CULTURE HEROES

[In America] murderers are more valued, certainly more admired, than
their victims. (Clancy Sigal)

In many films from Hollywood the violent killing of another person is an
achievement, an indication of strength of character. For British films it is
more likely to be an awkward necessity or a sign of incompetence. (David
Canter[11])

Many civilizations romanticize their outlaws; but the stories that are told of
them "act as a magnifying glass to show us the psycho-logic of violence in a
country." Writing of nineteenth-century Italy, Patrizia Guarnieri understood that "people wanted to read blood-curdling stories and to hear about
ferocious almost abnormal criminals," especially if "the murderer was
someone who had seemed to be above suspicion – a decent citizen or one
who appeared to be incapable of violence against weak, innocent victims."
What matters is *which* of their qualities are admired and imitated; for
stories told with too much of a positive emotional charge can be "a direct
source of 'inspiration' for violent men." American mass culture continually
asserts that criminal violence is noble and beautiful, itself a justification for
action. English culture tolerates violence only when there are no alternatives; and nothing in English culture compares with the American veneration for "small-time losers [who] can achieve a fiery incandescence, an
existential flowering, through the pain they inflict on others."[12]
     Such virulent notions are propagated in all the powerful mass cultural

forms of the twentieth century, including films, television, print and advertising. Joel Black asks questions we cannot yet answer regarding why "characters produced by the mass media [are] able to engage impressionable and
even critically sophisticated readers and viewers in ways that real-life
human beings cannot? What, in short, makes fiction even more powerful
than 'reality' in shaping – and destroying – people's lives?" He notes that
"only the victim knows the brutal 'reality' of murder; [while] the rest of us
view it at a distance, often as rapt onlookers who regard its 'reality' as a peak
aesthetic experience." Exactly: and that is why the manner in which our cultural forms portray violence and homicide is so critical, because they have
the capability to *aestheticize* and sexualize aggression.[13]

In modern mass-culture societies, the media – prime organs of cultural
transmission – are particularly cogent agents for the formulation of beliefs
about human nature. The process is a fascinating one, and ill understood.
An image, a personality, an action, is presented to the public; the act and the
actor are glamorized, made reasonable, even perfect, and we share their
feelings and their rationalizations. Even in violence-affirming cultures, the
majority of people are not violent; but a minority, the most vulnerable,
with the most limited emotional repertoires, responds to the violent
images, and the boundaries of acceptable behaviour are further degraded. If
we doubt the extraordinary power of films, or that many violent persons
model themselves on them, listen to British gangster Reg Kray describing
the grand entrance of a colleague into prison: he "arrived at Parkhurst
handcuffed to a screw and escorted by two others. He stopped at the gate,
jutted his jaw out and said, 'I made it, Ma!,' splaying out his arms à la James
Cagney in *White Heat*."[14]

If the American intoxication with aggressivity is a consistent cultural
theme, replayed in the classic western films throughout the century, the rate
and intensity of such messages appear to have accelerated since the mid-
1960s. The foundation for this was especially evident in the western films of
Sam Peckinpah, in which death was lovingly etched in slow motion, the
bullet and the resulting splattering of flesh portrayed with an aestheticized
sense of awe. As one analyst noted: "Peckinpah's gory scenes, blood-bags
and all, falsified the usual experience of death by gunshot, using visual

syntax to make it lyrical and garish rather than genuinely ugly," all this "at a time when the war in Vietnam was projecting lethal bloodshed wholesale on to television screens all over America." By the 1980s, Lewis H. Lapham records, "most of the important protagonists in the Hollywood action films had become paramilitary figures," "paranoid and enraged – angry at anybody and everybody to whom they could assign the fault for the world's evil," utterly lacking in "patriotic" or "ideological motive." Violence can be merely amusing in such a morally bankrupt milieu.[15]

An American Cultural Analysis: Primacy of the Self *Rambo*

First Blood was the first "Rambo" film: it appeared in 1982, in the aftermath of the withdrawal from Vietnam, and dealt with the humiliations of both country and soldier. The film orchestrates the wounds that all human beings experience, here intensified by war, and conveys the message that there is only one manly response to the frustrations of life – to respond to any provocation, against anyone who draws "first blood." This is necessary, the film reiterates in its theme song, because in the chaos of modern urban life "it's a real war outside your front door, I tell ya out there they'll kill ya."[16] If the social significance of the film transcends its limited aesthetic qualities, it is nevertheless a fundamental text for the explication of American mass culture's fascination with – and justification for – aggressive responses to a wide range of stimuli.

The text

A man is walking along a dirt road that cuts through wooded hills, past a collapsed barn (the barn, a symbol of honest values, is disused and decayed). The man is obviously poor, since he is wearing an army surplus jacket and blue jeans, and carrying a sleeping bag. He arrives at a farm, smiles and politely asks a middle-aged woman if this is the home of his friend, Delmar. Delmar's mother bitterly responds, "He ain't here." The man identifies himself as Delmar's Vietnam army comrade, John Rambo. "Delmar's gone," says the mother. "He died. Died last summer. Cancer, brought it back from 'Nam, all that [Agent] Orange stuff, they spread it around. Cut him down to nothing. I couldn't even lift him off from the sheet." Sombre music swells in the background. "I'm very sorry," a heart-broken Rambo tells the mother, and walks away.

In the next scene we are introduced to the idea of the legitimization of confrontation and violence. Entering a small town, an obese and vulgar sheriff drives beside Rambo – "Mornin' . . . you visiting somebody around here?" Then, with a hint of threat, he adds, "You know, looking the way you do, you're asking for trouble around here, friend. Jump in, I'll make sure you're headed in the right direction." Rambo asks the sheriff where he can eat. When the sheriff replies, "There's a diner about thirty miles up the highway," Rambo escalates the confrontation by asking, "Is there any law against me getting something here?" "Yeah, *me*," the sheriff replies.

Emphasizing that it is society drawing the first blood, Rambo asks, "Why are you pushing me? I haven't done anything to you?" The sheriff becomes aggressive: "*What* did you say? First of all, *you* don't ask the questions around here, *I* do, you understand? Secondly, we don't want guys like you in this town, drifters." Instead of heading on as the sheriff commands, Rambo defies authority and walks back towards town. Emotional music accompanies his challenge – "Where the hell do you think you're going?" Silence. "Hey, I'm talking to you, goddammit. Lemme see some ID." He shoves Rambo, drawing first physical "blood." "All right, you're under arrest. Put your hands on the car, and spread 'em." There is no response from Rambo, so the sheriff escalates the aggression by touching the pistol in his holster. Rambo stares defiantly, but finally moves slowly to the police car. The sheriff kicks Rambo's legs into place, then discovers Rambo's knife. "Well, what do we have here? Why would you be carrying a knife like this?" "Hunting," says Rambo, ominously. "Don't be a wise guy. What do you hunt with a knife?"

A handcuffed Rambo is brought into the police station, prompting an evil cop to begin abusing him, and intensify the "provocation": "Talk about your sorry-looking humanity," says the evil cop, and books Rambo on patently false charges of vagrancy, resisting arrest and carrying a concealed weapon. "See if you can clean him up a little bit," the sheriff tells his colleague. "He smells like an animal." When the evil cop asks him, "Name?," Rambo has flashbacks to when he was imprisoned and tortured in 'Nam.

Indifferent to his suffering, the evil cop threatens him: "Hey, if you're looking for trouble, you come to the right place, buddy." They discover Rambo's military identification: "Well, what do you know about that?" says the old cop after examining the dogtags. "Old Harry here is a soldier. Rambo." Rambo remains silent. "You gotta talk to me . . . I promise you got to talk to me, soldier. I'm starting to dislike you. A lot," he says as he brutally slams Rambo's chin with his club.

In the jail's showers, a good cop is shocked to notice the terrible scars all over Rambo's body. The evil cop smashes Rambo in the kidneys with his club, then kicks him – "The man said clean him up. Clean him up," and they turn a fire hose on Rambo. One cop chokes Rambo from behind, which produces more flashbacks to his tortures in 'Nam. The good cop begs his evil colleague to leave Rambo alone, while in Rambo's troubled mind, the evil cop becomes his Viet Cong torturer, slicing his chest with a knife. Rambo frees himself from the evil cop and assaults him. We are delighted. Rambo runs through the police station, kicking one officer and knocking another through a window: he finds his Rambo knife, and escapes on a stolen motorbike. A chase ensues, weaving across fields and hills. The sheriff calls in other cars, all smashing through fences and down muddy hills till his car overturns, lands on its roof, and Rambo roars away. "I know you can hear me," shouts the sheriff into the forest where he knows Rambo is hiding. "You're finished. You've gone as far as you can go." Police dogs growl. "It won't be long before we have this one stuffed and mounted," says one of the cops. "Make him into a bear rug."

Rambo is trapped at the edge of a cliff just as the police helicopter appears. "We got him cornered," one cop shouts. The evil cop appears in the helicopter's door with a rifle, and, unprovoked, opens fire. In desperation, Rambo jumps off the cliff, miraculously surviving a fall of hundreds of feet. The helicopter appears over him: just as the evil cop is about to take an easy shot, Rambo throws a rock which strikes the windshield, causing the helicopter to buck and the evil cop to tumble out to his death on the rocks below. We are delighted. Rambo picks up the cop and stares with hate in his bloodied face, then grabs his rifle. Rambo runs, and while stitching his wounds, shouts, "It's not my fault. I don't want any more hurt. I didn't do anything." The police open fire.

Now Rambo's true identity is revealed. A policeman on the wireless shouts to the sheriff, "Listen, Will, you sure picked one hell of a guy to mess around with. It just came over the teletype a few minutes ago. John Rambo is a Vietnam vet! He's a Green Beret, Congressional Medal of Honor, the guy's a war hero." The good cop, with whom we identify, smiles with admiration and exclaims, "I *knew* there was something about that guy!" Another cop murmurs in awe, "Those Green Berets, they're real bad asses." Rambo is in the woods sharpening a stake with his knife, making preparations for the encounter with sinister forces who cannot acknowledge his heroism.

As darkness and a storm descend, the trackers grow apprehensive: the police see what they think is Rambo and open fire, but it's a scarecrow, a trick, and in the confusion one of the cops is hit in the leg by "friendly fire." They send a dog after him, but Rambo kills it. The cops are frightened: "We ain't hunting him," says one cop, "he's hunting us." Rambo leaps up from a pile of leaves and stabs one cop who is screaming for help; then jumps out of a tree on to another cop, who runs off howling in fear. Another cop walks into a 'Nam-style booby-trap shrieking in pain, while still other police are disabled. Rambo grabs the sheriff, holds a knife to his throat and says: "I could have killed them all, I could have killed you. In town you're the law, out here it's me. Don't push it. Don't push it or I'll give you a war you won't believe. Let it go," Rambo begs before disappearing into the woods leaving a terrified sheriff weeping with fear.

Dawn breaks on what has become a major assault base, with dozens of police cars, television personnel and ambulances, all set for the attack on Fortress Rambo. We cut to a TV broadcaster, a lying apologist for the authorities – he speaks of Rambo as "the fugitive," and claims "he allegedly killed one deputy sheriff and tried to kill six others": worse, he covers up their incompetence (as the media did in Vietnam), saying "only their skilled training in police enforcement techniques saved their lives," and boasts that "the fugitive will be in custody in a matter of hours."

"Whatever possessed God in heaven to make a man like Rambo?" the sheriff asks. "God didn't make Rambo," says Rambo's beloved Colonel Trautman from Vietnam, who suddenly appears in the doorway, "I made him. I've come to get my boy. I recruited him, I trained him, I commanded him in Vietnam for three years." The sheriff asks why the army has offered to help. "I don't think you understand," says the colonel. "I didn't come here to rescue Rambo from you, I came here to rescue *you* from him. I'm just amazed that he allowed any of your posse to live. You're lucky to be breathing. You don't seem to want to accept the fact that you're dealing with an expert in guerrilla warfare, with a man who's the best with guns, with knives, with his bare hands, a man who's been trained to ignore pain, to ignore weather, to live off the land, to eat things that would make a billygoat puke. Rambo was the best." Somehow the colonel agrees to help, and we see Rambo in hiding, listening to a two-way radio. The colonel calls Rambo using old Vietnam squad codes. "Come in," urges the colonel. "We can't have you running around out there wasting friendly civilians." "There *are* *no* friendly civilians," replies Rambo. "There wouldn't be no trouble except for that King Shit cop. All I wanted was something to eat. But the man kept pushing, sir. They drew first blood, not me; they drew first blood."

After dark, Rambo hijacks an army truck and its machine gun and races to town, crashing through the police barricade and a wall of unprovoked gunfire. He sets on fire a petrol station for a stunning visual effect, and dodges through town in his famous pose – carrying his machine gun with its heavy ammunition belt wrapped around his shoulders. Now The Revenge begins. Police and soldiers flee in confusion, while the sheriff prepares for his Last Stand: "Everybody dies," he says, and shoves a loaded magazine into his assault rifle. Rambo opens fire with his machine gun, exploding the glass and buildings, pouring a trail of gunpowder to burn the entire town, preparing for the Final Confrontation. To re-emphasize Rambo's "second blood" justification, it is the sheriff who sees him and fires first: Rambo replies with a burst from his machine gun, which wounds the sheriff. Rambo appears to have decided to kill him: despite his pain the sheriff manfully urges him on. "Go ahead, go ahead, go ahead, you crazy son of a bitch, finish it." But the colonel appears and orders him to stop: "This mission is over."

This gives Rambo the cue for his monologue, which switches between Vietnam and the contemporary U.S., between his loss of purpose, status and respect, and the wounds that justify his behaviour. "Nothing is over, nothing. You just don't turn it off. It wasn't my war. You asked me, I didn't ask you, and I did what I had to do to win. But somebody wouldn't let us win. Then I come back to the world, and I see all those maggots at the airport, protesting me and spitting, calling me babykiller and all kinds of vile crap. Who are they to protest me, huh? Who are they, unless they've been me and been there, and know what the hell they're yelling about? For me civilian life is nothing. In the field we had a code of honour – you watch my back, I watch yours. Back here it's nothing. Back there I could fly a gunship, I could drive a tank, I was in charge of million-dollar equipment. Back here I can't even hold a job. Jesus, oh God, where is everybody, God . . . All those guys there . . . all those fighting guys, they were my friends. Back here there's nothing. You remember Danforth? [They] fucking blew his body all over the place, he's laying there, he's screaming and pieces of him all over me, my friend is all over me, he's got blood and I'm trying to hold him together. I put him together, his fucking insides keep coming out and nobody would help. Nobody would help. He'd say, 'I want to go home, I want to go home.' But 'I can't find your fucking legs, I can't find your legs.' I can't get it out of my head, it's been seven years, every day I have this, sometimes I wake up and I don't know where I am. I don't talk to anybody, sometimes [for] a day, sometimes [for a] week. I can't put it out of my mind." Sobbing, he hugs his trusted Colonel Trautman, as the music rises. The colonel and Rambo leave the building together, flanked by state police as if by an honour guard.

This extraordinary text is an explication and transmission of a *basic cultural code* still lost in a fantasy of primitive vengeance – that extreme violence is the appropriate response to a specific stimulus, in this case, frustration and humiliation. Its script provides a violence-validating inspiration for the most vulnerable citizens of the U.S., and assists in the construction of aggressive social identities.

An English Cultural Analysis: The Primacy of Authority

If Rambo rages righteously against authority, James Bond works only on its behalf. His violence is only deployed when it is necessary, and it is never personalized: indeed he never loses his cool detachment. Bond first expressed this message in 1962 in *Dr. No*. Bond and the stunningly beautiful foreign woman are escaping from Dr. No's private army when Bond dispassionately kills one of the soldiers. The woman wonders why Bond killed him. "Because I had to," Bond replied pragmatically. When the woman describes how she herself once killed a man who had molested her, Bond shudders and is visibly shocked at the primitive vengeance of the foreigner. "Did I do wrong?" she asks. Bond replies unemotionally, "Well, it wouldn't do to make a habit of it." Primitive personalized vengeance is not in his culture's script.

The Bond film that is contemporary with *First Blood* is the 1983 production, *Never Say Never*; and it retails a profoundly different cultural mystique. If Rambo was a study in raging frustration, Bond continually emphasizes that life should be viewed as a game, where stratagem and personal detachment are the thing. Violence is the last resort of a brute and a foreigner. Early in the film, the foreign female villain arrives at the secret meeting of Spectre – the Special Executive for Counter-intelligence, Terrorism, Revenge and Extortion – whose insignia is a cast human skull. The foreign Spectre leader is an unscrupulous arms dealer. "You will note," he says, "that we have supplied both rebels and government forces: in matters of death, Spectre is strictly impartial." He then reveals his diabolical plan, to steal NATO nuclear warheads and use them to blackmail the world. When they have successfully stolen the warheads, the female villain shouts "Bravo" at their accomplice, then hurls a poisonous snake through his car window: foreigners love evil and death.

Spectre announces to the world that they now have the warheads, threatening a "terrible catastrophe" which can only be avoided "by paying a tribute to our organization, amounting to 25 per cent of your respective countries' annual oil purchases. We have accomplished two of the functions that the name Spectre embodies, terror and extortion. If our demands are not met within seven days we shall ruthlessly apply the third, *revenge*." "If this gets out," shouts one European diplomat, "it will cause worldwide panic." Bond is set on the trail of the foreign arch-villain, Largo, now at home on his yacht, watching his beautiful girlfriend exercising. She shows her love for him, but asks ambiguously, "What would you do if I left you?" "Cut your throat," he says with an evil foreign smile.

At HQ, Bond is issued a clever new invention, a poison dart-throwing pen with the U.K. flag on it. "We're both humble servants of the Crown,"

Bond tells the inventor. "Good to see you, Mr. Bond," the inventor tells Bond. "Things have been awfully dull round here. Bureaucrats running the old place, everything done by the book, can't make a decision unless the computer gives you the go-ahead. Now you're on this," the inventor says, with a level of self-parody of which Rambo would be incapable, "I hope we're going to have some gratuitous sex and violence." "I certainly hope so too," says Bond.

In Nassau, Bond is met at the airport by a pompous official from the British Embassy, who briefs Bond on Largo: "He's charming – I mean *foreign*, but charming nonetheless." The female villain, Fatima, encounters Bond and they athletically make love on a yacht. Afterwards, they don frogman gear, and she places a shark-attracting beeper on his air tank before sneaking away. The sharks attack Bond, but he escapes into the arms of yet another beautiful woman. When Fatima notices he has survived, she plants a bomb in his bed. Ever alert to foreign perfidy, Bond changes hotel rooms and the ensuing explosion harms no one. Always, he responds to violence with clever strategy.

The film's centrepiece is the great electronic game played at Largo's lavish party. "Are you a man who enjoys games?" Largo asks Bond. "It depends with whom I'm playing," says Bond. Largo leads Bond to the game, called Domination. "I designed it myself," he tells Bond, "but my problem is I've never yet found a worthy adversary." With appropriate understatement, Bond replies, "No doubt I shall disappoint you too." "This game has one objective – power," Largo explains. "We will be fighting for countries, chosen at random by the machine," and the penalty for losing is to receive severe electric shocks. They begin to play. "Thank you, gentlemen," says the computer. "The eternal battle for the domination of the world begins." Bond loses the first round and the second but he is getting better, though the shocks visibly shake him. "Perhaps I didn't explain," says Largo; "as the stakes increase, so does the level of pain. Rather like life."

The game continues: Bond has the hang of it now, but the electric shocks drop him painfully to the floor. "I think it is better that you don't continue," Largo suggests patronizingly. Bond responds with British pluck, "Can we play one more game for the rest of the world?" The tension is now overwhelming, and a large audience gathers to watch the battle. "Danger level!" says the computer. "Repeat, danger level." Now it is Largo who is receiving intense shocks. "Pain level 70 per cent," says the computer. "Danger, danger, danger." Largo remains cool but the pain finally forces him to concede. "It seems I underestimated you," he says. "Do you lose as gracefully as you win?" "I wouldn't know, I've never lost," Bond replies, then dances with Largo's girlfriend, and tells her that Largo is "certifiable."

Returning to his apartment, he finds his colleague has been murdered by Fatima, who jumps into a sports car and hurries away, laughing maniacally. Bond follows on a motorcycle. The usual chase scene follows, ending with him pursuing Fatima into a warehouse, where he is knocked off his bike. Fatima points a revolver at him and demands that he spread his legs so she can shoot him in the genitals. "You're quite a man, Mr. James Bond, but I am a superior woman." Witty sexual repartee follows in which Bond suggests Fatima may not have been the best lover he's ever had: she is enraged, and demands that he "Write. Now write this: 'The greatest rapture in my life was afforded me in a boat in Nassau by Fatima Blush, signed James Bond 007.'" Bond pulls out his Secret Service dart-throwing pen, then drolly says, "I just remembered: it's against Service policy for agents to give out endorsements." He fires the pen as she fires her pistol: the rocket takes a moment to explode in her chest.

Later, on board the yacht, Bond kisses Largo's girlfriend, knowing the insanely jealous Largo is watching them through one-way glass. Enraged and out of control, Largo begins smashing things with a fire axe. Imprisoned, they miraculously escape, and are eventually rescued by a British submarine. Showering together, she asks, "You're going back after Largo, aren't you?" "Well, I have to," says Bond. "I want him as much as you do," says the beautiful woman. "*Probably more*," says Bond, but "I can understand you hating him," emphasizing his dispassionate Englishness. The classic English cultural messages never validate personalized violence, and provide an entirely different script for its most vulnerable citizens.

THE GROWTH OF THE ANTI-HERO

By the 1960s, not long before the English homicide rate began to rise, a new theme began to receive attention: now the sermon on the moral decline of society was given by a succession of murderers. A significant change seemed to occur in the public perception of major crimes and criminals – always romanticized, perhaps, but now progenitors of a violence-justifying ideology.

Kray twins

The image can be more destructive than the man, as when the Kray twins were celebrated as grotesque working-class heroes. Certainly that was the way they portrayed themselves, prompting one journalist to marvel at the mystique generated by "these unrepentant murderers," whose admirers could merely claim that "when the Krays ruled the East End, old ladies and children could walk about without fear because Ronnie or Reggie would 'sort out' anybody who threatened them." Still, several hundred people rallied in Hyde Park in October 1993 to demand the release from prison of the gangster twins, once "the capital's most powerful and feared criminals."[17]

Many books have been written by and about them, but the most fascinating document is Reggie Kray's "autobiography," *Born Fighter*, in which he stakes his claim to greatness. The illustrations accompanying the text are artfully chosen; their task is to catalogue his public case. It is the very stuff of image making and cultural transmission: twenty-five photographs in manly poses, surrounded by celebrities and business associates.

Appropriately to his pretensions, Reggie's opening chapter takes its title from the Bible – "In the beginning," he writes, and focuses on the adulation he now enjoys. He is "exhilarated" to be driven in a prison bus through the capital – "I was pleased to be back in London for a week. It's still the best city in the world, still a great city of glamour." Briefly returned to Wormwood Scrubs after a long absence, he revels in his status as *patron*: "They all asked how Ron was and sent their best wishes," and "all through that week, my friends there really went out of their way to make me welcome. People were coming to my cell to shake hands or to tell their different stories, and this made me feel touched and very humble." His career and his celebrity give him a sense of eternal youth: "Though I was the oldest in the coach, I did not feel older than the rest. It was as though I had not aged. We all laughed aloud. I felt really good to be with people who were so happy, even though they faced part of their future in adversity. I will never forget them. They were a smashing bunch." Transformed by this attention into a kind of prison sage, he is generous with his time and wisdom: "One young coloured kid who had just got a life sentence came to my cell to seek my advice on how to get through his time, and also asked me to sign a photo to his parents. I made the kid a cup of tea and I gave him advice in the hope it will help him."

To show us his credentials as a human being, he comforts us with sentimental images of family and friends, accompanied by a photograph of his adopted son. "Time has taken many of our old friends from us, through death, and we are left with just the memories . . . and the dreams." Remembering their childhood, he writes of the warmth he felt when his mother would sing Vera Lynn songs: "Ron and I used to sleep in the back room, and sometimes we would lie there in the mornings listening to my mother. As I listened, I used to get great comfort and a feeling of belonging, as though we were in our own mansion and not just a terraced house." To complete the rewriting of the family's history, he emphasizes that "it's not true that Ron ever struck the old man, although there used to be many arguments, just like most families in the East End had in those days. My old man was on the run from the army for twelve years, so he had some excuse to turn to drink, seeing that his family life had been so disrupted, but I never forgot that he went on the run in the first place to look after us when we were young," thus implying that those men who joined the wartime army had abandoned their children to fend for themselves.

Ultimately their use of force would enable them to buy *everything* they admired: "In the war years, we stayed at a place called Hadleigh, near Tring, where there were big fields of red poppies and a mansion owned by the Rothschilds. We used to play in the grounds there with the frogs from the ponds and wish that one day we could own a place like that. Twenty-five years later, we did. We bought a mansion and a cottage with eight and a half acres of land." Difficult philosophical contradictions, such as his deep reverence for royalty and his anti-establishment posture, are presented as a kind of defence of the family: if he and his brother were very rebellious, it was "because of the police hounding and searching for my father." Moreover, if they "have always been anti-authority, through my Dad's teachings I have also been a royalist and have never had anything against the upper class. This is because my old man always spoke well of them."

He used the short-lived wartime social solidarity as both analogy and justification for his own "war" on society. "These were days of camaraderie, of closely knit groups of people who were truly at war with the dictator Hitler. In later years, when I had this same type of feeling, I guess we were at war in a way with the establishment." Thus changing London's gambling regulations becomes somehow comparable to stopping Hitler: "I always considered that drinking and gambling clubs should be legal for the poorer classes as well as for the rich. And it would really needle me that exclusive clubs were run in the West End of London for the rich, while in the poorer areas, these same type of clubs were closed down and said to be illegal. That's another of the reasons why Ron and I were so anti-authority."

But there was no evil ambition in them, he claims, and he professed to be embarrassed to find he and his brother had "become notorious." Yet the celebrity can be a burden: "Sometimes today I'm asked how Ron and I can cope with our notoriety. I can only answer that we have grown so used to it over the years that the almost daily occurrence of seeing our name in print does not affect us at all." After offering the reader a list of their early appearances in newspapers, he remembers visiting a dance hall in Finsbury Park when he was eighteen, and an impressionable youth inquired, "'Have you heard of the Kray twins?' And I said, feeling a little embarrassed and trying to be as modest as possible, 'I am Reggie Kray.' He looked shocked."

Years before that, he admits, the brothers "were becoming notorious in the East End of London, mostly because we had our own gang, and we had been barred from most of the cinemas and dance halls in the areas round East London as a result. We used to keep choppers, machetes, knives, swords and all kinds of weapons beneath the bed that Ron and I slept in at Vallance Road." But such weaponry was necessary because of the neighbourhood, and the neighbours: "It was a very rough area, Bethnal Green. There were a lot of gang fights, and we had to have weapons of some kind. Ron and I usually had a knife on us. We got our first gun off some criminal at this age. Ron always guessed that he would shoot somebody some day. He guessed he would have to. Before long, we had an arsenal of guns." This may appear cruel, but it was necessary because other "gangs had at times attacked their rivals in their own households, sometimes even when they were in bed, and Ron and I were determined this would not happen to us. We had no intention of being caught unawares." But it was all for the best: "We were following in the footsteps of so many others from East and North London who had turned to villainy as a way of making money."

He and other celebrities have much to share, and he seems equally at ease with the company of – imaginary or otherwise – the Queen Mother, the president of the United States and celebrated rock stars. When he assisted in the compilation of a book on slang, "I sent copies of *Slang* to Ronald Reagan, because I always believed in reaching high, and on the same day, I sent one to the Queen Mother. I'm a big fan of hers." Later, indulging "my new interest in writing lyrics for pop songs," an article appeared in *Melody Maker* "about this new interest of mine," and he "began to receive inquiries from musicians I had never met," including Nasty Suicide and Das Psycho Rangers. Indeed, a demo tape was recorded "which includes my lyrics on a song called 'Retribution,' about the killing of Jack 'The Hat.'"

He comments on social issues from a lofty platform: he is against capital punishment, and despises "football hooligans who get this country a bad name." Moreover, he laments the loss of traditional values: the many "rapists and child-killers" in one prison "served as an indication of what the cities, towns and even villages are like today, with rampant rape and child killings. This is a sad reflection on society, and when I think of the fighting men I knew in the past, I yearn for yesterday and the principles that went with it." Moreover, his spiritual sensibilities are such that he claims to have psychic powers, to heal the sick and to influence events by his prayers. "I can reveal that I became close to God in Parkhurst. I prayed for a friend who had cancer. This friend was cured in return for me being born again as a Christian. I could not and cannot become a saint overnight, but I leave it all in God's hands."

The spirituality is striking, but the values he dispenses are most apparent in his comments on his own "heroes," those he and his brother admire the most. His brother "looks for loyalty and politeness in his friends. He doesn't like arrogant or rude people." One man they respect is Mike, considered by Ron "to be the bravest in Broadmoor. He attacked a screw, not in the wards but in the punishment block where the screws have everything their own way. He bit a screw's ear half off." Another with estimable personal qualities is a "feller called Trevor who's very tall and slim, with big bony hands. He once strangled a man with his bare hands, which is what he's in Broadmoor for. And he massages Ron's neck once a week! He's a very nice feller, apparently," and is "always helping the sick people."

As for the murders they committed, he admits to having "complex thoughts" regarding whether he should feel remorseful; and wonders "why the establishment expects criminals to feel remorse for murder while at the same time expecting the soldier at war to feel victorious. Let's put it this way: if I had not killed Jack McVitie, he might be writing this instead of me, and I might be where he is." Ron apparently developed this theme with a "researcher," who asked "what his feelings were about our violent acts towards other villains in the fifties and sixties." "His reply was this, 'I never felt sorry for anyone who got hurt. They deserved it, otherwise it wouldn't have happened. We didn't enjoy violence, we tried to avoid it, but we had to use it sometimes. One feller called me a fat slob, so I had to do him. I went in the toilet and told someone I wanted to speak to him. As he came in, I cut him with a knife. He had to have plastic surgery. We've both been violent in our time, me and Reggie, but we never liked it. It's like soldiers in the war, SAS and that. They're not violent people, really, but they have to use it.'"[18]

THE YORKSHIRE RIPPER

Just as the Krays claimed to use violence for vengeance, so did the Ripper, who later saw himself as God's avenging angel, pontificating on the decay of society – "It's depraved – all they think of is money and finances – there are no moral values," he said. Moreover, he exonerated himself in court, claiming he was essentially innocent because he had killed "on theological grounds." Indeed, his astute biographer, Barbara Jones, was overwhelmed by his obsession with being seen as a good person. As he told her, "I suppose the public believe what they've read in the newspapers – that's all wrong. I'm not a beast. That isn't me at all. I'm concerned about other people – I've always been good to my neighbours, particularly when they're in trouble. No one seems to understand what it's like when a person is taken over, given a mission. It's really awful for anyone to be in pain. I wouldn't be responsible for anyone's agony, ever. Those people I attacked, well it wasn't really me, I mean the real, caring me. That me was in conflict – a good Catholic fighting an avenging angel acting on orders from God. I'm no mass killer. I'd been told what my mission was, like a soldier in a war. I couldn't disobey my orders. They came from the highest authority." The orders had come in a revelation he had experienced, he said, while he worked as a grave digger. "The mumbling voice had a strange effect. I felt I was privileged to hear it. It had started to rain and I remember looking from the top of the slope over the valley and feeling I'd just experienced something fantastic. I looked across the valley, and all around, and thought of Heaven and Earth and how insignificant we all were. But I felt so important at that moment. I had been selected."

By his own admission, he was "not a violent person by nature." Indeed, the good neighbour and Catholic was merely doing his duty: "There have been crusades, holy wars, ever since history began. Thousands and thousands have been killed. I was on a crusade too – against prostitutes. But I thought I was saving their souls. Like I said, the instructions came from God. Really, it could have been anyone with the same religious beliefs. If I'd not been brought up a good Catholic this might never have happened. From the start I was taught the difference between right and wrong. It stands to reason that sex for money, sex without love, is wrong." Moreover, he was offended by his media title, this man who masturbated over the woman whose skull he had hammered: "They're wrong to call me the Yorkshire Ripper. I didn't chop up any of those women. But the newspapers seem to be able to print what they like about me. There was only one of them where I acted like Jack the Ripper," he admits, but even here, "I had no choice." "I believed I had to carry out the orders, and tell no one. That was the real tragedy," not the deaths of the young women, "not being able to tell anyone."

Moreover, he thought he had been merciful: the killing "was always over quickly, most of the time it was less than a couple of minutes. I don't think any of them felt any pain. I would always strike them first on the back of the head before they had a chance to experience any fright. That would stun them, then I usually dragged them out of sight and finished them off by stabbing with a knife. I didn't actually wish any of them harm in a personal way. I didn't know any of them, so I couldn't have anything against them personally. I didn't even speak to most of them." Sadistic sexual assault and humiliation of an object/victim were never his motives, he claims. Indeed, it was really he who suffered the most: "I were in agony for the few days before the attack, I were really suffering. I were compelled to plan every detail, then set off with one thing in mind. Nothing could stop me, and I could not stop myself. Anyone with a grain of common sense can see that I believed God was telling me to do it. There was no other motive."

Occasionally a trace of insight, even honesty, emerges, as when he discussed the aftermath of the first murder: "I carried on as normal, living with my wife. After that first time I developed and played up a hatred for prostitutes in order to justify within myself a reason why I had attacked and killed Wilma McCann." After the second murder, he "went straight home to my mother-in-law's house and had a feeling of satisfaction and justification." By then, he had begun to "brood and blame everything on prostitutes," and felt himself chosen to "clean up the streets." "It was my calling and I had no qualms about it." Only once did he admit, when he was reminded he had killed people who had nothing whatever to do with prostitutes, that "I just wanted to kill a woman."

When he finally confessed to police, he naturally painted his capitulation in self-justifying colours. "I realized that this was the time to tell them, because they were saying, in other words, that they had found the weapons I had hidden. I had been given the signal from God, through the police, that now was the time to tell them." Even at the end, God did not abandon him, he claimed: "I had guidance from God, for my mission. I didn't need a solicitor. God was aware of everything that was happening and it was in His hands." Now, in his characteristic self-absorption, he absolved himself of all evil: "I believed I were doing the right thing, and I had to do it. Nobody seems to realize what it took out of me. Look at the absolute moral decline of society. Every aspect of it is one of decay and corruption."[19]

Bombarded with such propaganda justifying violence in a hundred different ways, the most disordered members of a great civilization lumber in the wrong direction, sometimes with coaching from the most articulate members of the society: one catches a note of reverence for the killer and his mentality in more recent British books on multiple killers. David Canter notes with alarm that such work contributes to an atmosphere of "endemic acceptance of borderline morality," and provides "a fertile breeding ground for many forms of depravity."[20]

---

1   1982, *The Great Code: The Bible and Literature*, Toronto: Academic Press, p. 37.

2   W. A. Belsen, 1978, *Television Violence and the Adolescent Boy*, Westmead: Saxon House, p. 520; L. A. Joy, Meredith Kimball and Merle Zabrack, "Television and Children's Aggressive Behavior," in Tannis MacBeth Williams (ed), 1986, *The Impact of Television: A Natural Experiment in Three Communities*, London: Academic Press, p. 334; Osmo Wiio, 1995, "Is Television a Killer? An International Comparison," *Intermedia* 23: 26–31.

3   See *The New York Times*, Oct. 23, 1994, p. 16.

4   David Canter, 1994, *Criminal Shadows: Inside the Mind of the Serial Killer*, London: HarperCollins, pp. 232–233, my italics.

5   Maurice Keen, 1977, *The Outlaws of Medieval Legend* (revised edition), London: Routledge & Kegan Paul, pp. xvi, xvi–xvii.

6   J. C. Holt, 1982, *Robin Hood*, London: Thames & Hudson, pp. 7–8, 10–13.

7   Quoted in Ronald Rompkey, 1989, "Heroic Biography and the Life of Sir Wilfred Grenfell," *Prose Studies* 12: 159–73.

8   Quoted in Rompkey, 1989; Rompkey, 1989, pp. 160–161, 171.

9   F. C. Selous, quoted in Peter Hathaway Capstick, 1992, *The African Adventurers*, pp. 23–24, 49; J. G. Millais, 1919, *Life of Frederick Courtenay Selous, DSO*, London: Longman, Green & Co., pp. 340, 344–345. For similar late nineteenth century inspirational literature, see also Lt. Col. J. H. Patterson, 1907, *The Man-eaters of Tsavo*, London: Macmillan; and Capt. C. H. Stigand, 1913, *Hunting the Elephant in Africa*, London: Macmillan.

10   Hailey, introduction to Corbett's *Tree Tops*, 1955, Oxford U. P., p. vii; R. E. Hawkins' introduction to *Jim Corbett's India*, 1978, Oxford U. P., pp. 7, 8, 9, 3, 4, 5, 28. Corbett is long dead, but his gene pool lives on: in the spring of 1994, when my son and I were white-water rafting in northern Canada, the superbly athletic adventurer minding our safety from his kayak was Corbett's grandnephew, Peter Gordon.

11   Clancy Sigal, in the *Guardian Weekly*, Sept. 11, 1993, p. 28; David Canter, 1994, op. cit., p. 233.

12   David Canter, personal communication; Patrizia Guarnieri, 1993, *A Case of Child Murder: Law and Science in Nineteenth-Century Tuscany*, Cambridge: Polity Press, p. 88. "During the second half of the nineteenth century a new literary genre based on the exploits of bandits and criminals was gaining great success. Originally French, it quickly took hold in Italy, finding fertile ground in the credibility of the populace and the already existing ballad tradition." Sigal, op. cit., p. 29.

13   Joel Black, 1991, *The Aesthetics of Murder: A Study in Romantic Literature and Contemporary Culture*, London: The Johns Hopkins U. P., pp. x, 3.

14   *Born Fighter*, p. 145.

15   In *Times Literary Supplement*, #4703, May 21, 1993, p. 21; Lewis H. Lapham, *Harper's*, April 1994.

16   By Jerry Goldsmith, sung by Dan Hill, Anabass Investments.

17   *Guardian Weekly*, Oct. 17, 1993, p. 8.

18   *Born Fighter*, 1990, London: Arrow Books, pp. 2–8, 10, 12, 16, 20, 24–27, 146, 163, 156–57, 150–151, 166, 175, 120–121.

19   In Barbara Jones, 1992, *Voices From an Evil God*, London: Blake, pp. 255, 3, 38–39, 10, 6, 14, 19, 20, 77, 105, 86, 89, 92, 95, 128, 100, 153, 163, 270; Gordon Burn, 1990, *Somebody's Husband, Somebody's Son: The Story of the Yorkshire Ripper*, London: Pan, p. 360.

20   David Canter, personal communication.

THE EVOLUTION OF
A SENSIBILITY

Revenge belongeth to the magistrate.
(Sir Edward Coke, 1552–1634[1])

ORIGINS

ALTHOUGH THE STATE has long ago seized the monopoly of violence, each generation thinks it lives in uniquely violent times. This perception is so ancient, J. S. Cockburn wrote, that "most nineteenth-century Englishmen were convinced that crime was increasing as never before; eighteenth-century commentators were thoroughly alarmed by what they saw as a rising tide of violent criminality; and complaints of the imminent break-down of law and order punctuated the Middle Ages." Indeed, in 1582, William Lambard, magistrate of Kent, was moved to complain that "sin of all sorts swarmeth and ... evildoers go on with all licence and impunity." Yet the English homicide rate has for centuries remained among the lowest in the urban industrial world: how did it achieve and maintain such a comparatively pacific equilibrium?[2]

Little is known about the pre-literate civilization that preceded the Roman conquest of Britain, but it seems to have been similar to what existed throughout western Europe – clan- or tribe-based local groups based on hunting and primitive agriculture and pastoralism. Their rule of law would have been a mixture of early kingship and the sacred law of the blood feud, the near-universal kin-based form of dispute resolution. Like much of western Europe, England inherited the influence of Graeco-Roman civilization. The Athenian laws encapsulated and expressed the dominant mentality of blood vengeance implicit in primitive societies:

99

Douglas MacDowell observed that when a homicide had been committed in classical Athens, it was the responsibility of the victim's family to seek revenge according to the ancient laws of the blood feud. It was necessary for the victim to be avenged; and the killer, who had polluted himself and society by his actions, required "purification."[3]

In England, the ninth-century recorded laws of King Alfred reflected a society in which kinship was still the basis for identity and status, and relations between unrelated kin were regulated by vendetta. By 1012, following the Danish conquest, a land tax was already being collected, and the Danish kings "were expounding the law" on honour and blood vengeance. Thus, a man was permitted to "fight on behalf of his lord if the lord is being attacked"; and "a man may fight on behalf of his born kinsman, if he is being wrongly attacked, except against his lord; that we do not allow."[4]

Susan Reynolds notes that until the twelfth century, "legal procedures and the ideas they embody seem to have been very similar in England, France, Germany, and at least the northern part of Italy." It was only thereafter that the systems of law "began to diverge like species on slowly separating continents." The emerging *Englishness* of legal practice was an emphasis by the late twelfth century on "precise form and rules of application by a monarchy with the power to enforce them," a system, Reynolds thinks, that "fostered intelligent collective activity." This system "gave people the habit of arguing and agreeing and acting together to maintain the peace and to fulfil their responsibilities to their rulers." As English government grew ever more powerful and centralized, leaving behind the political fragmentation characteristic of much of Continental Europe, and as the weight of jurisprudence bent the common law towards reason, not revenge, the vendetta receded into history. "More and more crimes came to incur formal punishments, inflicted by the authority of the ruler, instead of being left to mutual negotiation by feud and wergeld." If much of "the maintenance of law and order still depended in large measure on collective self-policing, it was now the king's (or sometimes the count's or duke's) peace which the law-breaker broke."[5]

Thus the primary social developments in the three centuries following the Norman conquest were the construction of what was by European standards a "strong royal government"; the emergence of a distinctively English common law increasingly intolerant of blood feud and personal violence; and the establishment of Parliament. Asa Briggs argues that "the presence in Parliament in the reign of Edward I (1272–1307)" of a commons, not just nobility and clergy, "encouraged the merchants and feudal elements, divided in many political societies, to think of their common interests": moreover, a nascent sense of social responsibility was fostered in the common people by an expanding set of community obligations. But medieval English villagers were no longer simply European peasants, slaves to feudal power and tied to some "all-powerful" custom. By the thirteenth century, the individual was no longer submerged in the group. Indeed, Alan Macfarlane argues, the English "peasantry" was fast emerging as an assemblage of individuals, capable of perceiving their personal advantage in the social and economic market-places, and acting upon it – constrained only by a powerful and widely accepted system of law. The bottom of a complex but comparatively open social hierarchy, they learned to absorb the values and beliefs emanating from the élites.[6]

A BRIEF HISTORY OF HOMICIDE

England's criminal history is better documented than that of any other country, with the possible exception of Japan. Ted Gurr's masterful overview reminds us that "the post-1960 increase in violent crime in most western societies was preceded by a much longer period of decline." He noted that the British "incidence of homicide has fallen by a factor of at least ten to one since the thirteenth century," a time when "men were easily provoked to violent anger, and were unrestrained in the brutality with which they attacked their opponents." Like most contemporary authorities in the field, Gurr attributes the historical downward trend to *cultural* changes, "especially the growing sensitization to violence and the development of increased internal and external controls on aggressive behaviour." The increase of the homicide rate that occurred in England in the last few decades is comparatively small, was "preceded by a much longer period of decline," and is a common historical peculiarity in times of social and economic dislocation.[7]

Lawrence Stone admits that data between 1250 and 1800 are sometimes

"skimpy," but "reveal an unmistakable trend": "homicide rates in thirteenth-century England were about twice as high as those in the sixteenth
and seventeenth centuries, and those of the sixteenth and seventeenth centuries were some five to ten times higher than those today." These statistical
data, which even their harshest critics agree are "broadly correct," are also
buttressed by anecdotal evidence. Stone offers an illustration from one
unexceptional life:

> John Aubrey, the son of a squire in Wiltshire in the seventeenth century,
> was nearly killed three times in his life by the thrust of a sword: once in a
> London street by a drunk he had never seen before; once during a quarrel
> among friends in legal chambers in the Inner Temple; and once by the Earl
> of Pembroke at a disorderly parliamentary election at Salisbury.

Most homicides in that period "were by neighbours, friends or total
strangers, often the result of drunken barroom brawls or village quarrels."
Homicide rates were very high by modern standards: Hanawalt's estimate
for fourteenth-century London is between 36 and 52 per 100,000, five times
the current U.S. average; and Hammer's estimate for Oxford in the 1340s is
over 100.

The explanation for this decline, Stone suggests, is the "civilizing
process slowly seeping down from the upper classes to the violence-prone
poor"; the "transformation of manners in the late seventeenth century,
and then by the humanitarian ideology of the Enlightenment." If these
ideas were "first launched by intellectuals, lawyers, nobles and bourgeois,"
the civilizing attitudes they contained "penetrated all sectors of society,"
leading to a profound and consistent decline in levels of interpersonal violence. Parallel with this were sociological shifts: the transformation of
society from a feudal one "in which honour and status are the most prized
attributes" (and assaults on persons therefore the appropriate revenge) to
a bourgeois society, in which "money and market relationships form the
basis of social organization, and crimes are therefore directed against
property."[8]

By expunging the vendetta, England was evolving in quite a different
direction from the Continent, where notions of personal vengeance con-

tinued to hold sway, and "brutality" still marred "all social behaviour." Cyprus, for example, was deformed by "ceaseless wrangling between aristocratic kinsfolk – contested successions, fraught minorities and quarrels between cousins." Robert Irwin comments on the triviality of murderous provocation:

> On the day before his murder, Peter I imprisoned his steward and threatened to execute him for not providing enough oil for the asparagus. The King's murder which followed was the result of a separate quarrel which had its origins in a dispute over greyhounds. A few years later, blood flowed in the streets of Nicosia as the Venetians and Genoese quarrelled over who should hold the stirrup for the newly crowned King Peter II. It was a quarrel which led to the Genoese invasion of the island and fierce fightings, at the end of which the Genoese occupied Famagusta.[9]

The Thirteenth Century

The general tenor of the time was, by current standards, exceedingly violent, with a homicide rate from ten to twenty times that of modern-day England. James Given estimates a rate so high that virtually everyone "knew of someone" killed. The vast majority of killers (91.4 per cent) were males, but unlike the present where male and female victims are nearly equal, 80.5 per cent of the medieval victims were also male, often killed by strangers in casual encounters. These quarrels of the common people, often steeped in the consumption of large quantities of alcohol, utilized as weapons the ordinary tools of agricultural and personal life – knives, sticks, axes, forks, spades and scythes. The dominant culture of the time everywhere offered approved models for violent behaviour. Severe corporal punishment was used by parents, teachers, masters and husbands; and popular games – "from the exalted tournament to the lowly village wrestling match" – emphasized violence.

But, if blood feuds would be endemic on the Continent (and even in Scotland and Wales) for centuries, the thirteenth-century English ruling élites had already begun to disengage from violence as a means of dispute resolution. The institutionalized blood feud – that most homicidal of structures, in which a simple insult or injury demands retaliation and counter-retaliation in an unending cycle of killing – had virtually ceased to exist in England. Even when the nobility did quarrel, there was a surprising reluctance "to push matters to a violent conclusion." Given cites the dispute over a pasture in 1269 between the Earls of Surrey and Lincoln: "Both earls assembled their armed retainers and prepared for battle, but, as the chronicler who recorded these events noted, 'they feared to come together.' Ultimately the issue was settled by royal justices in a royal court."

These royal courts already had the authority to bind over offenders to keep the peace, leaving the nobility occupied primarily with the *pretence* of violence – aggressive posturing and the uttering of physical threats. Moreover, and conveniently, "if it appeared that a dispute was about to come to a physical resolution, there was almost always someone present to step between the two combatants," a posture that satisfied honour without risking actual assault and the king's displeasure. Failing that, there was the highly structured violence of the tournament, sometimes fatal, but a socially approved means for dissipating aggression.

Given emphasizes that this "reluctance to engage in direct violent conflict with their fellow nobles contrasts startlingly with the behaviour of other European nobles" of the thirteenth century. This profound difference was largely a consequence of the fact that the English state was "the most developed" legal and administrative machine in Europe. Thus the gentry and aristocracy had "access to a nearly ubiquitous, flexible, and, for the age, sophisticated system of courts," which left them with far less need "to turn out with arms to defend their interests," and wary of the monarchical consequences that would be provoked by attempting to do so. Except in political crises, "the English nobles appear to have preferred to settle their disputes" through alternative means.

This defusing of violence occurred because "by the thirteenth century the English kings had managed to establish a virtual monopoly of the right to judge crimes that involved the possible loss of life or limb as a punishment," and homicide had become a royal preserve. This surprising regal concern was undoubtedly motivated less by any sensibilities about the sanctity of life than by the fact that the king *profited* directly from homicide, not just in the extension of his power over the lives of the people, but through punitive fines and the confiscation of property. To ensure the king's treasury was not impoverished by any under-reporting of homicides, the office of coroner was created in 1194, charged with the responsibilities of investigating all violent deaths (accidental or otherwise), and arresting suspects whenever it was appropriate.

Thus judgement belonged increasingly to the state. The wealthy used that state, as did the more prosperous peasants and freeholders, who in addition to the more informal means of mediation (of friends, relatives and neighbours) also "had access to courts, whether royal or manorial, in which to settle their conflicts." Like the gentry and aristocracy, they had too much to lose by confronting the power of the state. Violence was the weapon abandoned to "the poor and the impotent," who produced the vast majority of killers; for the poor, violence remained "one of the few available means of influencing the behaviour of one's antagonist in a dispute." Given continues:

> Indeed, a poor peasant had relatively little to lose by resorting to violence. Should his victim die and he be forced to flee for safety, his lot might not have been materially much worse than before. He simply became a labourer in a different village. A wealthy peasant, on the other hand, would have had to give up his home, his animals, his tools, his land, and accept a catastrophic loss of social position.[10]

The Fifteenth Century

By the fifteenth century, the "rules of disorder," the cultural constraints upon violence, were clearly established in English society. Charles Phythian-Adams notes how the "maximum level of acceptable violence" had by then been radically downgraded, how "in incident after incident" physical aggression was diverted – by the intervention of kin and neighbours, by the reciprocal exchange of verbal taunt and insult, and most of all by the omnipresent fear of "the troublesome and costly entanglement in Law which will inevitably follow the serious shedding of blood." In a few centuries, the English had gone from a nation regarded by outsiders as "emotionally labile and easily excited to uncontrollable rage and violence," to a tightly controlled people for whom the blood feud was a distant memory, people who expressed their hostility in an "exaggerated" language of threat but resorted to the courts for resolution of their conflicts.

Philippa Maddern's researches in fifteenth-century East Anglia emphasize this point, that it was the *rhetoric*, not the behaviour, of the gentry that was steeped in blood. Their talk of aggressive acts was "surrounded by so great a cloud of laudatory adjectives – worthy, worshipful, manly, doughty, invincible, fierce – that no disapproval could touch them." Yet it is clear that they much preferred a ferocious image to its reality; while they "liked to picture themselves as the heroically bloodthirsty knights of chivalric romance," actual violence in their lives was already relatively rare. Indeed, there is "little hard evidence that assault, riot or murder were even commonly *alleged*," let alone committed, in fifteenth-century East Anglia.

Even when there were purported incidents of violence, Maddern notes, the charges "have a disturbing tendency to shrink, dislimn, or metamorphose when subjected to historical scrutiny": thus many of the charges were concocted political stratagems between rivals. "Litigation, arbitration, and non-violent debate" were part of winning a case in court – slandering a rival, not engaging him on the battlefield. Moreover, all this took place in a social context in which "the constant competition for livelihood and prestige" could be "worked out by subtle means in the law courts." This was a society already so steeped in non-violent litigious behaviour that the vast majority of gentry could expect to appear in court, "as either plaintiff or defendant . . . at some time in their lives." How could it be otherwise in this mercantile society in which property and status – not outdated notions of familial honour – were the primary sources of dispute, especially among the gentry? When violence did occur, it "seems generally to have been a last resort."

Maddern concentrates her analysis on the cultural deployment of violence "in constructing and maintaining systems of authority." The power to use violence against evil-doers was "an integral part of the authority of the greatest ruler of all – God," and basic to the fifteenth-century English world view was the notion "that God delegated to earthly knights and magistrates the sword to punish miscreants and protect the innocent." If violence "was thought to be essential in the maintenance of moral and civil order," it was justified "by analogy with the ultimately salutary violence suffered by Christ, which brought peace to all humankind." Thus the threat, and occasionally the reality, of violence gave a divine sanction to the social hierarchy: "the power to judge and execute descended from God to kings and knights, and kings in their turn delegated this authority to their judges, justices, and lieutenants."

Much of the violence in this period was assumed to be "on the side of the angels; peace, justice, and order were restored, not destroyed, by it." So long as violence was perpetrated by authority against the wicked, the right to do so was God-given. All that was necessary was that this "just violence must be done for a good motive," to protect the weak and vulnerable. Therefore the acts of the most popular culture hero, Robin Hood, were fundamentally "moral" in the fifteenth-century world view: "he punished the wicked, was a manly and successful fighter, and claimed to be a supporter of the king's law." Any killing that was not on behalf of the authorities was already an offence against both God and the king, and those who committed it "had to come dutifully to the king's courts to have their actions examined and categorized."[11]

The Seventeenth Century

By the seventeenth century, the English experience of violence was already approaching its modern form. As "the first 'modern' centralized nation-state," and "the first to establish the rule of law and to control violence," Alan Macfarlane argues, there was no longer any comparison with the experience of most other European nations. In eighteenth-century Brittany, for example, where the French regime "had governed largely by not governing," Le Goff and Sutherland write, "gangs of thieves" still roamed the countryside; and because local communities tenaciously resisted the law and its officers, "much of rural crime went unpunished." Indeed, the state hardly bothered to intervene so long as crime did not "interfere with the collection of taxes and general order." Similarly, Hufton's study of a diocese in Languedoc emphasizes the constant "bitter friction between seigneur and vassal, the frequent baiting of the parish priest," and "the over hasty recourse to the gun and the steadfast ignoring of government decrees." So intense were these tensions that "public hatred was the most constant and powerful expression of community solidarity," perhaps the only "binding force in a society often otherwise marked by private altercation and fragmentation." The French nation state would not reach its centralized maturity until the end of the nineteenth century.[12]

England went through a much earlier revolution, and experienced no comparable period of violence. If Continental social life often was riddled with physical assaults and homicides, such crimes were virtually absent in rural England. In Westmoreland, Macfarlane found "less than half a dozen persons suspected of murder or homicide during" the second half of the seventeenth century, and very few "serious and brutal assaults involving the loss of limbs or serious injuries." Even notorious bandits were relatively mild in their assaults: "in their worst attack, on Henry Preston, they left a man unable to walk for three weeks, but normally they just pricked their victims on ears or nose."

Neither was there any comparable hostility between "town and country or between social classes," "no hints of battles between peasants and 'landlords,'" "nor of anything similar to the seigneur-baiting of Languedoc, or the running battles between poachers and gamekeepers described for nineteenth-century France." Nor was there any evidence of vendettas: "the answering of blood with blood" had utterly disappeared from the English record. National justice kept the peace, making redundant – and illegal – the primitive justice of the kin-based blood feud. If matters were not dealt with in the criminal courts, they were referred to alternative courts or to informal negotiators: everywhere amongst this litigious people, "we find people hiring attorneys and taking each other to the civil courts, or settling matters out of court for the payment of cash, after influential local inhabitants had been called in to arbitrate."

Moreover, because bandits did not work for social justice, they made no claim on the evolving English sensibility, and they were not idealized as they were on the Continent. Nor was there any "popular opposition" to the national authority – whether its laws, courts or officials. Since "most adult men were themselves minor legal officials," there was a real measure of "self-policing," a concomitant and widespread sense of personal responsibility, and "a very considerable awareness of how the laws worked, what the laws were, and a general consensus that they were locally applicable and to be observed." The peaceable consequences of the distinctive development of the English common law were already in place.[13]

J. S. Cockburn's work confirms Macfarlane's judgement: those homicides that did occur in the England of this period were not the consequence of large-scale social disturbances, but "acts of sudden, unpremeditated aggression [that] resulted from attacks" – provoked "at work, in drink or at play" – and using any weapons that fell readily to hand. Fully 5 per cent of the recorded homicides were from "injuries sustained while playing or arguing about games of various sorts." Then as now, domestic violence was prevalent, and wives were the most common victims.[14]

The Eighteenth Century: The Death of "Honour"

The incidence of homicide continued to decline: Ian Gilmour quotes the Swiss, Msiter, who "believed there were fewer affrays in London in a fortnight than there were in Paris in a morning." Even the English highwaymen, travellers noted, "were more humane than those abroad," and indeed the "gentlemen of the road" rarely killed those they robbed. "Visitors to England throughout the century were struck by the rarity of murder." The century's grisly catalogue of capital crimes, the "bloody code," was "fettered, fortunately to a uniquely liberal criminal procedure," Gilmour notes: torture was prohibited and the vast majority of offenders escaped execution. This laid the foundation for an increasing public sensitivity about any form of violence, state or individual. By 1800, the homicide rate had fallen to below 2 per 100,000, and England "probably had fewer murders in proportion to its population than any other country in Europe." In London and Middlesex, "the most lawless part of England," eighty-one people were convicted of murder in the years between 1749 and 1771, when in "half that period Rome, a city only a quarter of the size of London, had 4,000 murders."[15]

Perhaps the primary social engine behind this reduction of all forms of state and personal violence was the social opposition that crystallized around the Continental custom of duelling, imported to England only in the late sixteenth century. James I may have thought of it in romantic terms as "the bewitching duel," but it was the aristocracy's belated "violent assertion of the right to private vengeance." Like the primitive tribesman, "the gentleman's 'honour' was sacred," and he was duty-bound to avenge any insult by challenging his opponent to a duel. Popular revulsion for the duel would spark a middle-class social movement that would go far beyond opposition to the duel, and become one of the bases for the assertion of a new bourgeois moral code based on civility and politeness. Indeed, "the debate about duelling" would play a major role in the "gestation of middle-class culture."[16]

Donna Andrew concludes that with the widespread opposition to the duel came a radical social ideology, a new "body of thinking," which articulated a "vision of society based on reasonableness, Christianity and commerce." Although such popular ideology had only a limited impact on the Continent, where duelling continued through the nineteenth and into the twentieth centuries, the last anachronistic English duel was staged in 1852. The feudal code of honour, the great class privilege that licensed the nobility to kill, was finished. Such a massive ideological shift, "the replacement of the code of honour by what might be called the code of Christian commerce," Andrew argues, necessarily entailed the ideas that "class privilege and immunity from the Law should give way to a strict and universal application" of an impartial law blind to social rank. Thus the bourgeois opposition to duelling was not merely about this issue: in fact, it was an opposition "to an entire [discredited] vision of society," and "in the process formulated a new idea of a society bound together by the equal subordination of individuals to Law and to the market place."[17]

What were the philosophical changes that underwrote this decline of violence? Even rioting and mass violence were of a "limited and ritualistic" kind, aimed at specific political goals – such as ending food shortages – and sometimes even encouraged by the authorities, Linda Colley notes. Frank McLynn describes the late eighteenth century's "revolution in attitudes" as including "less tolerance" for the physical abuse of women and children, and an "increasing distaste for slavery, blood sports, and capital punishment." McLynn thought the rudiments of mass education began to replace "instinct with intellect," and the growth of Methodism helped constrain "the popular taste for violence." Moreover, the needs of commerce made it clearly "in the interest of the State" to establish a sole monopoly of force, to "clamp down on all manifestations of individual violence and to reinforce pacific attitudes." Indeed, Colley thought that what was "most striking" about English society in this period "was not the violence its members inflicted on each other, but the *limits* of that violence in comparison with what was practised elsewhere in Europe, and in comparison too with what had been common in England itself in earlier periods."[18]

Paul Langford concluded that the aristocratic code of honour associated with feudal and agrarian economies was meaningless in a society now dominated by a "commercial middle class," a class which "required a more sophisticated means of regulating manners," forever directed towards the "pursuit of harmony within a propertied society." The emerging middle class was now free to develop, through its elaborate code of "politeness," a universal set of physically non-aggressive manners and behaviours, particular to no social class, but essential for the smooth functioning of a supremely commercial society. Britain was in the forefront of this new European commercial age, and *politeness* was a "logical consequence" of the imperatives of commerce. Thus the promulgated doctrine of "politeness conveyed upper-class gentility, enlightenment, and sociability to a much wider élite whose only qualification was money, but who were glad to spend it on acquiring the status of a gentleman." Politeness was ostensibly about morals, but its prime function was the "social control of the individual" that "permitted and controlled a relatively open competition for power, influence, jobs, wives, and markets."

Langford thought this "sentimental revolution" expressed "the middle-class need for a code of manners which challenged aristocratic ideals and fashions," and provided an alternative means for "the pursuit of genteel status." Mass education emphasized "the acquisition of useful skills and social graces," while "much attention was paid to the control and discipline of servants." This politeness became the hallmark of "an immensely vigorous but also a remorselessly snobbish society." Politeness progressed far beyond formal public social encounters to "the everyday routine and rules of social life, from matters as trivial as the time at which one dined, and the way one ate one's dinner, to matters as important as the expectations and arrangements of partners in marriage. There was no shortage of manuals and advice on all such questions. The essence of politeness was often said to be that *je ne sais quoi* which distinguished the innate gentleman's understanding of what made for civilized conduct."

Underwriting these developments in manners, Langford writes, was an "acute anxiety about the indiscipline and immorality of the lower classes," which constituted a serious threat to social harmony. As if in response to this grew a new concern with social problems, especially disease and crime; and the consequent development of charitable and "philanthropic experiments in the grand manner": sagaciously, much of this charity was "devoted to the discipline as well as the relief of the labouring poor." The cult of "sensibility" extended its sympathies to "children, animals, and non-European peoples"; and this growth of institutionalized compassion provided the cultural foundation for the further reduction of violence.[19]

The Nineteenth Century: The Great Pacification

> [The criminal] is nowadays a milder, and more civilized person than his predecessor of thirty years ago who was too often an ignorant, truculent, and intractable monster. (Judge Quinton, 1895[20])

Many commentators feared that the unprecedented wealth flooding into Britain might increase crime rates, but the opposite proved to be the case. A continuing decline in homicide accompanied the rising industrial prosperity, the rates almost halving from the mid-century to the First World War. This consistent decline continued until the Second World War, by which time the rates had halved again. Some thought this further decline was a consequence of the increased levels of police surveillance of the working class, but the vast majority of homicides are spur-of-the-moment "crimes of passion," and "impulsively violent offenders are not likely" even to consider let alone "be deterred by the threat of arrest or punishment."

V. A. C. Gatrell concludes that Victorian society "was in a wholly exceptional state of balance." As respect for the rule of law deepened, public and judicial intolerance for a wide range of offences increased still further: parallel with this, the public became "less critical of police oppression," and more enthusiastic about police intervention. Similarly, the peculiarly

English passion for litigation accelerated, Gatrell notes, intensified by the increased efficiency of prosecution, and "the growing readiness of an increasingly urbanized people to discard informal retribution in favour of formal." Violent crime continued to decline throughout the century, and "the rate of homicide trials dropped by 70 per cent from the mid-1830s to the pre-war years."[21]

This continuing slide away from violence was orchestrated by a sustained and blatant cultural campaign. Not for nothing was the new code of nineteenth-century civic virtues etched in great letters into Leeds Town Hall – "HONESTY IS THE BEST POLICY – GOODWILL TOWARDS MEN – WEAVE TRUTH WITH TRUST – TRIAL BY JURY – EXCEPT THE LORD BUILT THE HOUSE, THEY LABOURED IN VAIN THAT BUILT IT – FORWARD."

The cultural change that was occurring was a further refinement of sensitivities, and not just in the compassion (or realistic self-preservation) demonstrated by the progressive expansion of charity for humans. While French veterinarians as part of their training skinned horses alive in order to glimpse the formation of musculature and organs (the screams of the tortured animals disturbing whole neighbourhoods), a profoundly different sensibility was evolving in England. Erasmus Darwin argued for a mentality which acknowledged the feelings and rights of all living creatures:

> Does not daily observation convince us that they form contracts of friendship with each other, with mankind? When puppies and kittens play together is there not a tacit contract that they will not hurt each other? And does not your favourite dog expect you should give him his daily food, for his services and attention to you?[22]

A criminal registrar of the time was right to speak of "a decline in the spirit of lawlessness" in the country, and the increased tendency of the public to substitute "words without blows for blows." We can only begin to speculate on the manner in which these inhibitions were transmitted to the masses, but Gertrude Himmelfarb is surely right to point us towards the new sense of *respectability* that transformed Victorian society.

Respectability was *the* key notion conditioning behaviour in the Victorian era. Its dictates were clear, whether it was signified by the wearing of clean clothes, or providing for a proper funeral, or belonging to a friendly society, or attending a mechanics' institute, or reading edifying books, or not being on relief, or *not getting drunk and rowdy*. If this respectability, Brian Harrison argued, was "an anxious state of mind," leaving each individual forever obsessed with appearances, it was given a positive emotional charge "by the companionship available in respectability's institutional framework."[23]

Jose Harris records that domestic tranquillity seemed so assured that a criminologist could argue in 1901 that all crime would cease in the country "if seventy habitual criminals known to the police could simply be locked up for life." Personal control and order had become the rules of the day, and a 1914 study of international crime "found that for safety, decorum, and public order London resembled a gigantic 'open-air cathedral,' in stark comparison with other European capitals." Much modern social criticism has been devoted to exposing the "concealed" purpose "of Victorian social benevolence," as an exercise in domination in which the poor were socialized with the "self-serving values of the rulers." However cloudy its motivation may have been, the new climate helped reduce the rates of homicidal assaults on all citizens to the lowest possible levels.[24]

The Twentieth Century

The English homicide rate remained among the lowest in the world throughout the twentieth century, although – like homicide rates virtually everywhere in the western world – it rose during the cultural upheaval that followed the 1960s. Why the homicide rate should have increased in the mid-1970s is still a matter for speculation; but the phenomenon was worldwide, not confined to Britain. Some scholars argue that the worldwide rise was linked to the desensitization to violence that accompanied television's gift of the Vietnam War to every sitting room; others argue that the unprecedented prosperity of the 1960s created a whole new class of the bitter and disenfranchised. In any case, it was a modest increase, and the English rate remains in the world's lowest stratum. Sir John Macdonnell's famous judgement passed

TABLE 4 Offences of homicide initially recorded by the police, per 100,000 population, England and Wales.

Year	Homicide rate	Year	Homicide rate
1860	1.44	1930	0.75
1870	1.43	1940	0.70
1880	1.52	1950	0.79
1890	1.17	1960	0.62
1900	0.97	1970	0.81
1910	0.81	1980	1.26
1920	0.83	1990	1.32

Source: Home Office. Includes infanticide as well as murder and manslaughter. Rates "initially recorded by the police" are typically higher than other rates, such as those for convictions.

almost a century ago is still true: Murder remains "an incident in miserable lives in which disputes, quarrels, angry words and blows are common . . . domestic quarrels and brawls; much previous ill treatment, drinking, fighting, blows; a long course of brutality and continued absence of self-restraint."[25]

Terence Morris and Louis Blom-Cooper note that there were fewer than 7,500 murders in the first half of the century in England and Wales combined, only one-third of the number killed by drunken drivers. Not only are the numbers low, but there is a remarkable constancy about the type of persons who are killed – "murder is overwhelmingly a domestic crime," in which men kill their wives, lovers and children, and women kill their children. Half of the killers are linked to their victims through family ties, "and up to two-thirds of all have had a personal relationship of some duration and/or intensity with the victim." Two-thirds of killers are between fifteen and thirty-four and one-quarter of them are strangers to their victims. The types of murders which cause the greatest public alarm – those committed in the course of other crimes, such as robbery or rape; and those involving shooting – have *not* increased; they continue to occupy the same modest proportion of homicides (each about 8 per cent) as they have throughout the century. These unchanging characteristics inevitably lead Morris and Blom-Cooper to conclude that murder is not a planned and calculated event, but one in which "emotion (often passionate), panic, or

TABLE 5 Rate, per 100,000 population, of homicide offences tried, England and Wales.

Year	Rate (average)	Year	Rate (average)
1834–35	2.0	1876–80	1.1
1836–40	1.7	1881–85	1.1
1841–45	1.7	1886–90	0.9
1846–50	1.6	1891–95	0.8
1851–55	1.7	1896–1900	0.8
1856–60	1.5	1901–05	0.7
1861–65	1.6	1906–10	0.6
1866–70	1.5	1911–14	0.6
1871–75	1.3		

Source: Gatrell *et al*, p. 187. Gatrell's rates differ slightly from those of the Home Office because the former's use five-year averages of cases which actually went to trial.

mental disorder play a role disproportionate to that which they play in any other crime."[26]

The social origins and qualities of the majority of killers also remain unchanged: Barry Mitchell's recent research notes that killers are overwhelmingly male, young, unemployed or non-professional, single or divorced, and have previous convictions in court. Victims were almost equally divided between men and women; and the most common provocation is a dispute or quarrel. Much of the remainder of this volume will try to flesh out these characteristics.[27]

---

1   Quoted in Ian Gilmour, 1992, *Riot, Risings and Revolution: Governance and Violence in 18th-Century England*, London: Hutchinson, p. 265.

2   J. S. Cockburn, "The Nature and Incidence of Crime in England 1559–1625: A Preliminary Survey," in J. S. Cockburn (ed), 1977, *Crime in England 1550–1800*, London: Methuen, p. 49; Lambard quoted in Cockburn, p. 49. The historian Amos C. Miller has provided a most helpful overview after reading the first edition of *Men of Blood* (personal communication): "Because England's insular position gave her considerable, not total, protection from foreign invasions and large-scale immigration, her people enjoyed a greater sense of security than the nations that developed on the European continent and elsewhere." Moreover, "under Anglo-Norman rule after 1066, this sense of security was enhanced by the most efficient feudal government in Europe. The nobility never gained the independent power exercised by the French and German feudal nobility. But the

relative absence of foreign threat and the willingness of the Norman monarchs to use and build on Anglo-Saxon legal tradition led to the development of the Common Law and the evolution of government by consent expressed through the jury system, popular participation in local government (especially policing) and the development of Parliament. This combination of strong monarchy limited by Parliament created an environment more peaceful and law abiding, but one that allowed greater individual liberty. A gentler society evolved because Englishmen were less subject to the brutalizing effect of feudal conflict or Wars of Religion."

3   Douglas M. MacDowell, 1963, *Athenian Homicide Law in the Age of the Orators*, Manchester U.P., pp. 1–5, 144; C. F. Kolbert, 1979, introduction to *The Digest of Roman Law: Theft, Rapine, Damage and Insult*, Harmondsworth: Penguin Books, p. 7; d'Entreves, quoted in Kolbert, p. 8.

4   Asa Briggs, 1987, *A Social History of England*, Harmondsworth: Penguin Books, pp. 50–53.

5   Susan Reynolds, 1984, *Kingdoms and Communities in Western Europe, 900–1300*, Oxford: Clarendon Press, pp. 7–8, 36–39, 50.

6   Briggs, 1987, op. cit., pp. 60, 67, 76–77; Alan Macfarlane, 1978, *The Origins of English Individualism*, Oxford: Blackwell, p. 197.

7   Ted Robert Gurr, 1981, "Historical Trends in Violent Crime: A Critical Review of the Evidence," in *Crime and Justice: An Annual Review of Research* 3: 295–353, p. 295; Alfred Soman, 1980, "Deviance and Criminal Justice in Western Europe, 1300–1800: An Essay in Structure," in *Criminal Justice History: An International Annual* 1: 1–28, quoted in Gurr, p. 300. Among these social dislocations, Gurr refers specifically to periods of "warfare, which evidently tends to legitimate individual violence," and to "the stresses of the initial phases of rapid urbanization and industrialization; economic prosperity and decline; and changes in the demographic structure."

8   J. A. Sharpe, "The History of Violence in England: Some Observations," in *Past and Present* 108: 206–215; Hanawalt and Hammer quoted in Lawrence Stone, 1983, "Interpersonal Violence in English Society, 1300–1980," *Past and Present*, 101: 22–33.

9   Marie-Therese Lorcin, quoted in James Buchanan Given, 1977, *Society and Homicide in Thirteenth-Century England*, Stanford U.P., p. 34; Robert Irwin, 1991, *Times Literary Supplement*, June 28.

10 Given, pp. 40, 70–71, 74, 77–78, 82, 90, 135, 188–192, 199–201, 210.

11 Charles V. Phythian-Adams, 1991, "Rituals of Personal Confrontation in Late Medieval England," *Bulletin of the John Rylands University Library of Manchester*, vol. 73, no. 1; 65–90; Philippa Maddern, 1992, *Violence and Social Order: East Anglia 1422–1442*, Oxford: Clarendon Press, pp. 78, 226–227, 19, 171, 33, 228, 12, 84–85, 108, 128, 177.

12 See also, e.g., Edward Muir, 1993, *Mad Blood Stirring: Vendetta and Factions in Friuli During the Renaissance*, London: The Johns Hopkins U.P.; Alain Corbin,

1992, *The Village of Cannibals: Rage and Murder in France, 1870*, Cambridge: Polity; and R. Po-Chia Hsia, 1992, *Trent 1475: Stories of a Ritual Murder Trial*, Yale U.P.

13   Quoted in Alan Macfarlane, 1978, *The Origins of English Individualism: The Family, Property and Social Transition*, Oxford: Blackwell; 1981, *The Justice and the Mare's Ale: Law and Disorder in Seventeenth-Century England*, Cambridge U.P., pp. 1, 177–180, 186, 188, 192–194, 195–199.

14   J. S. Cockburn, 1977, "The Nature and Incidence of Crime in England 1559–1625: A Preliminary Survey," in his edition of *Crime in England 1550–1880*, London: Methuen, pp. 55–57.

15   Gilmour, 1992, op. cit., pp. 13–14, 148, 152–153, 156.

16   Gilmour, 1992, op. cit., pp. 263–265; Donna T. Andrew, 1980, "The Code of Honour and Its Critics: The Opposition to Duelling in England, 1700–1850," *Social History*, vol. 5, no. 3: 409–434.

17   Donna T. Andrew, 1980, ibid., p. 434.

18   Linda Colley, 1991, in *London Review of Books*, vol. 14, no. 17, pp. 15–16, and personal communication, 1992, my italics; Frank McLynn, 1989, *Crime and Punishment in Eighteenth-Century England*, Oxford U.P, pp. 307–309. For a darker view of the eighteenth-century law, see Douglas Hay, Peter Linebaugh, John Rule, E. P. Thompson and Cal Winslow's masterful *Albion's Fatal Tree: Crime and Society in Eighteenth-Century England*, 1977, Harmondsworth: Peregrine Books.

19   Paul Langford, 1989, *A Polite and Commercial People: England 1727–1783*, Oxford: Clarendon Press, pp. 1, 2, 4–5, 59–60, 71, 461, 123, 461–462.

20   Quoted in V. A. C. Gatrell, "The Decline of Theft and Violence in Victorian and Edwardian England," in V. A. C. Gatrell, Bruce Lenman and Geoffrey Parker (eds), 1980, *Crime and the Law: The Social History of Crime in Western Europe Since 1500*, London: Europa, p. 323.

21   Ibid. 337, 240, 244, 249–251, 286.

22   Gurr, 1981, op. cit., pp. 310, 314; Erasmus Darwin, quoted in Keith Thomas, 1984, *Man and the Natural World: Changing Attitudes in England 1500–1800*, Harmondsworth: Penguin, p. 121. Special thanks to Janina Bauman for refreshing my memory about these quotations.

23   Quoted in Gatrell, 1980, p. 293; Gertrude Himmelfarb, 1991, *Poverty and Compassion: The Moral Imagination of the Late Victorians*, New York: Alfred A. Knopf, p. 9; Brian Harrison quoted in Himmelfarb, 1991: 9–10.

24   In Jose Harris, 1994, *Private Lives, Public Spirit: Britain 1870–1914*, Harmondsworth: Penguin, pp. 209–211; Gatrell, 1980, 256–257.

25   Quoted in Terence Morris and Louis Blom-Cooper, 1967, "Homicide in England," in Marvin Wolfgang (ed), *Studies in Homicide*, New York: Harper & Row, p. 33.

26   Morris and Blom-Cooper, 1967: 29, 32; Terence Morris and Louis Blom-Cooper, 1979, "Murder in England and Wales Since 1957," *The Observer*, pp. 10, 11, 6, 8–9, 12.

27   Barry Mitchell, 1990, *Murder and Penal Policy*, London: Macmillan, p. 58, 44ff, 60–61.

LOVERS, SPOUSES AND KIN

MURDERS ARE USUALLY personal and domestic crimes, a consequence of uncontrolled personalities struggling to cope with troubled relationships – lovers and spouses, friends and acquaintances. This chapter contains cases illustrating some of these predominant forms. In one, a loving alcoholic wife strikes out after years of abuse and, without meaning to do so, kills her equally alcoholic husband; in another, a possessive clerk stabs his estranged lover in an apparent dispute about the division of their joint property and his visiting rights to their child; and in the third, a drunken family dispute erupts into a brawl in which several are stabbed, and one dies. As Barry Mitchell says, the nature of murder in England has not changed: "the vast majority of murderers are male, they usually know their victims, killing with a sharp instrument is still the most common method, and nearly half of the murders are carried out in a fit of temper."[1]

Table 6 documents my own more recent examination of Home Office statistics, and shows that the basics remain unchanged: one-quarter are spouses or lovers, and only one fifth do not know each other.

TWO WHITE SWANS: VIOLET STABS HER BELOVED HUSBAND

Twenty-six per cent of the victims in my sample were spouses or lovers. Glaswegian *émigrés* Violet Watkins, a Protestant, forty-eight, and her husband George, a devout Catholic, fifty-seven, habitually drank to excess and periodically enrolled in Alcoholics Anonymous. The couple quarrelled incessantly, loudly and violently. Yet Violet seemed heartbroken after the killing, and she made no attempt to justify her actions. She thought their love had given a kind of glory to their marriage: she and her husband, she

TABLE 6 Victims: Relationship to offender (*where principal suspect identified*), England.

	Stranger	Friend or Acquaintance	Family*	Spouse or Lover**	Misc. Other***
1982	71	142	98	129	32
1984	62	163	95	123	33
1986	126	137	68	150	17
1988	125	102	109	114	19
1990	103	135	104	118	45
Total	487	679	474	634	146
	(20%)	(28%)	(20%)	(26%)	(6%)

Source: Home Office.
*Including children, parents, etc.
**Including former partners.
***Including other associates, police, commercial relationships, and terrorists.

remembered, had been "like two white swans." Having killed him – as is so common with English killers – she wished to die with her beloved victim.

The Orange and the Green

On the day of the killing, Violet and George had been in a pleasant mood in their council flat in East London. In those closing hours of George's life they even telephoned Violet's seventy-three-year-old mother in Scotland to discuss, among other things, the family Bible. As the mother remembered that final contact, "George said that he had just phoned to see how I was keeping and sounded quite cheery. He mentioned that everyone down there was getting on fine. George asked about a wee Bible that I always keep in my purse. He wanted to know if I still had it and I told him that it was still there. George then asked if he could have it and I told him he could get it the next time he was up. I wasn't too surprised at George mentioning the Bible as he has often asked me if he could have it. After I finished talking to George, Violet came on the phone for a wee while. She sounded cheery and was telling me what a fine girl her daughter was turning out. I didn't speak to her for too long as I was worried about their telephone bill. The telephone call must have lasted for about five or ten minutes and neither of them mentioned anything to me about any troubles they were having. After going to bed that night I was awakened by my grandson, who called at the house and told me that he had received word that George was dead. I can't understand what has happened."

What *had* happened in their council flat that spring evening? Sitting in the police station through much of the following day, Violet described the couple's gradual slide towards a tragedy. In truth, either of them could have become the victim, and Violet seemed the more likely candidate, since she was more often the victim of her husband's physical assaults. The only surviving witness is Violet. Murderers' versions of events are normally subject to self-serving distortions and fabrications, but Violet was overcome with remorse, and determined both to tell the truth and to accept her punishment. Her account of the previous evening has the ring of truth.

As she told the detective, "I said to George there was football coming on TV. Well, he intended to watch football, and I was going to do the washing and I put the immersion heater on; and then about half an hour later I said, 'I won't bother about the washing, I'll have a bath. I'll do the washing over the weekend.' So we were sitting down and we had a couple of drinks – whisky and soda – and I sort of dozed off [until] the phone rang and George answered it, and it was my sister. She said that my brother had burned himself on the arm with some fat and that Mother was quite concerned about him and I said, 'I'll phone Mum after you ring off.'

"So I rung my mother and she took time in answering the phone and George called from the living room, 'You can be fucking well *up* in Scotland by the time the old lady answers the phone.' I said to him, 'Don't be so nasty, maybe she's fallen asleep.' So just at that my mother answered the phone. I asked my mother the usual, how was she. I explained how Cath had been on the phone and [she had] told me about my brother, and she explained that his arm was quite badly burned and that she hadn't seen him since Tuesday but she assumed that he was all right. So I had a chat with her. And then George got up and he spoke to her on the phone; then he went on to ask her why she didn't come down here as he had a spare room and that he would get it done up to make it comfortable for her to come and stop with us. He said, 'Look at the time we can have, Vi's out working all day, Cath's out working all day,' he said, 'you and I can have a good bevy.'

"I said to him, 'Don't be so silly, my mother's too old to travel and got her own ways of living; give me the phone, I'll speak to my mother,' and he said to my mother, 'There's she getting upset or uptight.' I said, 'That's all I would need is for me to come home from work and find you [two] lying drunk.' So with that I took the phone and spoke to my mother for a couple of minutes. I then said, 'I'll ring off, Mum, take care of yourself, I'll ring you over the weekend.' I put the phone back and went back into the living room and we were sitting there talking and we had some more drink. So it must have been about half-eight, quarter-nine, he said he was going out for a pint and I said, 'What do you want to go out for a pint for, don't you think that you've had enough?' He said, 'If I want to go for a fucking pint, I'll go for one.' I said, 'You've got some beer in the fridge and you've got some whisky left, why don't you make that do?' He said, 'I'm going for a pint and that's it,' and I said, 'Oh well, please your bloody self then, because you've been in a funny mood since I've been home from work.'

"So off he went," Violet remembered, "and I finished the whisky that was there on my own.[2] He came in, I don't know what time, and we had a row, and he wanted some money off me, and if I can remember rightly he brought in a bottle of Martini and I believe I had a drop out of that Martini bottle. We then had a heated row and I went into the hall. I'd put my rollers in and he lifted his hand to me prior to me going into the hall: I could never, ever retaliate to George, [but] I'm almost positive I picked something up and threw it at the TV. I vaguely remember saying, 'You'll never hit me again, I'm going out!' And I remember going to open the front door and the next thing he was pulling at my hair and he wouldn't let me out, and then he socked me on the jaw and then I honestly don't know, I don't remember going into the kitchen, and then he was on the floor in the hall and I remember seeing the blood on his trouser legs. And I was on the floor holding his head and I kept saying, 'Dad, speak to me, Dad, speak to me,' and I didn't get an answer. I just remember George put my hand on his face. And then I was surrounded by people.

"Then I'm not sure. I think I heard Catherine's voice, that's my daughter, and I can't be rightly sure whether she called out, 'What's happened to my Daddy, what's happened to my Mummy?' And then there was a crowd standing at my front door and I was brought down here and I've been here ever since." A few days later, the forensic report would conclude that George had died from "a single stab wound" to the heart.

When the detective asked Violet what they had argued about when George had returned from the pub, Violet became confused: "I really can't remember. You see there has been so many rows about everything and over nothing in the past. *Money*! I remember now, money, because he wanted money from me. He took it from my bag. I vaguely remember him tipping my brown handbag. Prior to that he'd struck me in the living room, he'd punched me on my body. When I tried to get out the front door, he tried to pull me back by my hair."

With breaks only for tea and meals, the sympathetic interview continued late into the night in the police station, with the detective revealing his sympathy for Violet's predicament, and gently leading her away from any possible charge of premeditated murder. "Can you remember George asking you to kill him?" "No, I don't think he would say that." "Can you remember threatening George with the knife?" "I may have, I can't remember. I don't remember how I got the knife; I don't remember going into the kitchen. The only thing I can remember, I went to go for the door handle and George pulling me back by the hair and punching me, and I screamed. The next thing I knew he was on the floor."

With what must have been a mounting sense of frustration at Violet's unwillingness to assist in her own acquittal, the detective painstakingly searched for any extenuating evidence: "You have indicated to me that you were very much under the influence of drink last night." "Yes, yes." "Do you often drink to this degree?" "Yes, quite recently I have." "Is there any particular evening when you drink, or is it every night?" "Not every night, mostly weekends with George." "How long have you been drinking to this degree?" "The past nine months it seems to have got worse." "Have you ever sought any help to get over this problem?" Violet remembered that "quite some time ago I attended AA meetings in Glasgow, but then at that particular time George was drinking heavy and I took a drink with him. I'm not putting it all on George but I can take a drink or leave it, but George, if George didn't have a good drink on a Friday and Saturday night, if he didn't get it he would play up [till] I would drink with him."

The detective turned to their stormy marriage, and the mitigating circumstances surrounding the killing. "What was it like when you were both sober?" "It was all right, but we had our rows." "Over the time that you have lived with George, did he often assault you?" "Yes." "How did he assault you?" "Bodily," Violet replied. "What did he use?" "His hands, his feet," Violet recalled. "Did he ever use any implement on you?" "Yes he did, a plate." "Did these beatings take place up until you were divorced from him, or since you went back to him?" "Before our divorce," Violent explained, "which I got for cruelty, and since I've been back with him."

Searching for a medical history to use on her behalf in court, he asked, "Have you ever received any treatment after he had assaulted you?" "Once, before we were divorced, when we lived in Glasgow, he hit me with a Wellington boot. The police thought he'd broken my nose and sent me to the hospital." "Have you ever complained to your GP about abuse that you have suffered from George?" "No." "Have you in the past received any form of medication from your doctor?" "A few months ago," Violet replied, "I had some tablets from him but I never took them because a few years ago I had a nervous breakdown. There was no drink involved and George was driving me off my head." "Have you ever attempted to commit suicide?" "Yes." "How long ago?" "When I was admitted to Castle Clinic twenty, twenty-three years ago. I took an overdose."

Continuing his search, the detective asked, "Over the years that George has been beating you, have you ever retaliated and hit him back?" "No. I beg your pardon, *once* I pulled his hair and left a bald patch." "Were you frightened of him?" "Yes." "When you were telling me about last night, you mentioned that you retaliated in a way by throwing something at the television?" "Yes, that was the only way I could retaliate over the years, was to throw something at something else." "Can you remember last night feeling desperately angry because of all this abuse you had suffered all these years?" "When George and I rowed I often said, 'George, you have dragged a lot of things out of me over the years, and we are now getting too old for it.'" "Are you conscious of the fact that possibly last night the whole matter came to a head in your mind and that you had to do something to stop him?" "I don't know how I felt, I know at times I really felt hatred when he started on me, but never to the extent I've wanted to kill him." Now the detective warned Violet that she might be charged with an offence.

Social History of the Family

George, like so many of our victims and offenders, had neither educational nor professional qualifications, merely a history of periodic unemployment, chronic alcohol abuse and a record of petty criminal offences. At the time of his death he was living with his wife on social security benefits in a council flat. In the fourteen years leading up to his death, his behaviour had brought him to the attention of the Metropolitan Police on five separate occasions. In 1968, he was convicted of assault on his wife and admonished by the court; in 1970, he was convicted again on the same charge, and offered the choice of thirty days in jail or a fine of £15; in 1973, he was convicted on charges of burglary and theft, fined £15 and ordered to pay £4.50 in compensation; in 1975, he was convicted once more on charges of burglary and theft and fined £25; and finally, in 1977, he was convicted of breach of the peace and assault and admonished again by the court.

Violet attended secondary school in Glasgow and left at the age of fifteen with no formal educational qualifications. In the two years prior to the killing of her husband, she was employed first as a cashier at a motoring centre earning £60 per week, and then as a packer for a local wholesaler at a still lower wage of £49 per week. Unlike most of our killers, she had no record of criminal convictions.

In the application for legal aid for Violet, the authorities briefly summarized the "facts" of the case. Violet and George were both from Glasgow, and were first married there in 1954, but the violent marriage had ended in divorce in 1962 – after four children had been born. Shortly after the divorce, Violet took a second husband, Jack Brown, who "also drank to excess and assaulted his wife." Brown died of natural causes in 1967, and Violet returned to her first husband. It was not long before George lost his job, began drinking heavily and abusing her once more: "Violet herself drank to excess and weekends became a regular occasion of alcoholism and violence between them," neighbours and relatives testified to police.

Violet's widowed mother later remembered her daughter's troubled life: "My daughter Violet is forty-eight years of age and is the third oldest in my family. She married George Watkins about 1953 and they had four children, three boys and a girl. At that time they lived in the Gorbals. They were divorced about twenty years ago – the divorce was due to George's cruelty towards Violet. She quite often in the early years of their marriage would arrive at my house in tears, saying that George had assaulted her. She would stay with me for a few days and then go back to him. If I can remember correctly, on one occasion years ago, Violet finished up in hospital after taking an overdose of drugs."

Violet's eighteen-year-old daughter confirmed the stories of continuing drunken abuse: "Ever since I can remember there have been violent arguments between them and on many occasions my father would beat my Mum. Sometimes Mum would retaliate but most times she just took the beating. When I was old enough I left home three times because I couldn't bear to see my Mum get beaten. Most times that these took place both Mum and Dad had been drinking. About a year ago Dad was made redundant and then his temper became worse and the arguments became more frequent. Despite these arguments I know both loved one another very much and when they hadn't been drinking they appeared to be the ideal couple. Dad would help around the house and do the cooking. It was only when they had been drinking that these arguments occurred. At times he became violent towards me and on occasions had slapped me; on two occasions my father took small amounts of money from my pocket without my permission. Apart from his drinking he had a lot of good qualities, and when he was sober you couldn't have met a nicer man, but he changed in drink. My mother's a kind lovely person and I think the world of her. I cannot see my mother purposely stabbing Dad, she must have picked up the knife to frighten him and it must have happened by accident. When sometimes Mum and Dad argued and he hit her, Mum would scream and shout, and neighbours must have heard her: in some cases they would get the wrong impression but they didn't see what Dad was doing to her to make her shout."

One neighbour told police, "I knew they were called Violet and George and that they were Scottish, but that's all I wanted to know, because they were always arguing and causing trouble for my wife and I. Only four days after they moved in we had to call police. The arguments were very regular, from the time they moved in, we could hear shouting. As far as I'm concerned I only really heard her shouting and she was regularly swearing at the top of her voice. I very rarely ever heard him shouting. I'm not saying he wasn't arguing, but he was never shouting. The arguments would always be during the night but I've never seen him cause any trouble. I've spoken to him many times and he always seemed a pleasant bloke to me. I've been up the flat on a few occasions to tell them to be quiet and they've stopped, but if I shouted from my flat up to them to be quiet she would start banging or turn their record player right up, then I'd go up and they'd be quiet. Violet has come to our flat a couple of times complaining about George hitting her and she has asked me to go up and calm him down. Then when I'd go up, he'd be sitting in a chair in the lounge rolling a cigarette as calm as anything. She never showed us any bruises. During the last three months things have been pretty quiet upstairs, in fact no big arguments, we've been able to go to bed and sleep. About a fortnight ago it started again every two or three nights. The arguments seem to be about money, I've heard her accuse him of stealing her money."

Another neighbour testified: "About 10 P.M. I heard a bashing on the front door and when I opened the door I saw Vi leaning up against the wall crying. She said, 'George is dead.' I tried to take her into my flat but she kept crying and saying, 'George is dead . . .' [After I went to her flat] Vi knelt down over George and kept shaking him and saying, 'George' over and over again. She kept crying. We pulled Vi off George and took her into my flat. She was thoroughly distraught. I took her into my sitting room and she said, 'He was pulling my hair. He took my money. He got me so mad that I stabbed him with the knife.' I did my best to comfort her. She kept saying she loved him and wanted to be with him. She seemed a bit drunk to me. She kept repeating herself. She said she had bought a bottle of whisky and some cans of beer for him. During the time that I have known the Watkins I have often heard them having a row, and my husband has been asked two or three times by Vi to go into their flat and help sort out an argument. I remember one time round about Christmas on a Saturday night, she knocked on our door, she was holding her hand to her forehead and I could see blood on her forehead. She said that George had broken the kitchen window and had hit her."

At the first news of the killing, Violet's sister rushed to the flat and found Violet and heard her say, "I've done something terrible." Clad only in a dressing-gown, her hair in rollers, her jaw swollen, sobbing and visibly drunk, Violet said that George had attacked her. A few moments later, when police arrived, she said, "I knew you would come, he told me to kill him, so I done it." The sister recalled, "I took hold of her hand and said, 'Are you all right?' Violet replied, 'What have I done? Tell me the truth: has George gone?' I said, 'I don't know.' Violet said, 'I didn't mean to do it; he made me do it.' I asked her what had happened. She said, 'He took my bag to get the money out of it. He tipped it up over the floor. We had words and he hit me. I was going to run out the door, George grabbed my hair and wouldn't let me go. I told him to let me go and George said, "You'll have to kill me first."'"

Violet also told her sister that "it all started over him calling me an Orange bastard." "What she was referring to was the fact that George was Catholic and Violet was Protestant. Violet also told me that they had argued over the television. George had said he was getting up early to watch the Pope's arrival and she had broken the television. Violet kept saying to me, 'He made me do it, he drove me to it, I'll pay the price but I'll always love him.' Violet also said, 'We are like two white swans, we will go together.' I gathered from this comment that she wanted to die. Violet kept on saying, 'I want to see him and talk to him, please let me see him.' She was obviously very confused and upset."

Given the obvious ameliorating circumstances, Violet was acquitted of murder. She was sentenced to eighteen months' imprisonment for manslaughter, but since there seemed so little evil to extirpate, the sentence was suspended.

"PASSION TOOK OVER": A CIVIL SERVICE CLERK STABS HIS ESTRANGED LOVER

Jennifer was reared in a council house with her mother's succession of husbands, and her natural father took no interest in her. As if in search for him, she formed an affection for an older man – a brief union that resulted in the birth of a son (her second child), and her death at twenty-three. Her neighbour, a widowed cleaner named Eileen, found her body: "On Monday about 9 A.M. I began to think it was a bit unusual that there was no activity at Jennifer's house. I heard a tap at the back door. On opening it, I saw little Kathy in her dressing-gown. I asked her what was wrong and she told me that she had been trying to wake her Mum up, but that she had been unable to do so. I told Kathy to stay downstairs whilst I went up to her Mummy. The bedroom door was wide open and I saw what appeared to be a lot of blood on the bedclothes. I felt instinctively that Jen was dead. The little boy, Alex, was at the side of the bed trying to get on to it. He was wearing a vest and nappy and he was covered in blood. I took both children back to my house and then asked for the police and an ambulance."

Police found Jennifer's blood-soaked body lying in her bed. One deep stab wound ran from the bottom of her mouth to a corner of her chin, there were two wounds to her right breast, and puncture wounds in the centre of her chest, the left breast, and her kidneys. She also had defensive wounds to the inside of her hand, as if she had put up her hand in a futile attempt to stop the blows. Jennifer's eighteen-month-old son, Alex, was also in bed but not harmed, and her six-year-old daughter, Kathy, had awakened naturally and seen that her mother was in distress.

Jennifer's mother, a chambermaid, described her daughter: "She was normal and happy, although I know she didn't get on with my third husband, 'cos she didn't see him as her proper father. She tried to contact her natural father but he had married again and showed no interest in her, which upset her. When she was sixteen she decided to leave school, about twelve months after I divorced my third husband. She lived in a council house. Also working in the same office was a man called Ray Richards and Jen formed a relationship with Ray, but they didn't live together." Jennifer's new lover seemed volatile, even aggressive: "Jen would phone me from time to time," her mother remembered, "always when Ray wasn't there. I was sure she was frightened of Ray. Several times she said that he had assaulted her. He had got hold of her arms and thrown her against the wall. He used to throw things at her. She once said to me she felt she was walking on eggshells as she was so frightened of saying or doing something which might cause Ray to hit her. He was so unpredictable – violent one minute, quiet the next. In August of this year she met another man called Andy, and she seemed happier," although that relationship did not endure.

The Killer

The killer was Jennifer's forty-four-year-old estranged lover, Raymond Richards, a civil service clerk. Richards stabbed to death his former lover while his son – for whom he professed much love – lay on the bed beside them. Leaving the baby on the bed beside the corpse of his mother, showing no apparent concern, he went home to tidy up his personal and financial affairs.

The only person who testified on Raymond's behalf was his former wife, who spoke about him in surprisingly affectionate terms. "I would describe our family life as being very happy. At Easter, Raymond disappeared with his car for the weekend. I didn't know where he'd gone but I began to suspect he was seeing another woman. After that weekend, a letter came to the house addressed to Raymond. It was a card: as I was becoming suspicious of Raymond, I decided to open it. Inside I found a 'Sorry' card with a short letter inside. This card was a shock to me. That night when he came home from work I confronted him about the card. He didn't argue, he just ignored me and went out. I felt very hurt by what was happening, but it took him a long time to admit he was having an affair with this woman." As is so often the case in these matters, Mrs. Richards blamed herself: "I used to do stupid things and that obviously provoked him. He used to not come home for periods of time. I wanted him to come back to me, but I couldn't make him see sense. I believe he was very much in love with this Jennifer. During this time I would describe Raymond as being volatile: he'd lose his temper when he argued and maybe shoved [me] now and again, but he never beat me or anything like that. He did break a few things in temper but that's all. I wouldn't say he was violent at all."

The Police Interviews

Raymond never admitted that he had killed Jennifer: his tactic was to maintain that she had attacked *him*, and that she had fallen upon her own knife during his attempt to defend himself. The pathologist's revelation that she would have had to fall on her own knife at least seven times did nothing to change his story. Neither did he find anything odd in his abandonment of his child on the bloody bed beside its dead mother. A series of skilful police interviews over two days had no discernible impact upon him, and he continued to insist that he had acted only in self-defence.

Raymond's preliminary version of events was: "Well, I'd visited Jennifer last night at about ten-ish to have words with her about our situation, which in my view was getting out of hand. It took about, I don't know, ten minutes give or take, for me to persuade her to let me in. I don't think she was going to let me in but at the end of the day, the exact words I used were something like, 'Well, I'll be here all night then.' Anyway, she did let me in and we chatted for hours, in fact I was surprised what time it was when we'd finished, two or so in the morning it was. We hadn't really got anywhere, just going round in circles. She was adamant about what she was going to do; before I was going to go, I was going to go and see Alex. She said he was asleep upstairs 'cos he sleeps in the back bedroom. I said I wasn't going to wake him. She wasn't really happy about it, I will be honest. So I went upstairs and sat on the bed there and was just sort of stroking his head. She came up and said, 'about going,' and I said, 'give us a couple of minutes and then I'll go.' Then she went down again and came back up.

"This time she had this knife and she threatened me and said I was to get out and she was getting quite het up about it, raising her voice. And I said, 'In a minute' sort of thing and this knife went across the back of my hand. And then when I was just sitting there and still stroking him, she lunged forward and this knife went through me, actually went through me hand and that's when I made a lunge for the knife then. I was still sitting down at the time and we just struggled, it seemed like hours. I remember getting up eventually on the bed, I had hold of the knife. We fought for this knife and the next thing I knew she just went still. She lay on the bed and this knife was sticking in her. Although I've never seen a dead body in real life, I just sort of knew, and pulled this knife out. I thought it was a bit of a dream, but I remember walking backwards just looking at it. I didn't feel so well so I went into the bathroom and realized my hands were all covered in blood. I remember dropping the knife in the sink and turning on the cold tap and sitting there washing my hands. I came back into the room to see if she was really dead. I could see she was dead, and the little one was in the corner still snoring. I came home and I was in a terrible state for hours. I had a bath, got these clothes off and then I went to the solicitors and told them."

Not unnaturally, the detective found this story quite remarkable: "How would you describe your relationship?" Feigning sentimentality, Raymond responded: "First met Jennifer 10th March, I can remember the date because we were on a course together. We got on like a house on fire and the only fly in the ointment was her mother. She was from day one against me. Her prime objections were to do with the [difference in our] age – it's twenty years – and cultural differences: she's from Lancashire, and I'm from the south, the two cultures are different. I could never seem to do anything right and then towards the end we just didn't speak at all." Claiming a deep affection for her and their child, Raymond insisted, "I've always loved Jen and I always will. It's difficult to explain but it's a bit like a drug, she gets into your bloodstream and that's it. In fact I accepted that she had found some-body new and that we had finished, but I just got this feeling I was being cut out from Alex as well."

The detective searched for the motivation regarding the killing: "What specifically were you discussing [the night of the murder]? Access to the child, or . . .?" "There was two main things, one was access for Alex. I accepted that you were looking at nothing more than a day, probably sort of pick him up in his pram and go to the park. I get the feeling that what she was trying to do was eventually just to sort of shut it off so I would never see him again. 'I want to sort of see him on a regular basis, weekly, fortnight, or whatever' – it hadn't really come to any firm conclusion." "Is it fair to say the conversation was friendly when you first went in?" "It was friendly but cold. It was conducted on what I would call business terms."

"I'm a little perplexed," the detective astutely observed about Jennifer's purported sudden change of mood, "that from 10 o'clock until 2 A.M. – accepting the fact that you say you've been arguing round in circles and things have been a bit cold – I'm just interested in what particularly changed her mood from one of discussion into one of aggression, where she's gone downstairs and brought a knife to you? I mean have you gone upstairs sort of threatening, saying, 'Look, I'll make sure I'll get Alex, I'm going to take him with me'?" "Oh, no. The first thing is that of course Alex needs her still and I don't think there is any court in the land that would give me Alex. He needs his Mum on a day-to-day basis. All I wanted was access to see him on a regular basis."

Returning the interview to the murder, the detective observed, "Right, she's got the knife, and you are in the bedroom?" "I was, yeah. Sat on the bed, and Alex is sleeping in one corner of it, against the wall so he doesn't fall out. I was sitting on the bed and I was just stroking his head, with me back to the head board." "So she's come into the room with the knife: how was she holding it?" Raymond replied vaguely, "She had it in her hands, sort of on a level with her body. She said to me, 'Get out now' and indicated with the knife and I remember saying to her with me hands, 'Yeah, in a minute' type thing, 'Just a few more minutes with Alex,' and this thing went across the back of my hand. She was just sort of using it like a pointer, to say, 'You, out.'"

"So, having been lunged at and the knife sticking in the second time, that's when you made a grab for it?" "I must have caught it. I got hold of the knife and her hand and then we was sitting. I remember grabbing hold of her hand and at the same time trying to get to my feet, and then we backed against the wall at the top of the bed. I think I was trying to push her face away, or her body, I was trying to keep the knife away from me. All I knew was I'd been attacked, I'd been stabbed, I just wanted to defend myself. It was as simple as that." "Did you at any stage get the knife from her?" "I don't think I actually had the knife in my hand. I can remember I had an awkward grip on the knife and whilst we struggled, I managed to get the knife and twist it so that she would have to drop the thing. The knife was still looking at me and I was trying to bend the knife downwards. We crashed against the wall once or twice and then we fell on the bed. There was a bit of a struggle and then she went still, this knife was sticking in her chest. When she went still I leaned back a bit, see it sitting in her chest there. Having defended myself against any further attack, I suppose there was relief, but I just couldn't believe it, that this knife was sticking in her. I just pulled this thing out. It was just one of those accidents. I was defending myself during the tussle. I have no idea of how long all this took, it could have taken thirty, forty seconds. I couldn't even see the knife half the time. All I know is I had my hand on her hand and my only concern was to keep the knife away from me."

"Where was Alex all this time?" Unconcerned, Raymond replied, "He was in the corner asleep. I can see her lying there and he was in the corner and I could hear him snoring, as though he had a cold. When I left he was asleep. I just didn't know what to do next. I truly didn't and the only thing I wanted to do was just get out of there."

The detective expressed his disbelief: "An incident occurs about 2 A.M. You've gone back to your house, and you've left a woman apparently dead, and her eighteen-month-old child in the bed to fend for itself, and a six-year-old daughter in the house as well?" Richards could only reply with a "Hmm," and a demonstration of his inability to process anything but bureaucratic details in his life. "Don't you think that could be regarded as a little bit callous?" "It may well be. *I just never thought about it again.* I had a couple of weeps, I realized my hand was hurting. After having the bath I did feel a bit better and I bandaged up my hand; and it was only then that I realized that 'I'll go see the solicitor.' That was the first thing, before I do anything else. And then I thought it would be down to the police station first and then, I presume, hospital. Then I thought, 'I've got to make sure the kids are all right,' so I remember saying to Paul, 'You'll be all right here'; and he'd also got an investment thing, and for ages I've been telling him that as soon as he gets a date for the army he's going to have to send it off to cash it because he'll lose the tax thing."

"Raymond, the pathologist says your explanation of how things have happened with the wounds isn't possible. Have you any comment on that? She's also got a gash at the base of the thumb, which is a defensive wound, which would render your explanation impossible. Can you explain that?" "No, I can't." "There's no way she could have come about the injuries she'd got in that way." Raymond insisted, "Well, all I'm saying, we struggled with that knife and she ended up on the bed with that knife sticking out of her." "You're not accepting that at some stage you've had the knife in your own hand and you've caused some of those injuries, because it's impossible the way that you've said for her to have received all those injuries?" "All I'm saying, we struggled with that knife. My recollection is that we shared the knife." When Raymond's solicitor objected that the detective was merely repeating the same question, the policeman admitted, "I'm trying to probe his answers, because I don't believe him, you see, and I think there's something more sinister to this than the way he was telling us." Raymond held fast.

The detective tried another approach: "What's emerging, Raymond, is a possible motive for you attacking Jennifer. There's presumably been an upset about the division of the property, and she's been refusing to return some items to you?" "She originally refused to give me back any of my property," Raymond complained. "So there's the dispute over that and there was obviously a dispute over access to Alex?" "My purpose of seeing Mrs. Brown [as he now called Jennifer] was to avoid any of this unpleasantness and court action. I was certain her attitude would probably become more intransigent, and I was going to have one last go at trying to persuade her that we should settle it amicably."

"I've got to tell you that the police surgeon who examined you yesterday is of the opinion that the injury from the base of your index finger towards the centre of your hand is self-inflicted. Have you any comment?" "It wasn't self-inflicted." "You've gone up there, you've caused her some harm, and then you've faked these injuries to your hand and made this whole story up about the struggle."

Then the detective read aloud from a letter Raymond had written his daughter on the day of the murder: "'By the time you read this you will no doubt have heard stories about me. To put the record straight I was attacked first and then I lost my temper – passion took over.' What does that mean?" "What I've always said, I was attacked first and then I went out to defend myself." "But you said, 'I lost my temper – passion took over.' You didn't say anything about losing your temper earlier?" "Well, I mean that's just a figure of speech. Not necessarily in temper, no. Poor choice of words. But there's nothing sinister in what I did before the event."

At this point the detective merely allowed himself to express his utter disbelief, bringing the tape-recorded interviews to a close. The court did not believe Raymond's fumbling protestations of innocence: he was found guilty of murder, and sentenced to life imprisonment.

SORTING JOE OUT: TOM IS CAUGHT IN A FAMILY FEUD

Twenty per cent of the victims in our sample were related to the killer through "family" ties – they were parents, children, grandparents, brothers and sisters, aunts and uncles or cousins. In this "family," however, it is often impossible to ascertain the precise relationship because there were so many overlapping ties of incest, marriage and divorce and bizarre sexual relations. Even the police were confused by the cast of characters. Long before the killing, the family's behaviour was well known to both local social workers and the police. Indeed, its members were infamous for their suspected incest and other forms of sexual deviance, and for the complex history of feuds between its alcoholic and unemployed members. Most members of the family were living in council housing on social assistance, and the majority of the men had long criminal histories.

The council flat in which the killing took place was littered with pornographic pictures, and one witness described one photograph in the family's collection, which showed Valerie Grimes, the mother of both killer and victim, "with her tits exposed, and a couple of men showing their pricks, and one of a baby holding his [penis] in his hand." Indeed, Valerie bled all over many of the photographs after she was stabbed in the ankle during the drunken mêlée. The ensuing police report noted that "the majority of the witnesses at the scene are alcoholics who engage in deviant sexual practices," and "weekly sex and drug parties [allegedly] take place at the home." Both the Grimes and Gretsky families were "well known to the borough's Social Services Department," and there had been "cases of alleged incest reported between Susan Donahue and [her brother] Joseph Gretsky, and more recently her seventeen-year-old son, Tony Donahue."

In the actual implosion, at least three men and one woman were stabbed (the mother, stepfather, half-brother and half-sister's biological father, of both killer and victim), apparently because they were there and automatically embroiled in the affray; and others were beaten and shoved. The provoking incident appeared to be a remark, made by fifteen-year-old Michelle's mother and her current boyfriend, Joseph Gretsky, calling Michelle a "slag" for having an affair with the family lodger; and threatening to evict her from the family's council flat unless she ended the romance.

After the killing, the first act of several family members was to appear at Whitechapel police station, where they promptly reported the events to the proper authorities.

Losing Control

As police reconstructed the events of that day, Michelle, who was sleeping with the family lodger, Peter, complained bitterly to her natural father and two half-brothers that her mother and her mother's current boyfriend, Joseph Gretsky, had insulted her and demanded she end her liaison with Peter. Enraged by this affront, the lodger intended to see Gretsky and "sort him out": in addition, Terrence White, the father of Susan Donahue's (Joseph Gretsky's sister) most recent baby, was known to be very angry about the pornographic photographs that included their child, and intended to demand satisfaction. Thus Peter and Terrence appear to have decided to visit the family flat in order to discipline the family members.

Acting in this capacity, and fortified with alcohol, Peter armed himself with a twelve-inch carving knife, and accompanied by Michelle's natural father, Ronald (who seems to have been armed with a small knife), Terrence White, and Michelle's half-brother Nick Brown (the victim), headed towards Michelle's home in order to avenge themselves upon Joseph Gretsky, the current boyfriend of Valerie Grimes, who was considered the primary provocateur in this matter. Quite drunk by this time, they burst into Valerie Grimes' council flat, and immediately attacked Joseph Gretsky. Long accustomed to anticipating danger, Valerie Grimes appears to have thrown herself bodily across Joseph Gretsky to protect him: for her gallant effort she was herself beaten and stabbed in the skirmish that followed.

At the moment the avenging group burst into the flat, the killer-to-be, Tom Grimes, was in the kitchen peeling potatoes with a small vegetable knife. Seeing the fight raging in front of him, he rushed to help his mother, and was attacked by Terrence and Ronald. "Tom then stabbed Nick with the knife, five times, in the chest, back, neck and eye," police reconstructed. "Nick staggered from the flat and collapsed outside on the ground floor, adjacent to the entrance of the building. Thomas then stabbed Ronald Jordan in the stomach as the fight between Valerie Grimes and Jordan continued. Tom then fled from the flat and saw his half-brother Nick in a collapsed state outside, but failed to assist him. He returned to the flat, where he stabbed the lodger, Peter Grant, in the back, stomach and shoulder, before running away again."

Apparently so drunk that they were unaware of the seriousness of their own injuries, Peter and Ronald continued kicking and punching Joseph Gretsky and Valerie Grimes: Peter was later arrested at Whitechapel hospital, where he was receiving first aid, and police found Ronald hiding in his own flat. When Tom Grimes learned that his half-brother had died, he surrendered to police, "and immediately claimed he had acted in the defence of himself and both his mother and Joseph Gretsky."

The investigating detectives were struck by the fact that "at no time has Tom Grimes shown the slightest sign of emotion in relation to his brother's death. From evidence gathered thus far, there would appear to have been no love lost between them. For some time prior to the incident, the Grimes family had been living with Susan Donahue, the ex-lover of White and mother of his baby. Inquiries show that there has [also] been a sexual relationship between Donahue and Tom Grimes since he was fourteen years old, and he was in fact the current lover of Donahue."

The prosecution's case against Tom was based on the suggestion that he knew the four would be coming to the flat to assault Joseph Gretsky, and "fully expected them to be armed with knives, having been told as much by his sister, Michelle." The prosecution also understood that Tom would "claim 'provocation' whilst in fear of his own life and that of his mother and Joseph Gretsky."

The Killer and His Victim

As is commonly the case, the social identities of both killer and victim were indistinguishable. The *offender*, Tom, at sixteen already had a string of convictions, including five findings of guilt for burglary, taking a conveyance and theft. At fifteen, he had first appeared in juvenile court on a burglary charge, and was ordered to pay £10 compensation and placed on a two-year supervision order; at sixteen, he appeared twice in juvenile court on additional burglary charges, was conditionally discharged, and given a one-year supervision order. In that same year, he was fined £25 for taking and driving away a vehicle; and later charged with theft and two counts of burglary, for which his supervision order was extended still further. He had attended secondary school and was a patient in an Intermediate Treatment Unit, but he left both institutions at the age of fifteen, without any qualifications, and had been unemployed since then. His parents had divorced long before, and his father lived in the Midlands. Tom lived with his mother, Valerie, sister, Michelle, and the Gretsky family in a three-bedroom council flat, sharing a bedroom with his mother and her boyfriend, for which he paid £25 each fortnight for rent and food. At the time of the killing, he was receiving £36.40 each fortnight in state benefits.

At the time of his death, Tom's half-brother, the *victim*, twenty-two-year-old Nick Brown, lived in a hostel in East London. He also had a number of previous convictions for dishonesty, possession of an offensive weapon and violent behaviour. His last prison sentence – he had served twenty-eight days for shoplifting – had ended six months before he was killed. Unmarried, he had received a form of secondary education, leaving at the age of sixteen without any qualifications. From time to time he lived at various addresses with his mother, Valerie Grimes, and he took casual employment to supplement his income from petty crime. "His family life," police commented, "to say the least, was very unstable," after his mother's many divorces. Nick was unemployed at the time of his death, and receiving state benefits. He spent most of his time in pubs in Stepney, drinking and smoking cannabis.

The Witnesses Remember

Mandy, the victim's twenty-year-old girlfriend, told police that Nick was upset that his sister had been called a "slag," and that Ronald thought Valerie Grimes needed "a good kicking." Seventeen-year-old Tony, who lived with his mother, Susan Donahue, told police that the men went into the front room with Nick in the lead. Tom was sitting in an armchair peeling potatoes with a kitchen knife. He told police he followed the men into the front room, where he heard Peter say to his uncle, "You had better fucking stop telling Michelle to get out of the house, and stop calling her a slag as well."

He remembered that the men started to punch and kick his uncle, and that Valerie Grimes tried to stop them. His mother, Susan Donahue, also told them to stop; and it was then that he saw Peter Grant pull a long black-handled knife from his trousers.

Tony then left the room because he did not want to get involved in the argument. A few minutes later, seated in his bedroom, he heard what sounded to him like someone slapping the bottom of his bedroom door. He thought at first it was the baby, but on opening the door he saw Nick lying on the floor: the back of his neck was covered with blood, and around his head a pool of blood widened. He went back into his bedroom, but saw Peter and Ronald looking at Nick on the floor and shouting at his uncle and threatening to cut him up. Tony closed his door and heard Peter shout, "Come on, let's go, come on quick!" He went over to Nick and put his hand on his back, but could not feel him breathing.

The intended victim of the assault, Joseph Gretsky, had a rather different memory of its origins. That afternoon, Tom had demanded to know, "Did you call Michelle a slag?" Although he denied he had said that, Tom told him, "Nicky's coming down to give you another stripe on the other side of your face." Joseph told police that soon after Valerie Grimes had returned with fresh supplies of wine and cigarettes, the assailants burst into the flat. Nick had shouted, "I've come to see someone," and Peter then pointed at Joseph Gretsky and said, "You, you cunt, I want to see you," and punched him on the right side of the head with his right fist.

Interrogation of the Killer

The morning after the killing, Tom was interviewed by the police. He made no attempt to explain, or even conceal, what he had done, and he seemed unaware of what precisely had happened – it was just one of those things that seemed to have developed in the course of a family argument, someone was cut, perhaps several were hurt, someone was killed. "I was preparing dinner, peeling potatoes, Nicky walked in and a man called Ronnie, and Peter. They walked in and started hitting Joe. Then Ronnie started hitting my Mum. And I tried to stop them hitting my Mum. I tried to grab them to pull them off. Nicky grabbed hold of me, and Ronnie and

Peter pulled out the knife. Then I used a knife to try and escape. Both of them grabbed hold of me. I don't know which one I stabbed. I just stabbed just to get them off me."

"Why was Ron hitting your mother?" "I don't know." "When you went to help your mother, did you say anything to them, like 'Stop fighting'? Something like that?" "I said, 'Leave her alone.'" "Are you saying Peter lunged [with] a knife at you?" "Yes, because when Ronnie and Nicky got off me, Peter pulled a knife out. As Nicky and Ronnie were hitting me, I must have stabbed Nicky and he ran out."

"Do you recall stabbing Peter?" "I don't know. Robin [a visitor to the flat] run out for the police. When I was fighting with Nicky and Ronnie, Peter was hitting Joe." "When you stabbed out at Nicky did you intend to kill him?" "No, just to stop him from hitting me." "Prior to this fight, how did you get on with your brother?" "All right," Tom lied, for there had been bad blood between the two of them.

In a second police interview seven hours later, after Tom had had the opportunity to collect his thoughts, he told police, "My sister, Michelle, she used to go over Whitechapel to see Peter. One night she stayed over there and when she came back over Joe and Sue were drunk and Joe told her to get out. And she went back and told Nicky and all them. That's why they came over. My sister said to my Mum that Nicky was going to do the other side of Joe's face." "Do you know who cut Joe's face previously?" "The one [scar] he's got? Nicky did." "Why did he do it?" "I dunno. They had an argument."

"You said this morning that you went to stop them hitting your mother. Can you explain who you pulled off your mother?" "Ronnie and I tried to pull off Peter, off Joe. Joe was sitting on the settee when Peter was hitting him. And Mum and Ron was on the floor." By now even the detectives were confusing the names of the participants: "So how did you get hold of Ronnie and Nicky? If one was fighting..." "Not Ronnie and Nicky – Ronnie and Peter." "How did you manage to hold [them] if Peter was fighting on the settee and Ronnie was fighting your mother on the floor?" "As I pulled Ronnie off my Mum, he went on to the floor because I think he had a bit of drink. As I tried to pull Peter off, Nicky grabbed hold of me. Then Ronnie got up and started hitting me and all. Nicky tried to get his arm round my head and as I pushed him, Nicky went on to the floor. When I was fighting Ronnie, Nicky got back up again. When he tried to put me in an arm lock, I must have stabbed him then."

"So when did you stab Peter?" "When I went back upstairs again. He had his back to me and hitting Joe again. And that's when I stabbed him in the back there. I stabbed him in the back about twice I think. That's when he pulled the knife the second time and chased me with it."

"Who was looking after Nick?" "Robin." "Had the ambulance been called?" "Yeah, because Robin had just come back from calling them." "What was your mother doing?" "Sitting down in the sitting room." "Did she ask what had happened to Nick?" "No, she was crying." "What happened next? Did you leave the flat or wait for the ambulance?" "When I left, Ronnie and Peter had already left. Nicky laid outside on the floor. Then I left." Tom went to a friend's flat: "How long did you stay at their flat?" "Fifteen minutes. Then they said Sue, my Mum, and Joe had all gone down the police station. Then the three of us went over to the flat."

When asked if he had been "upset" to learn that his half-brother had died, Tom could only say, "Yes." When asked what he had told his friends, he replied, "I said I had a fight and an ambulance had been called." "Did you tell them that you had 'done them all'?" "I said I had a fight and stabbed them with a knife." "During the fight last night, did you receive any injuries?" "No." "Had you been drinking last night or yesterday afternoon?" "No." "Had your mother been drinking, or anyone else?" "I think me Mum and Joe, and Robin."

Somehow, the court pieced together what had transpired, and who had done what to whom. Tom was found guilty of both manslaughter and malicious wounding. He was sentenced to serve a total of three years in youth custody, three years for manslaughter and six months for malicious wounding (to be served concurrently).

---

1   Barry Mitchell, 1990, *Murder and Penal Policy*, London: Macmillan, p. 128. Morris and Blom-Cooper, 1979, pp. 32–33.

2   In addition to what he drank at the pub, that evening at home George consumed three drinks from the whisky bottle, four cans of export beer and a portion of a bottle of Martini.

PARENTS AND CHILDREN

CHILDREN OF TWELVE AND UNDER, and the "elderly," sixty-five and over, seem inherently vulnerable to assault; yet *together* they constitute less than one-quarter of the total homicides in the sampled years between 1982 and 1990. Of these two, it is children who are more likely to become the victims of homicide; but, as Terence Morris and Louis Blom-Cooper have noted, the "vulnerability of children is still clearly related to the behaviour of their parents who are, *par excellence*, the prime category of child killers." In the sampled years between 1982 and 1990, 294 (11 per cent) of the 2,680 recorded victims were the "elderly." Children of twelve and under were slightly more likely to become victims (they constituted 355 of the 2,680 victims, or 13 per cent), but the vast majority (78 per cent) of these 355 were children of five and under, most commonly the victims of their own parents, acting out some deep depression – often triggered by marital separation, or sudden financial reverses. Sons and daughters are three times as likely to be murdered by a parent as the reverse: only 4 per cent of the homicide victims were parents of the killer, while 12 per cent of the victims were the children of the killer.[1]

PARENTS KILLING CHILDREN

It is the theme of this book that the immediate cause of homicide is neither the desire nor the technology (both of which are everywhere readily available, in the human psyche and in the landscape), but the presence in the culture of specific messages teaching people about the appropriateness of violence. To illustrate, examine a patricide in Oklahoma in the early 1990s, as told with elegance and grace by Beverly Lowry. Lonnie

Dutton, thirty-nine, was shot in the head by his two sons, Herman, fifteen, and Druie, twelve. The victim, a notorious abuser of his wife and children, had apparently himself been the victim of violence by his own father, Luther; Lowry reports incidents in which blood streaked from their heads to their ankles. One episode was so brutal that "everybody went and hid so they couldn't hear." Once married with his own children, Lonnie tortured them all, so sadistically that, Luther remembers, "Lonnie abused her [his wife] and beat her up so bad you couldn't tell who she was." Sometimes Lonnie threw darts at his wife, or beat her till she would sleep with other men, then beat her again for betraying him. When neighbours or family complained to the welfare authorities, or the police, of the savage torture and assault in the family, none responded: one neighbour remembered, "They told us there was nothing they could do unless we caught him red-handed and held on to him until somebody came." As Lowry rightly concluded, the social message was clear. "Be your own vigilante; do what you have to do." That is what *society* taught them all to do, to take justice into their own hands.[2]

Lonnie's familial culture taught him that violence was a manly and appropriate response to all frustration and insult. Then Lonnie specifically taught his sons to kill: he had seemed strangely possessive of his daughter, Alesha, and had introduced her, still a toddler, as "my little slut." Lonnie always told his sons that if *anyone* ever sexually abused his daughter, they must kill him. Lonnie even gave specific and emphatic instructions, how to pick up the deer rifle and shoot the offender in the head. Thus they did the right thing when they agreed to "kill Daddy," Herman holding the gun while Druie pulled the trigger, after ten-year-old Alesha ran out of the house shrieking that their father had molested her. That is what their society and their father taught them to do.

It was not the presence of the rifle that provoked the homicide: murderous technology is available everywhere, in every kitchen and every garage; an axe or a knife, a bottle or a car would have accomplished the same end. It is the will to use that technology that is culturally coded, the decision that is half-consciously culturally applauded; this is what shapes the numbers of homicidal assaults in a nation.

AN ENGLISH CASE: PETER KILLS HIS MOTHER

The will to murder a parent seems to exist everywhere, as occasionally does the act: in all of England in 1990, for example, there were twenty-two such cases, most commonly the result of a profound mental disorder in the killer (or, sometimes, a response to years of abuse), as when Peter Gotzeitis, twenty-one, beat to death his fifty-one-year-old mother in a northern city. A police report noted that there had been a family argument during which the young man had locked his mother out of the house. The quarrel seems to have begun when the mother, Greek-born Madonna Gotzeitis, had asked their family doctor to visit the house to examine Peter. On arriving, the doctor recalled, "I was met at the door by Mrs. Gotzeitis, who was in a worried state. I asked her what was wrong and she told me that Peter had been withdrawn for about three days and on one occasion had barricaded himself in his room. We went into the back living room and he was lying on the settee with some blankets over him. I sat on the settee and asked him what was wrong. He didn't make any reply but his face turned to a look of anger and he edged himself up over the settee until he was standing up. He raised clenched fists and told me to get out of the house. Mrs. Gotzeitis was trying to calm him down, but he was directing all his aggression at me. I just told him I was going and left, hoping to take the heat out of the situation. I got the impression from Peter's attitude that he meant harm."

The doctor waited outside the home for a few moments and then knocked on the door. "I was allowed in by Mrs. Gotzeitis. She apologized for her son and led me into the back living room where Peter was. He apologized for his conduct, and Mrs. Gotzeitis left us to go into the front living room. Peter appeared calm and collected, and was talking quite rationally. He was very apologetic for his aggressive behaviour. I asked him how he was, and if there were any problems, but he said he felt okay. From what Mrs. Gotzeitis described, and from what I had seen of him, I formed the opinion that he was acutely mentally ill. I suggested that the best approach would be for one of my colleagues to come and visit them. My idea was that there was a possibility that he would be admitted under the Mental Health Act. She seemed happy at that."

While arrangements were being made for a psychiatric visit, Peter locked his mother out of the home once again. "Eventually he let her in," the police reconstructed, "and a row developed. Peter Gotzeitis then struck his mother, pulling her to the floor, whereupon he hit her in the face with a vase. The struggle continued and he cut her throat with the broken vase. He then attempted to cut her head off but was unable to completely do this." He stabbed her in the head with pieces from the vase, and jumped on her several times before throwing her body down the cellar steps.

Shortly after this, Peter's sister, Maria, entered the home. When she saw the blood splattered through the living room, she asked about her mother: Peter told her their mother was "in the cellar," then added that he had killed her. When police were called, Peter left the house, saying he was going to the local pub for a drink. As Maria recalled the devastating events: "We have always been a very close family and my parents have always been very loving and caring, and when my father died of cancer, it left a very deep hurt in our lives. The death of my father brought the family even closer.

"On New Year's Eve, Peter still appeared to be upset about something, but he didn't say what it was. I put it down to him being depressed about my father's death, which he took very badly. On New Year's Day my mother and Peter came to our house in order to watch television with us. They wanted to watch the film, *The Ten Commandments*. Peter started to cry later in the afternoon and we asked him what was the matter. I asked him if he was thinking about Dad, and he said, 'Yes.' I told him we were all thinking about him. He stopped crying and then made us a drink of tea or coffee.

"The following day I called at Mother's with my husband to have a chat. I thought my brother Peter would be at work. I rang the doorbell and Peter answered the door. I asked him why he wasn't at work and I don't think he answered. I walked into the living room and Peter said something like, 'There's been a disaster.' I said, 'Why, what's wrong?' I then saw a blanket on the settee. My brother said, 'The doctor's been,' or something. I then saw what appeared to be muck and dark fluid on the carpet in the middle of the room. I looked at the ceiling and saw it had not come from there. I thought there may have been a burst. I asked Peter where Mother was and he said, 'She's in the cellar.' I then realized the mess on the carpet was blood and I shouted at him, 'Why, what's happened?' He said, 'She tried to kill me.'

"Peter said, 'Thank God, I love you.' He put his arms around me and said, 'We've got each other; look after me now.' Peter asked me not to look, but on looking down the cellar I saw my mother lying on her stomach with her head on the bottom step and her feet pointing up the stairs. I cried out and my husband ran away for help. I was about to go down the cellar steps, when Peter said, 'No, don't go down there. You don't want to see her like that.' He jumped in front of me to stop me going down: he did not use any force, but held me gently. He put his arms around me. I went down the cellar steps. I could see no sign of life and I realized that she was dead. I returned to the living room and I asked Peter what had happened. He said, 'I've killed her. She tried to kill me and she was going to bring a doctor because I was not well.' He put his arms around me in a gentle manner, and asked me to go upstairs to look at Dad's photographs. He said he wanted to look at Dad's eyes. I told him I didn't want to go upstairs and I asked him why he had done it. He said again, 'She tried to kill me.'

"Peter then asked where my husband was, and I told him he had gone for help. He said, 'We don't need any help.' Then he asked me if I wanted to go for a drink. My husband returned and told Peter that he had called for an ambulance. Peter said, 'We don't need one, there *are* no ambulances and no hospital.' I formed the opinion he was thinking about when my father was dying of cancer. He went against hospitals at that time."

Arrest

The first police constable to arrive at the house approached Peter and asked, "There has been an incident at your home and I believe you can help us?" "Yes, there has," Peter replied, "but I don't want to talk about it." When the constable told Peter he was being arrested for the death, Peter tried to run away: he was forcibly restrained, handcuffed and placed in the police vehicle. At the police station, the questions – and the bizarre responses – began.

At first, the detective simply tried to determine Peter's level of awareness: "Do you know where you are?" "I'm in the police station." "Do you know why you are here?" "It's because what happened at home." "How do you feel?" "Fine, thank you." "Have you been drinking today?" "I nearly got a drink, then they brought me here." "Are you under any medication from the doctor, tablets or whatever?" "No, I don't take drugs."

"Do you want to tell us about what happened today?" "No, I think it's the kind of thing I'd like to forget." "It might help you to talk about it: all we want to do is find out what has happened, get your side of it." "Yes, there is two sides, isn't there," Peter said. "So are we going to talk about it and get it sorted out?" "Maybe. I'd like to, because it's *amazing!*" "Do you feel all right?" "Yes, I'm fine." "How do you mean, 'It's amazing'?" "It just is!" "Well, why not tell us? We are good listeners." "Yes, I think I would feel even better to go through it." "Have you had an argument with your mother?" "I hit her, you know, in the face." "With your fist?" "No, a vase. A glass one with flowers on. I cut her lots of times and there is blood everywhere. I've washed and changed."

"What we are going to do is to talk to you at length, and any answers you wish to make will also be written down. Do you understand?" "Yes, that sounds fair." "You have heard why you have been arrested in the charge office?" "Oh yes! I feel bad about it." "Why don't you tell us what happened?" "I'd like to tell you, I'd feel better about it, I think, now you know. Well, first of all, my mother came to the house with the doctor. She thought I was ill but I wasn't, I was just tired. I frightened him away! I warned him and told him to get out of the house. I just shouted at him right loud, I said, 'Get out.' I didn't want to see him. He went out the back. I was laid on the settee. Then my Mam came back in and said, 'What's a matter, why didn't you talk nicely to him?' I said, 'What did you bring him for?' I had my life saved when I was four years old, you know. But I didn't need to see any doctor. I was annoyed with my Mam about fetching a doctor to me. She said she would bring another doctor, so I got upset again. My mother went out the front door and I locked her out. She came back once and I told her to get lost. I didn't want to see a doctor and I thought she had gone for another. She went away then came back a short time after and knocked on the door. I told her to get lost again. I might have said, 'Fuck off.' She was really dying to get in. She was knocking and ringing the bell five, six, or eleven times. I put the radio on loud. She came back again. I had turned the radio off, she shouted through the door that my sister was coming, so I let her in the house.

"She kept saying, 'Why didn't you let me in? Why didn't you let me in, you stupid thing?' I got mad, very mad. I grabbed hold of the cuffs of her coat and said, 'That's what I mean.' I pulled her down by the coat. She went down by the side of the settee at first. I got really mad by this time. She kept saying, 'Stop it, stop it, what are you doing, you're hurting me, Peter.'" "What were you doing to hurt her?" "Putting my fingers in her eyes. She had got up and we were in the middle of the room. I'll show you." With one hand, Peter grabbed the detective's lapels, and with the other jabbed towards her eyes. "That's how I did it."

Anticipating that this might be difficult for Peter to discuss, the detective asked if Peter was feeling well. "Yes, I am feeling fine in myself," Peter replied. "It is clear to me exactly what happened. I feel better talking to you. I dragged her to the floor. I was at the side of her: she was lying on the carpet on her back. I cracked her on the side of her head with my fist, I think my left. A punch. I then grabbed hold of that glass vase: I just grabbed it, it was on top of the gas fire. I was still knelt at the side of my Mam, I reached it easily. I smashed it over my Mam's face, and it broke into about forty-eight pieces. I kept cutting her face with different pieces of the broken vase. No, I mean her neck. I kept pushing the pieces into her neck. I just kept on cutting and cutting and cutting. I was trying to kill her. That's what I was trying to do. Because I thought she was trying to kill me. It was all really over the doctor thing."

"What else did you do to your mother after cutting the neck?" "I tried to twist it round. I tried to break her neck. I had a problem trying to break it. She was just laid there, but I know that she was not dead. She was groaning a bit and alive. Just laid there with her face towards the settee. I broke both her wrists, or I tried when she was on the floor near to the settee: before I did the second one I said in my mind, 'Goodbye to you, I love you.' I laid on top of her, put my arms around her. Then I stood thinking what I had done – but I knew all the time what I was doing. I hit her [with the] thick glass ashtray after I had put the forty-third piece of glass in her neck. That blow was to the back of the neck." "How many times did you hit her with the ashtray?" "About twenty times. I was sawing at the back of her neck trying to cut her head off but she was so strong. Her veins were up. I knew I couldn't do that. It was amazing. I was so worn out at the end. I said to my Ma, 'You're like a robot, you,' meaning she was so strong.

"I was still trying to break her neck to kill her. I moved it forward and backwards but couldn't. I started jumping on her stomach and blood was pumping out of her neck. I was jumping all over her body to get the blood out of her. I felt her face and legs and that to see if she was still alive, she was. So I grabbed hold of her and started kicking her in the back. Then I left her and went to go upstairs but I paused, came back, felt her face to see if she was getting cold. I did that four times. On the fourth time she was cool. I just waited and she got colder and colder. I knew then she was dead. As soon as I knew that, a postcard and a brown envelope came through the letter box. I dragged Mam to the cellar by her shoulders. Only to the top of the steps. I pushed her down the steps and she rolled down. I stayed at the top and then started to clean up. I got changed and had a bath to get the blood off me."

Then "My sister called, and her husband, too. I let them in. My sister seen the blood. She said, 'What have you done, Peter?' She was mad. I said, 'I've killed us mother, you'll be all right now, you've got me.' Her husband ran out of the house, then he came back and I said, 'I'm going to The Swan.' He said, 'No, you can't go.'" "Did your sister know where your mother was?" "I showed her she was in the cellar and she went down and came back screaming, grabbed hold of me. She went back down then, saying, 'She might need some help.' I told her she was dead. I insisted I was going to The Swan. My sister tried to stop me but I shouted at her – I frightened her, and ran out of the back of the house to The Swan."

"Why have you done all this to your mother?" asked the puzzled detective. Peter tried to explain: "It's been her. She's been getting at me. I've been trying to make her happy but she has been cutting me down." "What time did all this happen?" "It's in three sections: the killing, the letters coming and my sister." "Who else lives at the house?" "Nobody. Just me and my mother. My father died about one year four months ago." Still grasping for a comprehensible explanation, the detective asked Peter, "Do you have many upsets with your Mam?" "No – none." "Have you anything else to say?" Peter could only reply, "Merry Christmas and a Happy New Year. God bless you two."

The Aftermath

His co-workers and friends were mystified, as such acquaintances usually appear to be: the killing seemed so out of character. The personnel officer of the business where Peter worked reported that "I believed he was of a quiet personality and of smart appearance. I would also say from his file that he was a good, willing worker, of a conscientious nature. All the reports I had about him were good. He did not have any apparent time away from work."

A thoughtful twenty-two-year-old friend mused: "Since my schooldays I have known Peter Gotzeitis. Peter has always been a quiet, shy person, who has kept himself to himself. Peter's father died in the summer-time of 1984. He's never really got over this. Even in conversation, if people started talking about their father, Peter would go very quiet as if he was a bit upset. Peter started drinking each dinner and night-time from around Christmas. This was unusual for him because he was never usually bothered about drinking. He seemed as if he had things on his mind. [The day before the murder] I asked him if he had any problems and told him he could talk to me if he had. He just said that he would sort his own problems out and he left without saying anything. He was a person who would never discuss things."

At the magistrate's court, Peter Gotzeitis was found guilty of manslaughter on grounds of diminished responsibility. He was placed in an institution for an indefinite period.

"I JUST KEPT HITTING HER": MICK BEATS TO DEATH HIS INFANT STEPDAUGHTER

Mick Randell was ill educated and virtually illiterate, with a substantial list of criminal convictions, unemployed and living on state benefits in a council house. The child of one broken marriage, he lived in a common-law relationship with a young widow, taking partial responsibility for minding her two children while she went to work. On the day of the killing, Randell rained punches on thirteen-month-old Ellen Crotty when she annoyed him by pulling his hair.

Obfuscation

Mrs. Grayston, a housewife who lived across the road from the victim, answered a knock on her door. Randell was standing there, holding baby Ellen in his arms, and asking for help. Mrs. Grayston noted that Ellen looked a "terrible yellowy colour," and followed Randell back to his home. Here she examined the child, but was unable to find a pulse, and an attempt at artificial respiration was unsuccessful. She called an ambulance, and Randell told her that Ellen had fallen off the settee. When questioned by the examining doctor, Randell repeated this claim; but the doctor was suspicious and asked that the police be called. Randell then repeated this story once more to a police constable.

After a brief interview by sceptical detectives, however, Randell asked for pen and paper, and wrote a voluntary statement admitting that he had struck the child in the stomach and dropped her on the floor. After that admission, he was interviewed at length, and he slowly began to provide police with more details. He now claimed that he had twice struck the baby in the stomach after she had crawled too near to a gas fire.

Police noted that the child's injuries were far too serious to be accounted for by Randell's story. They continued questioning him till he "broke down," and changed his story once again. This time he admitted that when he picked up the child to stop her from crawling near the gas fire, she pulled his hair, aggravating an old injury. As a response to her hair-pulling, he threw her on the settee and heard a bang – which he assumed was the sound of her head hitting the arm of the settee. Infuriated still, he "rained blows in the area of the child's abdomen with his left fist and the heel of his right hand." Police thought "the injuries received by the child were entirely consistent with this form of attack."

At first the victim's mother sympathized with the killer. Melanie Crotty, twenty-two, told police that "Michael Randell, who I had known since schooldays, moved in with me and we began living as husband and wife. We were going to get married. I have never known him to show any violence towards my children. Indeed, when I have smacked them he has always told me off, saying that they were too young to understand. I have been working in the evenings seven days a week, Michael has been left in charge of the children. There have been occasions when Michael has lost his temper with me and given me a slap; although I must say that these occasions were always my fault. I can't believe that Michael would do it."

But in a second statement given to police four months later, Melanie changed her story. "I would like to tell you about the situation when Mick moved in with me. At first as I previously stated he totally accepted my two children when he moved in to live with me in January. Although he was out of work, our relationship worked fairly well at the beginning because financially I was in receipt of my widows' benefit and Mick had his National Assistance money. I suppose the only feelings I had for him were because I genuinely believed that he cared for my two children; but after the first couple of months he started to change and became jealous. For example, if my friends called he would make some nasty comment after they had left. He didn't like it if I dressed up to go out. Later, his attitude changed towards the children: he would say that they were not his, why should he care.

"Around about April or May of the same year, he would provoke an argument which ended up with him punching, slapping and kicking me. I have had a cut lip, black eye and bruises on my arms. I never reported any of these matters because he threatened me that if I did he would deny it, and say that because I would occasionally go out in the evenings I was not a suitable mother and he would have the children taken away from me. I would like to say that at that particular time I was still thinking about the death of my husband, and I had not properly conditioned myself to being a widow. Things got worse as time went on and his attacks on me mostly for no reason became more frequent. Some time in May, a man friend who I had known for some time came to stay for the weekend. On one of these evenings, Ellen was playing up, and Mick in the presence of my friend, Phil, said words to the effect 'they should have put her in the corner with razor blades to play with.' I was a bit shocked at this remark and Phil said it was a wicked thing to say.

"Phil stayed that weekend while Mick was at his Mum's. When Mick returned on the Monday I told him that I had slept with Phil. He became extremely jealous, and accused me of sleeping with everybody, even when I went out to the shops. I only ever saw him hit the children on their backsides, but I knew about his quick temper; and thinking about the whole period I am not now really surprised that he lost control and killed my child. I blame myself to some extent because I should have realized that with his quick temper and his attitude towards the children, he was capable of going the whole way. However when I started my work in June, I made a point of telling my neighbour's daughter, Lisa, to keep an eye on things during the evenings. I know that she was present when he did the baby-sitting. Unfortunately, the week of the tragedy, Lisa was on holiday. As previously mentioned, my feelings for him were because I genuinely believed he cared for my kids, but I now realize having sorted out my mental state, that this was all false."

The Killer's History

Mick was born in Birmingham and educated at a comprehensive school, which he left without qualifications at the age of fifteen. During the summers, he had been employed as a swimming pool lifeguard by the local council, earning £48 per week. Since then he had done casual work for his father, a self-employed painter and decorator. At the time of the killing he lived with his fiancée and her children in a two-bedroom council house, and received £52.50 per fortnight unemployment benefit, out of which he paid £10 per week hire purchase repayment on a vacuum cleaner.

His first criminal conviction was for burglary and theft of property from a shop display, for which he was given a two-year supervision order. Eight months after that, he was again in court for a similar offence: this time he received three months in a detention centre, and was ordered to pay costs of £46. Four months after that, he was convicted of robbery and placed for three months in a detention centre. Three months after being released, he was convicted on three counts of theft, and driving without a licence or insurance: for this he was fined £5 or ten days on each charge, and ordered to pay compensation. Two years passed before he was convicted again, for handling stolen property and absconding from bail, for which he was fined a total of £110. Within two months, he was convicted of taking and driving away, and driving whilst disqualified without insurance. He was sentenced to eighty hours' community service and six months' disqualification from driving, and fined £10. Only three months passed before he was at Snaresbrook Crown Court, charged with driving while disqualified with no insurance and taking and driving away, for which his Borstal training licence was endorsed. Almost another two years passed before he was caught again, once more for driving whilst disqualified without insurance: he was fined £10 or one day on each offence. Nine months later, he was in the Central Criminal Court, charged with the manslaughter of Ellen Crotty.

Psychiatric Interviews

Two months after the killing, the consulting forensic psychiatrist examined Randell in Brixton prison, and reported, "I asked him to give me an account of the events leading to his arrest. He said, 'Well, I've got two kids in the house and was taking one upstairs to her bed, and when I came down I saw the other baby near the gas fire, and when I picked her up she pulled my hair and then I went berserk.' It emerged on my second interview with him that he alleges that he is acutely sensitive to having his hair pulled, and that on one occasion he assaulted his sister for doing the same thing."

The psychiatrist reported that Mick had moved to London with his mother and sister when he was a child. Although he had "no knowledge of his natural father," he told the psychiatrist that "he gets on very well" with his mother and stepfather, with whom he lived till he moved in with Melanie Crotty. At school, he had been a "frequent truant and for a time hardly went to school at all," preferring to spend his time in cafés and amusement arcades.

Mick told the psychiatrist that he had not worked since leaving Borstal, and had been living on social security. There were peculiar psychosomatic complaints: "When he was about fifteen, he said, he had some illness in which he could not move his left side," although eventually the ability returned. "He also claims that during childhood he had fits but cannot remember ever being treated for these." The psychiatrist observed that Mick "became extremely weepy when discussing the crime"; but he did not consider Mick "clinically depressed," and he found no evidence of mental disorder. A week after his incarceration, Mick had attempted suicide and "inflicted multiple lacerations on his left forearm," but within weeks he

"had improved quite considerably and although still somewhat lugubri-
ous" could be "seen to raise a smile." The psychiatrist found him "fit to
plead, to stand his trial and to suffer any punishment the court may award."

Mick's First Confession

At first Mick had claimed he had "only dropped Ellen," but soon told the
detective, "I want to write down what happened. Ellen, how she died, it's all
my fault." When the detective cautioned him, Mick replied, "I know . . . I'm
just writing about Ellen," and began to cry. His initial written statement
admitted only partial responsibility:

> Ellen was playing near the fire when she nearly burnet her self. I rushed
> over and hit her in the stomach and put her on the sertee with her bottle,
> then I took Samantha up stair to her cot when I heard a bang. I went down
> and ellen was on the floor and near the Fire, I hit her in the stomach once
> again, and that when she stoped breathing. I slaped her on the face to see if
> she would start bereathing again but she never with shock I droped her,
> then I picked her up and went next door to see if next door could help, the
> reason I hit her was in rage that she kept going to the fire.

This statement provoked a second interview that day, in which Mick continued to maintain his innocence regarding the fatal blow. "I put her on the
settee and gave her her bottle. I took the other baby upstairs to her bed –
that's Samantha – and tucked her in. I heard a bang. I came downstairs and
saw Ellen near the fire. I picked her up the same way as before. I hit her in
the stomach. That's when she stopped breathing and I dropped her with
shock. I hit her twice altogether, that's with the other time." "How did you
hit her in the stomach?" "The same way as before. I can't clench my fist
because of my thumb, because I've got a scar and had an accident with a car.
That's why I can't write properly – but I can if I take my time.

"When I dropped her I picked her up and went next door and asked if
I should ring the doctor. There was no noise from her at all; and that's when
the lady over the road felt her pulse as well. I tried her pulse on the left of her
arm." "Why did you strike her in the stomach as you've said – it's not a

normal place to hit a child?" "I don't really know. It was just the first place that came to me. I've never hit children before." "Why did you hit her?" "'Cos of the rage I had because she kept going to the fire and I was worried that she might set herself on fire."

Each time Mick was asked to repeat the story, he edged closer to the truth. "I heard a sound, I don't know what it was. I came downstairs and saw Ellen by the fire and rushed over and picked her up and hit her in the stomach." "Why did you drop the baby?" "From the shock of her not breathing." "How did you put her down?" "By holding her under the arms and bringing her down hard on the floor." "What part of her body struck the floor first?" "Her backside. Then her head hit the arm of the settee. I can't remember after that." "What you've just described as a drop is a bit more than that, as you've deliberately put her on the floor?" "Yes." "How do you account for the mark on her face?" "It's been there for a few days. I don't know how it happened. I slapped her on the other side of the face. I wished I'd never hit her. I didn't mean it. It was in rage of her going near the fire and worrying that she would burn herself."

Now a second detective joined the interview, and asked for yet another repetition of Randell's story. "I was taking the other baby up to her cot and I thought I heard a bang, which made me come downstairs and see Ellen near the gas fire." "Was the fire on?" "Yes. I picked her up and then hit her in the stomach." "Why did you hit her?" "I never hit a child before," Randell lied, "that was my first reaction – I was worried in case she set herself on fire." "How hard did you hit her?" "I couldn't really say. I was in a temper because she kept going near the fire. She stopped breathing about five or six seconds afterwards." "This was in fact the second time that you had hit her that evening?" "Yes. About half an hour before, I was watching the television, she was crawling on the floor and worked her way over to the gas fire so I grabbed her and put her on the settee with a bottle. She didn't cry, just sucked her bottle."

"Going back to the second time when you hit her and she stopped breathing; what did you do with her?" "In the shock I dropped her." "Did you intend to do the child any harm?" "I loved that child as if she were my own," Randell claimed. However, when the detective told Mick that Ellen's mother had mentioned a bruised eye, and that Ellen's post-mortem examination revealed "over thirty bruises and a fractured skull besides her main bowel being ruptured," Mick retreated still further. "I poked her with my finger when I was telling her to behave. Just the first time I pulled her away from the fire: I shouted at her and poked her in the chest." "How do you account for the fractured skull?" "Maybe when I dropped her, I don't know."

When asked what he had done when Ellen first stopped breathing, Mick said, "I tidied these [toys] up before I went next door. I like a tidy house. I always clean up before anyone comes in." The detective was incredulous: "You mean to say you have a baby that's not breathing, and you were concerned about tidying up the room?" "There weren't many toys. I just picked them up and threw them in the box. I picked her up and ran next door and asked them if I should call a doctor." "When you arrived at the hospital last night, why did you tell lies about Ellen's injuries?" "I don't know. I was scared."

Exploring Mick's level of aggressive impulse control, the detective asked, "Do you normally lose your temper quickly?" "No. I lose it, but it takes a time." "I understand from Melanie that you lose your temper quickly with her?" "Yes, with *her*. Since we've been living together she's found all my weak spots." "Have you got a lot?" "Yes." "Have you hit her?" "Yes, I've slapped her but never done any damage." "I understand you lose your temper very quickly if somebody pulls your hair?" "Yes, just here [indicating left side], I've got some scars here from a car accident."

Capitulation

Having established what made Mick angry, the detective then returned the conversation to the killing. "Did the baby pull your hair last night and make you lose your temper?" Mick nodded yes, and burst into tears. "Yes." "Come on then, Michael, tell us what really happened?" Finally, Mick described the last minutes of Ellen's life. "She pulled my hair and I just kept on punching her with my left fist and my right hand, as she lay on the settee. I lost my temper. I'm not sure, I just kept hitting her. I don't remember anything after that. When I finally realized what I was doing she was just laying on the settee not breathing. I love kids. I didn't want that to happen."

The police report noted that Randell had punched baby Ellen "with such ferocity" that he had "severed the large intestine against the inside of the spinal column causing death." In court, Mick claimed diminished responsibility and a lack of intent to kill: he was convicted of manslaughter, and jailed for four years. Astonishingly, Melanie remained engaged to him after his imprisonment, and said she would marry him when he was released.

CHILDREN KILLING A PARENT

Three times as many parents kill children (often following a major life crisis such as marital separation, unemployment or psychological depression) as children kill parents. Of that 4 per cent of all homicides where a son or daughter kills his or her parent, the majority appears to be a response to abuse of some kind, physical or mental. When there is ambiguity, as there is in the case that follows, the courts typically, and quite rightly, tend to decide in favour of the weaker, more vulnerable actor.

"AN EVIL AND PATHETIC MAN": A YOUNG WOMAN STABS HER STEPFATHER

The police constable entered the semi-detached council house, and fastidiously noted that it was "poorly and sparsely furnished, in a general state of untidiness, and carried the smell that one associates with an unclean household." On the settee, she saw "a middle-aged man with dark hair, lying on his back, his eyes were closed, he was semi-conscious and moaning and I could see his mouth moving. He was fully dressed wearing trousers, a cardigan and a torn shirt underneath which something was protruding like a large lump on his left midriff near to the base of the ribs." She could not know that within hours he would be dead.

After confirming that an ambulance was on its way, she began questioning those in the house. Marie, the victim's nineteen-year-old stepdaughter, admitted that "we had an argument. We had an argument and he got stabbed." Having examined a knife that lay on Marie's bed, the constable arrested her on charges of "suspicion of wounding." Marie was placed in the Juvenile Detention Room in the town's decaying police station, where the interview continued.

"It's my Dad, well stepdad, Tony Maxwell," Marie told police. "Who lives in this house?" "My Mum, Joan Maxwell, Dad, Tony Maxwell, my sister, Carol, who is twenty-six years old and me. Me and Dad don't get on. When he's had a drink he always comes home and shouts horrible things at me, like 'I want you out of here,' or 'You're nowt but a slag.' He went out earlier in the evening, about eightish I think, leaving me and my sister in the house alone 'cos me Mum works in the evenings. We don't like to be around when he gets back, so me and my sister Carol went upstairs to bed. Then about elevenish we heard a loud banging on the door and Carol went down to see what it was. I then heard my Dad in the kitchen shouting and raving at me upstairs. I put my jeans on and came from my bedroom on to the top of the stairs. Me Dad was shouting upstairs to me calling me a slag and a slut. I don't know why, I have got a boyfriend, but he went home this after-noon, because Dad doesn't allow my boyfriend in the house. I went down-stairs and had a big argument with my Dad in the hallway, near to the kitchen. He always acts like that when he's had a drink.

"Anyway, I'd had enough and went back upstairs to my bedroom. I've got a box with things that me and my boyfriend have been saving for when we can get a flat, some pans and things for the kitchen. There was a box with some knives in, and I picked the largest one out of the box. I wanted to scare me Dad so that he would leave me alone, I'd had enough. When I'm in my bedroom I lock the door 'cos I don't want him coming in, he's already abused my sister, you know what I mean. I then went from my room to the top of the stairs, he was still ranting on at the bottom in the hall. I went downstairs, still carrying the knife from my bedroom and put the knife on the bottom step. I then went towards my Dad as we continued arguing. He called me a slag again, I don't think he knew that I'd had a knife. He came towards me and threatened to break a plate over my head and I went to the bottom of the stairs and picked the knife up.

"I just wanted to scare him, so that he would leave me alone. I had the knife in my hand, you know, pointing downwards and me Dad came and grabbed hold of my hand, the one holding the knife, so that I couldn't drop it, and tried to force my hand back so that I would be stabbing myself. I was saying 'Stop,' he said something like 'Trying that one, are you?' We struggled on the bottom of the stairs in the hall and I pushed my hand away so that I wouldn't stab myself and then somehow the knife turned and went into his belly.

"At first I didn't think the blade had gone into him, I thought it had just gone into his cardigan, but it went through his shirt. I pulled my hand back and he let go of my hand and held his side, he was pressing his side and said, 'That's it now, you've killed me now, go on, I'm done for.' I was crying and saying, 'Dad, let me help you.' I then dropped the knife, he went into the lounge and I shouted upstairs to Carol: I told her to run across the road to my brother's house and phone for an ambulance 'cos we aren't on the phone. She went across to David's and I went back to the bottom of the stairs and picked the knife up. There wasn't much blood, just a bit on the blade. I took the knife upstairs and threw it on to my bed. I went back downstairs and saw that my Dad had got on the settee and was lying down flat on his back holding his side. I ripped his shirt so I could see what his injury was and saw all that stuff, insides, coming out, then my sister and brother came back, then the police arrived. When he got stabbed I was sorry for what had happened, I wanted to help him. I didn't want to stab him, just scare him so he would stop shouting at me."

The Police Analysis

Both victim and killer were unemployed and in receipt of Income Support benefits, living in a council house. The victim was forty-five-year-old Anthony Maxwell, who worked as a window cleaner when casual employment was available. He had many previous criminal convictions, mainly for offences of dishonesty; but in 1978 he had been convicted of indecent assault on the eldest of his two stepdaughters, Carol. He was sentenced to 120 hours' community service for the sexual assault, but he did not comply with the terms of the order, and he was imprisoned for six months. After this conviction, his wife sought a divorce, but the proceedings were eventually dropped and Maxwell returned to the family home. Two years later, he was convicted of assault occasioning actual bodily harm against his wife, Joan: this was merely one of many acts of violence towards her, but she had not bothered reporting them to the police. Maxwell was a very heavy drinker who routinely became intoxicated twice each day, at noon and at night. When drunk, he became aggressive, even violent, and this caused "distress and friction within the family." Indeed, the police report summarized, "It is fair to say that few people have anything good to say of Maxwell."

In recent years the relationship between the killer and the victim had deteriorated dramatically. In particular, Maxwell objected to Marie's relationship with her boyfriend and refused to allow him into their home. Ultimately, Marie left home to live with her boyfriend's parents, but the cramped conditions there forced her to return to the family home: it was then that the frequent rows began between Marie and Maxwell, with Marie claiming that she was continually in fear of being either physically or sexually assaulted by her stepfather.

Marie had evidence. In the months before the killing, she had made audio tape recordings of their quarrels. On one of the tapes, which followed an intensifying three-minute argument, Marie could be heard to shout, "Tha' waint be here long enough!" "Why?" asked Maxwell. "Tha' fucking waint!" "Are you gonna fucking shift me?" "No, I'll fucking put thee in a coffin first." "Put me in a fucking coffin!" "Tha' fucking getting in one." In a second argument, Marie was heard shouting, "Do you think we're that fucking desperate? We'd let you fucking touch us?" Maxwell laughed, and Marie continued, "Try it, you'd get your fucking throat cut, you dense bastard." On yet another tape, Maxwell shouted, "Tha' can't get a fucking job!" Marie replied, "I can gerra job." "Tha' don't want a fucking job!" "I fucking do." This was followed by the noise of a physical struggle between them, after which Marie said, "Fucking bastard!" "Pack thee fucking clothes up." "Just fuck off." "Pack thee fucking . . ." "You're not gerrin me out of here." Later, an argument about Marie's boyfriend seemed to begin with an exclamation from Maxwell, "That hurt!" "Eh," Marie replied. Maxwell then claimed, "That *didn't* hurt," to which Marie replied, "It'll fucking hurt in a minute." "Has tha' gorra fucking knife in thee hand?" Maxwell asked. "I don't need a knife." "Tha' fucking does!" "I fucking don't." "Tha' fucking does." "Wanna bet?"

The police reconstructed the day of the killing: Maxwell had left home that morning to do some casual work in the city; at mid-afternoon, he visited his local and drank his customary eight pints of bitter. That evening he visited his wife at the Chinese takeaway where she worked and asked her for £20, which she gave him. He returned to the Pig and Whistle and continued drinking till 10:40 P.M. Not long after, a neighbour passing the family house saw Maxwell outside the front door, thumping on the door with his fist, while a "terrified-looking" Marie leaned out of her bedroom window. The neighbour heard Maxwell shout, "Open this door, you bastard. You know what you're going to get." Marie let Maxwell into the house, and the neighbour heard Marie shout, "I've had enough you picking on me. Get off, leave me alone." The argument continued for five or ten minutes before she heard Maxwell shout, "I think you've really done it this time, Marie."

Family

Mrs. Maxwell told police that her husband had "never really accepted his stepdaughters. I remember Tony made a remark about indecently assaulting my daughter, Carol, whilst he was drunk. I asked Carol about this and she told me he had been making her touch him on the penis. I asked her if he had done anything else and she told me she wouldn't let him. The main feature in my marriage to Tony was that he persistently got drunk both dinner-time and night. He always came home shouting and causing trouble. All the money he had was spent on his drinking habits. On several occasions he came home and threatened me and the children by holding his fists up and shouting. On one occasion about seventeen years ago, he came in and had me by the throat but I did not complain to the police. In 1980, he punched me in the face and I reported this to the police. My daughter Marie began courting a lad called Jason and Tony took an instant dislike to him for some unknown reason. He has been particularly nasty to Marie since this time.

"About two or three weeks ago Marie told me that Tony had been drunk and had asked Marie to get into the bed and take her knickers off and show him how good she was. I do not believe that anything actually happened on this occasion, but Tony could well have said this to Marie as he had a fixation about her. Marie has argued a lot with Tony and has stood up against him when he has been in a drunken stupor abusing her. Tony told

Marie never to bring her boyfriend into the house, and to appease him she agreed. Tony has on occasions had a knife in his hand, mainly a carving knife, and during his drunken state he has offered it to me and told me to stab him, as he knew we all wanted him out of the house. He regularly slept in the chair downstairs and I have found the knife under him in the chair."

Marie's sister, Carol, a shop assistant, told police, "My stepfather Tony Maxwell used to sexually abuse me. His abuse started just after my mother had married him. He would only abuse me when we were alone in the house. I was ten years old when he started to assault me, he would always wait until we were on our own. He would take my clothes off and push his fingers inside my vagina. I was very young and I can remember being frightened of him. He used to call me names like 'dirty whore' and 'prick teaser.' He used to tell me to masturbate him. I would do as he said so that my mother would never find out. I only used my hand to rub his penis until he came, he never asked me to suck him. I can remember having a biology lesson at school and finding out about some of the things that Tony had made me do. This abuse went on right up until Tony died: each time we were alone in the house, he used to come upstairs to my room, and close the door. I knew what he wanted and I let him do it because I didn't want my mother to find out. Tony only used his fingers to put inside my vagina, he never forced me to have sexual intercourse with him.

"This abuse was the cause of me having two nervous breakdowns and it carried on right from me being ten years old until he died. I remember on several occasions over the last four or five years Tony had asked me to have sex with him. He said, 'You can't get pregnant the first time.' I told him that was stupid and I never let him, he never forced me to have sex. Every time anything happened Tony would blame everyone but himself. Tony abused me because I think he was a pervert, I was not old enough, not like his other girlfriends, he only abused me in our family as far as I'm aware. Our family would never talk to each other about it. I didn't want to do what Tony wanted me to, I had to, I was scared of what he would do. I didn't tell anyone because my mother has suffered enough and I didn't want to upset her further. Tony made my life hell, as he did for Marie. He would always shout and insult us. It didn't matter whether he was drunk or sober, he was always the same. Tony was an evil, pathetic person, he used to use me and I hated him."

As Carol remembered the killing: "He kept shouting and swearing, accusing me and Marie of locking him out. I didn't say anything to him, I just went back upstairs to keep out of his way. I think this argument went on for about five or ten minutes. Suddenly I heard Tony's voice shout, 'I think you've really done it this time, Marie.' Marie said, 'I've hurt him, I've stabbed him, something's hanging out. Go and phone for the ambulance quick.' She was hysterical. Tony had threatened for a long time he was going to stab Marie. He used to call her a blonde bastard. He had said to me, 'I'm going to get the blonde bastard one day on her own and stab her.'"

Marie's unemployed boyfriend, eighteen-year-old Jason, testified: "On several occasions Marie has told me that Tony has been in her bedroom when she has been alone and has come out with things like, 'Why not get in bed with a man (meaning himself) instead of a boy (meaning me).' Also he has told her to get her knickers off and get in bed with him. About October, Marie rang me upset and told me she'd left the house in tears as Tony'd made suggestions to her and asked her to go to bed with him. She was very upset: she came to stay at my Mum's house [but] returned home due to overcrowding. Marie has always insisted Tony has never been sexually intimate with her, but I don't believe it due to her nervous reactions around me. She is openly frightened of Tony and she has told me he has threatened her life. She tells me everything and I believe her as she is very frightened. She was very upset about it."

Marie

"He usually comes in from work drunk. About five past eleven he came banging on't door and, well, I asked me sister Carol to go and open the door for him and I shut my bedroom door and put me jeans on 'cos he's sexually assaulted me sister before and I were scared he might try summat because I'm afraid he might try and assault me. So I shut bedroom door, sat on edge of bed, watching telly wi' dog, then as soon as he come through door he started to call me all names under sun like slags and whores and sluts and that. Me sister I think went back to bed and I opened door to listen to what he were saying and I went onto landing and he were saying some right nasty things and so I started arguing wi' him back, and I just stood there in doorway and he started, so I went walking downstairs, arguing.

"I asked him to be quiet 'cos me mother was coming in from work and she'd had it all w' all drunkards and that at shop, there's a baby next door and I asked him to keep his voice down and he wouldn't. He kept on and on, calling me names and he says why don't I start when he's not drunk – I daren't start when he's not drunk because I knows I'd gid a hammering, beat crap out of me. I went back upstairs and sat on bed a bit, took it for a bit longer, and he ended up carrying on, so I got a set of six kitchen knives and I picked the biggest one out then went downstairs. I put it on the bottom stairs and then confronted him again. Then he threatened to smash a plate over me head if I caused trouble when me mum come in. I told him it's not me who causes trouble, it's him, every time he comes in after a drink. He just started and he says he were gonna kill me and stuff like that so I just went and got knife to threaten him 'cos he got me that scared. I din't mean to hurt him and he come for it and grabbed hold of me hand, he tried to push it into my side first and I just went like, pushing me hand away, and I just put it into his right-hand side, I just caught it 'cos it came out with a bit of blood on and I saw his jumper were ripped. I just thought I'd cut side and he grabbed, he pushed knife away and he'd still got hold of me hand and I were like trying to get upstairs, 'cos he were trying to put it into me and he says, 'You've done it now, haven't you, you've killed me.' He says, 'I'm gonna do same to you now. Then that'll be both bastards out of way,' and I begged him to stop, I just said, 'stop, please,' and he were holding his side and he went into other room, he didn't fall or owt 'cos I think wi' all booze it din't hurt him. I tried to help him but he kept swearing at me telling me to get off and called me all names and stuff. I shouted and I told me sister to go and phone ambulance. It was an accident. I din't attack him, he came for me. Let's put it this way, I'd rather kill myself than kill him."

Marie was found guilty of manslaughter and placed on probation for two years.

---

1   See Appendix for statistics; Morris and Blom-Cooper, 1979, p. 12.
2   "Patricide," in *Granta* 1994: no. 47, pp. 177–191.

THEFT OR GAIN

[Murder] is not generally the crime of the so-called criminal classes. . . .
There is, however, a clearly marked class of murders, of rare occurrence,
the motive of which is robbery, committed by habitual criminals and
forming the climax, and usually the termination, of a career of crime. (Sir
John Macdonnell, 1905[1])

MACDONNELL WAS RIGHT AS USUAL; and his insights still apply. Murders
for financial gain are among those most feared by the public; but only 208
of our 2,680 representative homicides were motivated by what police call
"theft or gain." Such mercenary homicides thus continue to constitute less
than 8 per cent of the total, an *unchanging* proportion over the decades. In
the cases that follow, one was a simple robbery, the second a contract killing
and the third the murder of elderly relatives in order to conceal thefts from
their accounts.

"A LOT OF MONEY": A GANG ROBS A SUPERMARKET

Two singularly ungifted young men, with long prison records, blindly followed their leader, a vicious pimp: they called their gang of robbers "the
firm," after the language of the London underworld of the 1960s. The "vice-
president" of the firm, Anthony Bartlett, was resolutely courageous with
anyone clearly weaker than himself. To him, people seemed to be only
things, toys to use and manipulate, as when he savagely beat and threatened
his girlfriend till she agreed to prostitute for him; and as when the unarmed
man at his feet was shot. After an anonymous informant had identified the

pimp, his thirty-year-old Scottish girlfriend (whose Greek husband was himself in prison on drug charges) was interviewed by police.

Sitting in her council flat, she recalled her short-lived romance with Bartlett: "I worked in three hotels, part-time, as a receptionist; but due to my bad health I had to give up working. I receive £52 from the DHSS, and they pay all my bills. In December, I met Anthony Bartlett in a wine bar. We stayed there till the early hours of the morning, and the next thing I remember I was in Stoke Newington with him. It was a council ground-floor flat. When I woke up, I was feeling terrible with a hangover. I then asked him to take me back [home]. He asked if he could take me out that night. I agreed. We went to the pictures. We started to go out on a regular basis and one day he requested for my help. I agreed that he could use my flat for a few days. A few days later he was at my door with his baggage ready to move in."

Bartlett wasted no time in converting his romantic conquest into a commercial commodity. "In bed he said, 'There are lots of guys whose women give them money to help them out because times are bad.' I said, 'What did you mean?' He said, 'As I am in the music business I need a lot of money to arrange studios and all that.' I said, 'I am not doing anything like that' – meaning prostitution. He said, 'Well, I could find another woman to do it for me.' I said, 'You can do that if you like.' He said, 'I wouldn't ask much money from you, about £40, would be enough to help me.' I said, 'No.' He said, 'It's all right, we love each other, I'll help you too.' I said, 'No, I don't need your help.' [The following day] we were walking and Tony said, 'Look at all those men looking at you.' I said, 'What do you mean?' He said, 'You could make a lot of money.' I said, 'You're kidding,' or words to that effect. At this time he kept saying, 'I need money, I need money, I need money.' A couple of evenings later whilst having a meal he threw the dinner plate in the air and said to me, 'Get out there and get me some money, you are a lazy bitch.' I said, 'Do you really mean that?' He said, 'Yeah, I really mean it: you better believe it.' He then took off his belt and hit me with it on my right arm and right leg, twice or three times. I ran out of the flat and went downstairs. He followed me. I was outside near the side entrance. He said, 'What are you standing there for?' After he had hit me and [we had had] an argument, I said that I would do it.

"A car stopped: he was a white man, smiled at me, I smiled back, he said, 'Do you have a place?' I said, 'Yeah. Do you want to come back to my place? You'll have to give me £20.' He said, 'That's all right,' so he parked the car and we walked back to my flat. Tony was in the flat, in the toilets. I took the white man to the living room and I said, 'Can you wait a minute? I've got to go to the toilet.' In the toilet, Tony gave me a Durex and I went back to the living room. The man gave me £20 and we had sex. When we finished he got dressed and left. Tony came into the room and said, 'I told you it was easy, it didn't even take two minutes.' I felt angry and dirty, and wished to hit him. He then buttered me up and picked up the money from the table. He was in the kitchen making tea and said, 'If you do it again and ask for £30 and that will be £50.' He mentioned about the time being early to pick up customers. About two hours later I got another white man and £30 from him. That was it for the evening. After that I was forced to go on the streets for another four nights picking up men and having sex for money.

"After the fourth night, I said to Tony, 'I've had enough, I'm not doing it any more, I don't care even if you kill me.' He said, 'Oh, is that right? Don't you talk to me like that, just go out there and get the money.' I refused, and he dragged me into the kitchen, pushed me against the sink [and] punched me in the eye, causing bruising and a cut. I went down on the floor and he said, 'I'm not kidding, I'll put you in a hospital.' I was screaming and crying, my wrist was broken. Things got worse and I was still being beaten up, my health was going bad: I had a urinary infection and he would still force me out, even at times of my periods. He would say, 'I don't care: just get me the money. Just get in there and get the money.' During this period of two or three weeks one of the punters was robbed of a watch and on another occasion I remember bringing back an Egyptian, we had sex, he left paying £25. Tony followed and mugged him in the hallway: the guy was screaming."

Without letting Tony know where she had gone, she went to the hospital to have her injuries treated: when she returned a few days later, having only partially recovered from his most recent beating, she found another woman in their flat. "He said, 'Now don't get upset, Margaret, I thought you left me for good, and you know that I've been looking this week for a working girl – you need a break.' I said, 'You have a woman in here?' He said,

'Yes, she's going to work for me, don't spoil it for me.' I said, 'Are you going to stay here?' He said, 'Shut your fucking mouth.' He took his belt off and hit me across my chest. He said, 'Where were you?' I said, 'I was in the hospital, they kept me there and I signed myself out.' He said, 'You'll be going back.' He took his belt off and started to hit me with it. I was screaming: he stopped, put the belt down, I was on the bed facing the ceiling. He then jumped on me and put his knees on my shoulders and then punched me with his right hand on my nose. I felt faint. He stopped and stood up. I said, 'Please help me, I feel dizzy.' He said, 'I warned you to be here when I tell you, if you are not here I'll find you and put you in hospital.' I said nothing. He said, 'I'm going to the club and when I come back I want you here and don't move.' I crawled into the living room. He said, 'Don't move, I'm sorry for hitting you' and left." She knew nothing of his robberies, or the murder he would commit seventeen months later.

The Killing

Early on a February evening, supermarket manager Steven Aston, and his fiancée, Wendy Hughes, were alone in the rear of the supermarket. They were closing the store and preparing to leave through the rear exit when three masked men rushed into the store. Steven was shoved to the floor, and his spectacles spun from his face. One of the three masked men was unarmed, but a second, Baker, had a sawn-off shotgun, and Anstey brandished a handgun. Bartlett grabbed Miss Hughes and tried to take her jewellery. While Baker was struggling with Aston on the floor, the shotgun discharged, killing Aston almost immediately. Miss Hughes was then forced to go through her fiancée's pockets to find the keys to the safe, but the safe had a time-lock and could not be opened.

The "firm" then left, taking with them Aston's ring and credit cards. The three drove across the city in Bartlett's car, and forty minutes later, they entered a carpet shop. Threatening the shop staff with their guns – "the handgun was placed against the neck of one of the employees and the shotgun was used to smash the window of the cashier's office" – the trio made off with £800 in cash. An artist's impression of one of the men whose mask had slipped, combined with an anonymous tip to police, led the police to Bartlett. Intensive surveillance established that Bartlett was head of a robbery "firm," and that members of the firm "were concerned about a 'big job' they had been on with Nigel Anstey." Bartlett was arrested towards the end of March, and after much manoeuvring, he confessed and implicated the other two. Anstey was arrested one week later; after many denials, he eventually admitted his role in a further twenty armed robberies, many of them committed with Baker. Both Bartlett and Baker confessed to the series of robberies.

The Interviews

He described himself as a "singer": hoping to receive immunity from prosecution in return for his testimony, he maintained his innocence at first and insisted, "I'm not saying nothing. That's false what you are saying. I'm hungry. Can I have a cheese sandwich, please, and a cup of tea with four sugars because I've not eaten since two days? I've got nish to say: in other words, nothing. Anything you put to me, I'm not saying nothing, that's the last word." "You indicated to me last night that the other two men were Stanley Baker and Nigel Anstey," the detective commented. "Do you deny saying that?" "Yes, I deny it, that's bullshit! I've got nothing more to say. How can I help you when I know nish? Would you like me to lead you up the garden path?" "No, I would like you to tell me the truth and I would like you to assist me in apprehending the people concerned in this murder. I know that you want total immunity but that is something that is not within my power." "I want nothing more than my bed because I got no sleep last night," Bartlett claimed.

"Am I right in saying that Stanley Baker was the man who had the shotgun and Nigel had the handgun?" "How am I supposed to know that when I wasn't there?" "Because you *were* there, as you told me last night." "Do you want an answer for that? Bullshit!" "What I would like to know is why Steven Aston was killed as he lay helpless on the floor." "Ask the people who done it." "That is exactly what I am doing." "Bullshit!" "I am only saying that I know that you were the one unarmed person amongst the three, and it may be that you had no idea that the gun was loaded. It certainly seems to me that even the killing could have been an accident, because from what I know the gun was fired before the robbers had an opportunity to achieve their aims." "I'm saying nish: it's the third time I've said that I'm not saying nothing. I don't know nothing."

In a second and capitulating interview seven hours later, following consultations with his solicitor, Bartlett was again asked, "Were you involved in the murder of Steven Aston?" "Yes," he admitted. "As I told you earlier it is still my belief that you were the man who did not have a gun. Is that correct?" "That's right." "There were two guns there that night. Were they both real?" "Yes." "Are you prepared at this stage to tell me who the other two men were?"

At this, Bartlett was overcome with self-pity and began to sob. "Take your time," the detective soothed. "Yes." "Who had the shotgun?" "Baker." "Who had the handgun?" "Nigel, I don't know if his second name is Anstey." "How much planning went into the robbery?" "I don't know how much planning was done for it, but I was just told there was one in the supermarket." "Who asked you to go on it?" "Baker. He just said there was a lot of money there and we should go and take it. He said supermarkets usually carry a lot. We'd wait out the back till they come out and take them back in. I never see the shop until that day."

"What happened when you went in?" "We started asking for the money, 'Where's the money?' I went and held the lady. [Mr. Aston] was shot when he was standing up. There was a struggle between him. Can I rephrase that? There was a struggle first as he was going down. I turned to the woman to stop her from getting anywhere near the gun. [Then] I heard a bang and turned round again and the man was lying on the floor." The detective sifted through the details, and asked, "My witness also tells me that one of the gunmen told her to go through the pockets." "I can't remember that." "Did you take anything from the premises at all?" "No. I did. I think it was a purse or wallet. Some money and some papers and some cards I think. All I can remember of that time is of the man laying on the floor with blood pumping from his side, and steam coming up from the blood from where he was shot and the noises he was making." "Why did Stanley shoot him?" "I have no idea. He said it was an accident. I have no other idea, because he's never loaded a gun before."

A third interview was conducted the following afternoon. The detective asked, "Have you at any time had a discussion with the other two about this incident and been told anything specific by the other two about what to do?" "Burn my gear and don't tell no one." "If I called you a gang, is there a definite leader?" "Yes." "Who?" "Stanley." "As far as you're concerned, Stanley did all the organizing for this robbery?" "He said when to go out. He already had the guns. I still think he borrowed the shotgun, but the handgun is his. He called the shotgun the elephant gun."

Bartlett burst into tears again when he was asked for the details of the robberies. "We [just] went driving around looking for some money and ended up where the murder took place." The robbery of the rug shop was also spur-of-the-moment: "We went into the shop, can't remember if I had a gun, but if I had a gun I would naturally pull it out at that point. I had a few people up in the corner and said, 'Don't move!' Stanley then went to the back, looked for a room to lock them up in. We found the money. I took one double speaker cassette and one video, Stanley done the same – one video and cassette – then we walked out the shop, went around the corner and into the car, that was it. No planning. Ran back to the car. We got rid of clothes, cards, cheques and papers, took it in turn to count out the cash, and after that I went home."

The police interview with Nigel Anstey confirmed Bartlett's story. "There was nothing planned," said Anstey, "we just passed and saw the manager in there and the lights on and decided to do it and thought it would be easy. Waited till the shop had shut and the staff had left. Just waited for the manager to come out. As they opened the shutters they were confronted with the shotgun. That man just tried to rush me, we struggled for a bit, both of us fell on the floor. He started to say we could have the money. He was still lying down and I was getting up. I don't really know what happened after that. I saw the blood on the floor. I didn't even hear the gun go off. My mind was blank. I was looking at him, just looking at him. I wanted to help him, but I didn't know what to do. I never heard the gun go off. I didn't know it was even loaded. Stanley said in the car that it was not loaded, because he was messing about with it with Tony. He said don't worry about it, it's not loaded anyway. From what Stanley said to me he pressed it into his stomach to stop him struggling with me. Like his finger must have pushed the safety off, it must have gone off."

Stanley Baker had fled to the Continent, but was captured by police in Amsterdam. He dismissed all police questioning with a shrug and a "no comment" until he was told that Bartlett and Anstey had implicated him in the robbery and murder: "It happened, but it was an accident," he admitted. "What actually happened?" "Quite frankly I can't remember. Serious, I can't remember." "Were you holding the gun in one hand or both hands?" "Both." "Did you prod him with the gun?" "I think so." "What kind of gun did Nigel have?" "A small one." "Was it real?" "Yes." "Was it loaded?" "I'm not sure." "Where did he get the gun?" "I don't know. He wanted to use my rep[lica] but I didn't have it so I don't know where he got that one from. My one was borrowed, right, but for reasons I can't give a name who, because that will endanger my family."

We know nothing about their adaptation in prison, but from jailers' reports, they seem well suited to the environment. At their trial in the Central Criminal Court, the trio pleaded not guilty. Bartlett was found guilty of manslaughter, and sentenced to twelve years' imprisonment; Nigel Anstey was convicted of manslaughter and robbery, and sentenced to twelve years (concurrent) for each offence; Stanley Baker was convicted of murder and robbery, and sentenced to life imprisonment.

"A WHACK FOR ROY": THE CONTRACT KILLING OF A WIFE'S LOVER

The contractor, thirty-eight-year-old Roy Best, had once been a policeman, but he had been convicted of armed robbery and dismissed from the force. He spent three years in Borstal, but made good use of his detention time by training to be an electrician. When he was released, he established a successful electrical shop that supplied and repaired household electrical equipment. His comfortable income allowed him to drink as much as he wanted at The Hanover public house, an infamous underworld hangout.

Not long after his release from prison, Best met Christine Pentecost: their marriage endured for some ten years, but it was rarely tranquil. Christine eventually tired of her frequent beatings, and she began having an affair with Norman Carson. Soon after, she left her husband and moved in with Carson. Best's first idea for manly vengeance was to murder his wife and then commit suicide; and in fact when he realized the marriage was completely over, he purchased liquid Valium, handcuffs, chloroform and ankle straps. His intention was to kidnap her, take her to his house, make her confess to her unfaithfulness and give "good reason" for leaving him – since he could never understand why she had done so – and then kill her and commit suicide.

But after their separation and ultimate divorce, he made another decision: his obsessive "love" demanded revenge. In The Hanover he met Canadian-born Larry Simmons, fifty-four. Simmons had previously served a twenty-year sentence for armed robbery and shooting at the police. Even after Carson's murder, Best hounded Christine as she moved from council flat to council flat in a desperate attempt to avoid him. Eventually he hired others to assist him in this terrorist campaign: they broke into her home, stole her clothing and jewellery and smashed her washing machine, cooker and television.

The Killing

Larry Simmons was hired first to find, and then attack, Carson. Finally, Best found out that Christine would be visiting her brother in Colchester with Carson. Best passed this information to Simmons who drove to Colchester, lay in wait for Carson and beat him unconscious with an iron bar. Carson did not regain consciousness and he died in hospital nineteen days later. The police report noted that the attack on Carson had been particularly "vicious": so much so that the medical staff and police both assumed the assault had been a "gangland" attack, "because of the multiple head injuries due to sixteen blows to the head."

Recollections of the Estranged Wife

As Christine recalled the end of their stormy marriage: "Norman and I started to have an affair. We went to his house a couple of times and mine a couple of times. Roy used to stay in the flat above the shop on Thursdays, Fridays and sometimes Monday night: on Tuesday I had a row with Roy over a financial matter and he hit me several times, giving me a black eye.

All during my married life Roy has hit me. On Wednesday Roy left home, stating he wouldn't be home that weekend. I told Norman what had happened and on Saturday I left my home taking my clothes and two children to Norman's house. I should add that I had decided to leave home even before I had started the affair with Norman. After I'd been gone about a week I got a friend of Norman's to post a letter from London to Roy saying that the children were all right. He never knew where we were staying.

"I had meetings with Roy on a few occasions so that he could see the children – only once was there no one else present. Nothing untoward happened [for six weeks]. I can't remember exactly what was said or what started an argument but Roy said words to the effect that he was going to kill Norman or ruin him for the rest of his life, and that I'd ruined his life and that he was going to ruin mine. He said that he was going to do it tomorrow because it was my birthday. I said who was going to help him and he said no one. 'I don't need anyone, I'll do it myself,' and that he didn't care about the consequences, he said the only person he'd feel sorry for was his mother."

During this stormy period, what Christine called "a bizarre incident" occurred. "Roy had told me that he wanted to give me something. I wanted to talk to him about maintenance money and so I went to the shop to see him. As soon as I was in the shop, Roy locked the door behind me. He said he had some money for me. We went to the flat above the shop and he again tried to persuade me to go back and live with him. I refused. He then went to a wall unit and pulled out a short shotgun and pointed it at me. He said, 'Either you come back to me, or I blow you all over the room.' I didn't know what to do. I then stood up and threw a glass of vodka, which Roy had poured for me, in his face and tried to wrestle the gun from him. As we were struggling he said, 'Don't struggle because it's loaded.' I said, 'What do you want from me? You want me to make love to you, don't you?' He said, 'Yes.' So I said, 'Put the gun down then.' He opened the gun saying, 'I don't want to hurt you,' and placed it on a chair – which I was now bending over with my trousers down. Roy dropped his trousers and started to put his penis into my vagina. His penis felt hard but before he pushed it in he said, 'I can't do it this way. It seems more like rape to me and I've never raped anybody in my life. I can't do it.' Whilst we were talking I picked up the cartridge and put it in my handbag. Roy couldn't see me doing this because he had his head buried in my back, behind me. Roy then said, 'I love you and the kids so much.' I said, 'Can we go for a drink at the pub?' He said, 'You'll go for a drink at the pub with me?' I said. 'Yes.'"

When she returned to her flat that night, "I discovered that my bedroom window had been smashed. I saw a liquid all over the bed quilt. I left the bedroom and in the passageway I kicked something which was a bottle. I looked and saw it was smoking. I went into my front room and saw my television smashed on the floor, and a house plant knocked over. From there I went to the kitchen and saw the washing machine and fridge freezer had been tipped over."

Surveillance

Best and Simmons were only charged after a police operation of the very highest quality, which included extensive surveillance and the use of eavesdropping equipment – all aimed not only at solving the murder of Norman Carson, but also at averting the murder of Christine Best. The Hanover public house was known to be a watering hole for many who attracted the interest of the police. It was here that Best drank, made many friends, orchestrated his increasingly bizarre activities and regaled his comrades with tales of his connections. When Carson was assaulted, Best was immediately suspected. He was kept in custody for two days and questioned at great length. But Best had a strong alibi, that he was drinking in The Hanover at the time Carson was attacked; and there were some twenty witnesses to vouch for his presence there that day (although intensive interrogation eventually revealed that Simmons had attacked Carson and, on passing the pub, sounded the horn of his car as a signal to Best that the work was done).

Flushed with the apparent success of his contracted attack on Carson, and to demonstrate his power to an admiring audience, Best offered to help another of his drinking companions, Unsworth, whose wife was having an affair with a man called Colin. Unsworth offered £400 and shortly afterwards, Colin was hit over the head while walking home from work one night across Clapham Common, his skull so badly lacerated it required twenty-three stitches. With this exploit, Best's prestige grew even more

among the regulars at The Hanover, intensified by the common understanding that he had been responsible for Norman Carson's death.

Confessions of the Killer

It was the actual killer who first confessed. Police had extended their
inquiries till two of Best's friends were brought in and interrogated. Having
discovered the name of Lawrence Simmons, they interrogated him for two
days until Simmons capitulated after being confronted with the mounting
evidence against him. "I found out where he was at, and I beat him up and
he died. What else can I say? I was supposed to beat him up and he paid me
money to do this but that wasn't intended at all." He dictated his formal
statement.

> I want someone to write down what I say. I have lived in the Clapham area
> for some years and have got to know people including Roy Best from
> drinking in the local pubs in particular The Hanover which is his local.
> When we have been drinking together he had been moaning [about] his
> wife leaving him. I wasn't working at the time, I wasn't even claiming
> welfare or the dole as you call it, and I was living apart from my wife. He
> asked me if I would mind helping him out. He took me to the Colchester
> area and showed me where the man was staying with his wife and he
> pointed out the car the guy was using. It started out he was going to pay me
> £3,500 but it wasn't in a lump sum. Roy had phoned me and told me that
> the man was supposed to be there between 8:30 and 9. It was evening, it was
> dark, I went in and went up to the top, stood up there and waited and I met
> him as he turned to go through the door. I had [an iron] bar with me, and
> I was going to give him a couple of belts with that which is what I actually
> did in the end. I never said a word, I just give him a couple of real good
> clouts and he fell and I pulled him over and just left him then and took off
> along the landing. I don't think I hit him any more than three times at the
> most. The man was still alive, I know that I could hear him breathing. If I
> wanted to kill him I wouldn't have left him breathing.
>   [Best] paid me some afterwards, I think about five thousand includ-
> ing the money I got in Colchester. I was drinking like a mad fool. I went to

The Hanover and hooted twice, this was a pre-arranged signal, and he came out of the pub and waved to me and went back in. He had his alibi, didn't he? If he was in the pub surrounded by everybody then he couldn't have done it.

"Are you sure that the money wasn't to kill the man?" "No, just to beat him up, that's all. For £3,000 can you get a man killed or not, I don't know." "Is it right that Roy wanted you [also] to beat up his mother-in-law?" "Yes. That was at the time we were looking for his wife in King's Cross. We couldn't find her so he said I should beat up on his mother-in-law, her mother, because his wife would come to the hospital to see her and he would be able to follow her from there. This is only what I heard, that Roy intended to kill his wife and children. As soon as he asked me to beat up on his mother-in-law, I said that's it. I don't beat up on women and I've had nothing more to do with him. But he rang me up and threatened me over the phone, calling me every name in the book. My wife was there and I told her what he had said. We both thought he was completely crazy.

"When that thing happened up in the flat, I did not mean that man to die, and he wasn't dead when I left. I can't remember his name – it was the name you mentioned the other day. I would only like to say that I am very sorry that I was inveigled into doing this crime by being drunk and drinking with Mr. Roy Best and listening to his story."

Reluctant Confessions of the Contractor

After Best was shown Simmons' confession, he began to crack. Still, it took detectives fourteen interviews, spread over eighteen hours and twenty-nine minutes (entailing 256 pages of contemporaneous notes), to nudge Best to confess. At first, the interviews seemed merely astute conversations. "I'll tell you," said one detective, "the only thing that has ever puzzled me, Roy, really; did you want Norman dead, or did you just want him whacked?" "I never wanted Norman dead. I had a few words with him on the telephone once and he was all big and brave." "That is the only thing I've ever wanted to get straight between you and I – because you don't come over to me, and you never have done, like a killer."

"I've never been a killer in my life, sir, and you know what I'm like when something's bloody dead anyway. It's just a right fucking mess. I must admit, I don't understand some of it, don't for the life of me understand. It's just, I'm not being funny in any way, but she'd been back to me three times, so where am I so bloody bad? You know, let's be honest. All that you've got down there, with a good barrister that's going to be torn to pieces in court. I'm not even worried on that score at all. Um, but at the outcome, obviously, it's down to you. Domestic dispute and . . . even like on the break-ins, they're not. . . . If they are put down to me, they're not break-ins." "That's right. That's why it's strange that you prevaricate so much about them?" "What would you do in my place, sir?"

"Well, I know you've got to look after yourself, haven't you? That is the only thing I've ever had my doubts with you. Because the way he was done [was] to make a mess of him." "There was no way in this world I'd kill anybody like that," Best insisted. "Well, that's what I'm saying. What did you expect to happen, Roy? You just wanted him away from Chris?" "Well, let's put it this way, Inspector. If I'd paid for something to be done like that, I would not expect it done where it was done, because it's too obviously coming back to me." "If you're going to pay for it to be done, you ain't going to have the say-so where, when and how. The less you know the better isn't it, surely?" "But I could never, never agree to that. Obviously Chris and I talked a fair bit about him and I turned round to Chris and I said, 'If I was responsible for that, I couldn't live with it,' which I couldn't."

Demonstrating his inability to understand human relationships, Best confided: "The marriage is finished, Inspector. Can you just explain to me *why*, have you any idea why, Chris is treating me like this? Between you and me? You must have some . . . I'll tell you right here and now, Chris cannot deny that I bloody worked. I worked and I can assure you I can earn money. But I also had a good backer in Chris. Even after what's [happened], I won't fault her on [that]. She had to go through the hard times and she worked, believe you me. What savings I got, to my mind she's entitled to half of that, because if it hadn't have been for her I'd have been bust anyway. And I didn't go out robbing Tescos and nick the money. I've worked and I've provided for her." "It don't come down to anything else from your point of view at the end of the day, does it?" Not even comprehending the Inspector's remark,

Best continued: "Chris and I are finished. I've no doubt about that, Inspector. I'll always have feelings towards her, don't get me wrong and after all this is blown over – Chris knew [that] even when we was apart. She only had to pick the phone up to me if she needed money for something and it'd be there."

It was not till he was shown Simmons' written statement that he formally confessed. "I spent most of my time either working at the house or at my work in London. There was not much home life because of the work I was doing, but I made a point of seeing the children before they went to bed when I was in the area. The last weekend in July I'd had a row with Christine and I didn't go home. I returned on 2 August to find most of Christine's and the children's things had been removed. I believe it was on the third week that I saw Chris at her Mum's. She had written to me telling me she was well and the children were well. At the same time she had written to my mother, and in that letter she told my mother she was with somebody else. My mother had the unpleasant job of telling me.

"I asked her to come back, without success. I was very distressed, not sleeping or eating, and it felt as if my whole world had collapsed and whilst all this was going on I was still trying to sell our old house which I eventually did for a lot less than it was worth. I started to do a lot of drinking and things just piled on top of me. I saw my children I think every second week. On picking my son up on a Sunday at the tail end of October, he was very quiet which is very unusual for him. After a while he told me that Norman had belted him around the head. I managed to speak to Norman at his place of work where he was very cocky. I was paying Simmons varying amounts of money with the intent of giving Norman Carson a damn good hiding and to frighten him off. At one time he suggested using a gun but I wouldn't have this.

"In November I knew that Chris and Norman were visiting her mother. Although I was not there, Larry I gather waited at the top of the building and attacked Norman. I did not know with what until I was told by police officers, but I knew Larry had beaten up Norman because as I was in the pub he tooted so many times as he drove by. I was told by police officers how bad he was injured and was quite amazed. I paid Larry a considerable amount of money: the exact figure I do not know, but with cars, hotel fees it came to probably near £10,000. Norman Carson died in December. I am sorry that the man's dead. In a lot of ways he was no good but nobody deserves to die like that, and through me paying I caused that man's death. That is all I've got to say, sir."

At the Central Criminal Court, both Best and Simmons were found guilty of murder, and sentenced to life imprisonment, with a recommendation that they should serve a minimum of fifteen years. A detective warned the prison that Best would be "quite capable" of attempting either escape or suicide.

"I DIDN'T KNOW WHERE TO TURN": IAN KAPEL MURDERS HIS GRANDMOTHER AND GREAT-AUNT

At the age of twenty-four, Ian Kapel set fire to his grandmother's home, to burn alive his ninety-two-year-old grandmother, Mary George, and his infirm eighty-eight-year-old great-aunt, Jessie Thyme. To support his many business failures, and to maintain his cocaine and LSD habits, he had been stealing thousands of pounds from their building society accounts. When alert building society employees discovered the anomalies and tried to report them to Mrs. George, Kapel intercepted her mail and confiscated the damning letters. Eventually, however, his grandmother was apprised of what had happened. To avoid exposure and repayment, he killed them both.

Kapel lived with his sixteen-year-old girlfriend in a two-room flat above his recently purchased video rental shop. He had already been imprisoned twice – for unlawful sexual intercourse, and for inciting a child under twelve to gross indecency – and he had been fined for obstructing the police, and for driving without insurance. His family covered up his many dishonesties. His thirty-one-year-old sister reported, for example, that "at the time of my mother's death, myself and other members of the family had a disagreement with Ian, who disposed of Mother's car without permission, and additionally attempted to fraudulently withdraw money from her building society account by forging her signature on a letter." His sister was especially infuriated by this deceit "because it had only been some six months previous that Mother, as guarantor, had to pay out £12,000 to cover debts that Ian had got, following the collapse of a business venture." Ian attributed his financial collapse, his sister said, to squandering his money "at night-clubs and casinos."

After that, she had refused to see him. Yet only a few months before the killings, she discovered two shredded letters in a waste bin at their father's home. Suspicious of what they might be, she "pieced the letters together and saw that one was a letter to my grandmother from the Trustee Savings Bank and one from the Nationwide Anglia Building Society, both notifying her that cheques paid into her account from Ian had 'bounced.'" When confronted with these letters, Ian insisted it was all a misunderstanding, and that he had merely borrowed £10,000 from their grandmother to purchase his video rental business.

The Fire

When the fire brigade responded to an early-morning house fire at Mrs. George's home, they searched the house and found the remains of the two elderly women in their bedrooms. They had not been burned, but suffocating fumes had billowed throughout the house. The fire, which initially appeared to investigators to have started accidentally, had caused extensive damage to one corner of the front ground-floor room.

However, when the dead women's solicitor began to settle their estates, he noticed the anomalous withdrawals from their building society accounts. Large sums of money had been withdrawn – a total of £20,000 from the Halifax Building Society account in the name of Mary George, and £9,000 from a Nationwide Anglia account in the name of Jessie Thyme. Moreover, an investment bond belonging to Mary George had been cashed. All of these transactions had been performed by Ian Kapel, using forms which appeared to be signed by his grandmother. Several weeks later, police interviewed Kapel about the missing money.

The Interviews

During an increasingly tense series of interviews by two detectives working in tandem, Kapel at first protested his innocence, even to the charge of stealing his grandmother's mail – his explanation was merely that "some-times if the postman was coming down, he give me their mail to take in." Under interrogation, however, he eventually admitted having stolen money. His initial explanation was, "I was working for Sharp Video where my shop is now and the opportunity came up to buy that: the bank loaned me five thousand towards doing it and Grandmother did lend me some, but I can't remember the figure, but I obviously couldn't come up with the rest of the money to pay for it. So seeing how Grandmother had withdrawn from her account I did it without her knowing." The detective was unim-pressed: "So they're your property, but they were bought with this stolen money? How did you go about drawing these sums of money?" "Usually Grandmother was still full of sense," Kapel remembered, "but she wasn't with it fully, and rather than try and forge her signature, which was difficult, I often dealt with a lot of her mail while she was there and I'd just get her to sign a withdrawal slip. I don't think she realized what it was."

The detective asked what Ian had done with the remainder of the pur-loined tens of thousands of pounds. "I didn't know it was that much," Ian claimed. "There's been bills for this year in the shop, there's been rent for a thousand for a quarter, there's been a printing bill, that was just under a thousand, one of the film companies that I got films from, I owe them three thousand, but the rest I wouldn't like to try and account for." "Going out and boozing – wine, women and song? Do you think that she'd have let you have that much money, all her life savings?" "I don't think she would have done, but I think if I'd have asked she'd have helped out in one way or another, but not to that amount." "I mean, she's virtually spent her life savings?" "Yeah."

When the detective asked how knowledge of the withdrawals from the building society had been kept from his grandmother, Ian admitted, "The ones where I'd taken the money, I threw them away. The postman will give [any letters to] me to hand to Grandma, so I can bring it in for them." When the detective speculated that as much as £50,000 had actually been embez-zled from the accounts, Ian agreed: "I'd say that's about the right figure, yeah." The detective asked where this "considerable amount of money" was being spent. Kapel replied, "Over the past few months, since about February and March this year, I seem to have gradually gone on from smoking marijuana on to cocaine and acid, and most of the money's gone buying that stuff." "How much were you spending on drugs at the beginning?" "At the beginning I'd say only about maybe hundred, hundred and fifty a week. I was only earning a hundred and twenty a week, and I was spending more than that on drugs. To start with I did have a decent hi-fi and other things. I've sold all those off." "So initially you're using about a hundred pounds a week?" "Around that. But it soon built up. I'd say closer to three hundred or more a week. Some weeks I'd get some extra, I'd knock a bit out [sell] for extra cash. I've not sold much of the cocaine, it's mainly marijuana I've sold – you know, the little bags you can get with the sealed top." "What happened to the money that you were making?" "Quite a bit I lost in the casinos, some nights about two hundred quid." "You weren't making a lot of money; and it was helping to pay for your habit, helping to pay for your gambling?" An additional five thousand went to Kapel's drug dealer: "He reckoned I owed him for drugs that had been supplied, cocaine, marijuana and one day he got very abusive when he came round to my flat and said if I didn't start coming up with money he'd send the heavies round."

As his confession developed, Kapel mentioned he had left one of his grandmother's accounts untouched: "The only one I don't think I did touch was in Grandma's own Nationwide account." "And why didn't you do that?" "To be honest I don't think there was very much in it, if I remember right." "You didn't think that account was worth bothering with?" said the detective. "Yeah." "Otherwise you would have done?" "I imagine I would, yeah." "Because you'd no scruples whatsoever, had you, by this time?" "Not then, no." "Were you so dependent on drugs?" "At the time you don't think you are but ..."

Sensing a capitulation, the detective reminded Kapel of his mood at the time of the killings: "You didn't have the money to pay them then. There's no more money left in your Gran's account. No more money in your aunty's account. This time there weren't anything to pay the bills, was there? You couldn't rob Peter to pay Paul any more. There was bills to be paid as soon as possible so that the discrepancies didn't come to light. You'd still got your drugs problem, you're still wanting money for your drugs. Your business had no money coming in, you'd overdrawn on all your accounts, there's no prospect of you getting any money, was there? So you'd have been really at your wits' end that morning when you go up to see your Gran and there's some bills on the mat. It's a bit like a nightmare?"

"Yeah, but I always seemed to come up with the money before, I found some way of getting it," Ian mused. But the detective understood what had happened: "This time there was no other means. Before you always had other means, didn't you, Ian? There was your Gran's money, that had gone down. There weren't another answer without selling the clothes off your back, and that wouldn't have lasted until the following month when the bills came through again. You'd tried, I mean you'd tried hadn't you? Your grandmother spoke to the manager of the building society about the irregularities in the account. And she was informed about the cheques that you had made out that had bounced through your Aunty Jessie's account, and she told the building society's manager that she intended to take you to task about that matter the following day. When she saw you, she told the building society manager that she would get back to him and tell him what had happened. Unfortunately, there was a fire. And she was dead, which to say the least, solved a lot of your problems at that time. Would you agree with that?"

Kapel insisted he had spent the night of the murders in bed with his girlfriend, Kelly. "My brothers came and told me that Grandma had died, that they'd both died in a fire, and could I get up with them, so I followed them up in my van. The firemen were there and told us roughly what had happened – I think they said [it happened] about four in the morning, some time during the night anyway." "You see, you are someone who's got a clear motive for possibly not wanting your Gran to be around much longer?" "Yeah, with the finance stuff and everything, yeah, but my Gran was my Gran." "She was also to be the end of your little jaunt that you'd had, wasn't she?" "If she knew about the money, yeah. Which I'm not saying she ..." "Because she'd started to find out, it were obvious that she was going to find out, wasn't it? I've put to you certain circumstances that would point towards you having a motive, and the opportunity to have done something that someone in a desperate situation might have done." "Yeah, but I've been desperate for the last couple of months."

"We're nearly there," the detective said, encouraging Kapel, "and when it's all sorted we can sit down. I think we're pretty near the truth now. I do honestly. I don't think there's that much more. I don't believe that you've told us the full truth, not for one minute, I think you've told us 99 per cent of the truth."

The Confession

"I've told you the truth as it is," Kapel insisted. "The point is there's no way I'm gonna do that to my own bleedin' Grandma. All right, I've taken money from her, but . . ." "More like you've spent all her life savings!" "Yeah, I have." "There were no scruples then, were there?" "No, there weren't." "In view of what was said in the last interview, I must tell you that I've reason to suspect that you may be responsible for the death of your grandmother and your great-aunt. I must tell you that I'm arresting you on suspicion of the murder of those two people."

Astonishingly, immediately upon hearing he was to be charged with multiple murder, Kapel collapsed. When the detective asked, "Were you responsible for their deaths?" Kapel merely replied, "I was, yes." The detective reminded him that he did not have to speak without a solicitor being present, and urged him to be cautious.

But Kapel had made the decision to turn the remainder of his life over to the authorities. "First of all, I went Tuesday morning around nine as I normally would do. Grandmother had given me her passbook for the Nationwide with bills and that, said I was to take it straight in myself rather than post it as normal. She didn't say anything out of the ordinary about it, but I guessed something was up. Apart from the worry of that and God knows how many other things, I didn't know where to turn to. That day I just spent working in the shop like normal, I don't know, not really thinking I suppose.

"That night Kelly had gone to sleep, I don't think she knew I'd gone out. I went up to their house, parked at the bottom of the road. I knew quite often Grandma didn't even actually lock the door up at night. The door was unlocked like I thought it would be. Went in, and spent maybe ten or fifteen minutes just trying to work out what I was doing. I turned the gas fire on in the living room, picked something up, I don't know if it was a cardigan or a dressing-gown, something like that, put it right in front of the fire – I just bunched it up so it was close against the fire, just kinda picked it up, scrunched it up, and plonked it on there – some kind of man-made material that started smoking pretty quickly. It smouldered, but there were never flames jumping up, and I just hung around until it started smoking. Then I left, dropped the latch, shut the door behind me and went. Drove home. Went in, went to bed and spent half the night awake, fell asleep eventually early in the morning. And then I was woken by me brothers."

"Did you want the fire to spread into the house?" "Yes, and no as well. It's confusing. I mean yeah, I wanted to start a fire. The intention was my Gran and Aunt Jess should die, but inside as well I felt . . ." Kapel began to cry. "What you're saying is you wanted to kill 'em, but cause as little damage as possible? You wanted to kill them by smoke rather than them actually burn?" "Yes, that's right. I didn't want them to die by fire. The smoke. Without them knowing." "Did you expect it to go slow, smoke slowly?" "I don't think I knew how the fire would go." "And the reason for you doing this was due to the financial?" "Everything." "The financial disaster that you'd found yourself in?" "Yeah. By doing this it would stop everything coming to light." "We'll again ask you whether you want a solicitor present?"

In what may well have been the first courageous act of his life, Kapel replied: "*I've got myself in this mess*, I shouldn't rely on a solicitor to try and get me out of it." With that, the detective switched off the tape recorder. Ian Kapel was found guilty on two charges of murder, and sentenced to life imprisonment.

---

1   Quoted in Morris and Blom-Cooper, 1967, in Wolfgang (ed), *Studies in Homicide*.

STRANGERS

GANGS OF BULLY BOYS, young men fortified with alcohol and out spoiling for a fight, often find one. If they show too much enthusiasm for their task, or lose control of their anger, or launch their blow in an unfortunate direction, or their victim's head perchance strikes an unyielding surface, it can occasionally lead to a death. In the chaos of a brawl that may last only a few seconds, a shove or a punch is instantly criminalized as a homicide: frequently, the participants do not even know that someone has been killed.

Young men can be dangerous fools, too emotionally uncontrolled and physically powerful: two-thirds of all homicides in England are committed by men younger than thirty-five. Fewer than 10 per cent of our 2,420 cases where the suspect was identified were "strangers," people who met accidentally, confronted one another, and tried to face each other down. In five years, there were only 234 such events in all of England: 468 too many wasted lives (of victim and killer), to be sure, but a modest number in comparison with most other urban industrial countries.

For the sake of familiarity and convenience, we have categorized some of the killers in this volume according to their relationship to the victim; but these categories are merely descriptive and illustrative, not analytic: they merely show us who kills whom. They *conceal* the deeper reality that they are all much the same, regardless of whom they kill. Most of our killers (and so many of our victims, with whom they share both their lives and their deaths) came from disordered families and had criminal records, routinely consumed prodigious quantities of alcohol, were marginally employed or unemployed and living on state benefits in council housing.

They were limited and uncontrolled men, whose grasp of ethics in the social encounter did not seem to extend much beyond rules regarding the inappropriateness of certain forms of attack. Nevertheless, it should be noted that even here, at the lowest levels of self-control and education in the nation, there are unwritten rules governing fighting – some "don't approve" of knives, most genuinely "didn't mean to hurt anyone" (or at least kill them – a more plausible claim than in many other countries, where a hail of gunfire may be directed towards the victim). Moreover, which one of them will die seems purely a matter of chance.

"THEY WERE TROUBLE": AN AFFRAY IN A PUB LEAVES A STRANGER DEAD

The most dangerous social situation is the same anywhere in the world – when two males confront one another in a dispute, whether spontaneous or long-simmering.[1] Despite the reservations some of the participants in this drunken mêlée had about the use of weapons, knives were commandeered from the club's kitchen when the challenge was issued. At the end of the chaotic encounter, one man lay dead on The Nightclub's floor, and those who would ultimately be convicted fled to Spain. The dead man was Martin Catowski, twenty-two, stabbed by a stranger.

The Killing

The victim, Martin, himself had a criminal record and a history of minimal self-control: at the age of fourteen, he was convicted in a juvenile court for assault; at fifteen, he was charged in a magistrate's court with threatening behaviour; and at seventeen, he was convicted in the same court for possession of an offensive weapon. Police thought the victim's surviving brother, David, also unemployed, had been one of the catalysts of the fight, although David had suffered no serious injuries. David told police that they had arrived at The Nightclub just before midnight: "Both Martin and I were searched [for weapons] before we were allowed into the club. Once inside we both went to the first floor which is a bar area. There we met a couple of Martin's friends, Danny and Chris. We had a few drinks and occasionally one or two of the lads would go up to the second floor, which is a bar and disco, and see what was happening upstairs. I stayed downstairs until one of the lads – I think it was Danny – come down and said, 'Come and give us a hand, Mickey is having trouble.' Danny, Chris, Martin and I then went upstairs where I saw Mickey and a couple of his friends being faced by another group of youths, one of which was a black youth aged about twenty-four years, six feet tall, medium build, with Afro hair. I asked Mickey what was happening and he said it was the group with the black youth who were causing trouble.

"I went over to the black youth who had about six or seven white friends with him and said, 'Come on, mate, leave it out.' He said, 'Keep your hands off me.' So I just walked away. But I went back to him very soon after, to try and clear things up. The black youth punched me in my left eye. I head-butted him in his face. At this point all of his friends jumped on me and punched and kicked me to the ground. I have been told by my friends that I was struck on the face by a stool or a table that had been thrown. I cannot recall being struck, I must have been knocked out immediately. However, I was later seen by my own doctor and was treated for a broken left cheekbone and nose. I don't know where Martin, Danny or Chris was when this happened but they had come upstairs with me. One of the bouncers pulled me to my feet and I then noticed the black youth had a knife, the blade was about nine inches long. Also a short white youth in the same group had a knife of similar size. They were both waving the knives about in a threatening manner. I looked around and saw Martin was lying on his back behind the bar near the hatch door, but I couldn't see any blood on his clothing, his eyes were open but he wasn't making any noises. When I looked back, the youths with the knives had left the room. Danny dragged Martin from behind the bar and tried to give him the kiss of life. Shortly afterwards the police arrived, and it was then I found that Martin was dead – but I can't remember seeing any wounds on his body. Over the whole evening I had probably had about ten pints of lager. I don't know how much Martin had drunk during the evening."

Anon

Before the events had been sorted out, and anyone charged, when Bernard and Summers were still hiding on the Continent, police received information from a number of anonymous sources, presumably in repayment of previous debts. One who "grassed" on them, "Anon," was asked by the detective if he had seen the actual stabbing. Anon replied, "No, but Summers, Bernard and 'Bill the Pill' all had knives. When I saw Summers and Bernard afterwards, Bernard's hand was shaking. I reckon Bernard did it." When the detective asked, "Are you sure 'Bill the Pill' had a knife?," Anon said, "Yeah, I'm sure I saw him with one." "How sure are you that they're in Spain?" Anon replied, "They asked me mate to go with them but he said why should he go, he didn't murder no one. Anyway I heard Summers did the signature on a driving licence with brake fluid." The detective said, "What? To get a false passport?" "Yeah. Summers got hold of a driving licence, removed the signature with brake fluid and he fucked up the photograph on the passport."

The Killers

David Summers, twenty-four, who was charged with murder but found guilty of manslaughter and received the heaviest penalty for the affray, was sentenced to five years' imprisonment. He too had a criminal record, and his previous convictions included theft, "estreeting" bail and the consumption in public of "excess alcohol." He had attended a comprehensive school, but left at the age of fifteen without any qualifications. He worked briefly as a motor fitter in the dockyard, but was made redundant: at the time of the murder, he had been unemployed for five years, and lived at home with his parents. After the killing, he and his friend Bernard fled to Spain to avoid capture, but they were apprehended by the police and returned to the United Kingdom. Neither of the two men who fled to Spain, and who were ultimately convicted of the killing, would speak to police during their interviews. At Catford police station, the two simply sat silently, and made no reply to any questions that were put to them: they were returned to their cells.

Paul Bernard, twenty-seven, was found guilty of being in an affray and sentenced to eighteen months' imprisonment. Of all those involved in the brawl, he had the most extensive criminal record. His seventeen convictions included four counts of burglary; one of "going equipped" (for burglary); assault causing actual bodily harm; taking and driving away a vehicle; four counts of absconding bail; two charges of theft (one for stealing a leather jacket and aftershave lotion from a shop display; one for stealing dresses from a shop); possessing a firearm with intent to commit an indictable offence; and common assault. He had no known education at all, and his employment consisted of casual labouring jobs, although for one short period he was a stall-holder in Lewisham market. Unemployed at the time of arrest, he lived in a council flat with his common-law wife and two small children, one of whom was "unwell and in hospital."

A third offender considered by the police, but ultimately released, was William "Bill the Pill" Dalton, forty-one, of Camberwell, who had a history of fifteen previous convictions for burglary, theft, receiving stolen goods and assault. Dalton had worked on market stalls in South London, but had been unemployed for two years. He lived on social security benefits with his wife and three children in a council house, and his rent was paid by social services. A court official considered Dalton's role in the affray too marginal to take him to trial: "There is plenty of evidence to show that Dalton took part in the fight and kicked David Catowski in the head. Nobody, however, saw him with a knife and there is evidence to show that he disapproved of the use of knives during the fight. The high-water mark of the case against Dalton comes from the same witness who also says that when knives were produced, Dalton said, 'Do it outside.' Looking at all the evidence I interpret that remark to mean that the fight as a whole should take place in the street and cannot be construed as an inducement that anyone should necessarily be stabbed. Accordingly, I advise that the charge of murder be withdrawn." Dalton was interviewed, but not charged.

Dalton told police: "On the night in question I had been drinking in the bottom bar of The Nightclub with Dick and some other people who I'm not quite sure of their surnames; for most of the evening the bottom bar was nearly empty; I couldn't say at what time but it was within an hour of closing. Me and Summers decided to go upstairs after he had finished singing. We decided to go up to the top bar which still had a fair-sized crowd. We was drinking at the far end of the bar, furthest away from the dance floor. I believe Summers was talking to someone, I knew by face but not by name.

"I don't know exactly what time that the trouble started but the first thing I knew was that someone had been butted in the face, and I, along with Summers and some other people, was pushed into the bar by other people who were trying to get away from the row which seemed to be going on. I thought the row had stopped because everything seemed to go back to normal for a short period – twenty or thirty seconds. By this time we had moved back to our original spaces, about six feet from where the bar meets the wall. I was standing talking to Summers when something hit me across the back – I thought I was being hit across the back. I now know I wasn't but it was someone who had been hit and who fell on to me. But at the time I thought that I was being picked on, like a person I'd just seen getting head-butted. I turned round and kicked out with my foot but then realized that the person was falling to the floor and had already been struck by someone else. I also noticed that the person laying on the floor was the one that had done the head-butting in the first place. I shouted out, 'You're all trouble causers,' and also to another person who was standing up I give some abuse to – I believe it to be a friend of the person laying on the floor. Summers started to walk towards the stairs and I immediately started to walk towards them some five to ten paces behind him. I did not know that someone else at the other end of the bar was at the time being stabbed. I was told the next day that it had been on the telly and found it hard to believe that someone had been murdered there. I never ever saw the deceased and completely deny being anywhere near to this man when the crime took place. That's it. Finished!"

In a second interview the following day, police asked Dalton, "At about that time two men appeared armed with knives, one of whom shouted, 'Who wants some of this?' That man was Summers, wasn't it?" "I cannot answer that question," Dalton replied honestly, "because I don't know that to be fact. I never heard that shouted out and at no time did I see any men with knives." "Who told you, apart from the television, that someone had died in The Nightclub that night?" "Just the television, nobody else told me." "Who told you that you'd better disappear until the heat goes down?" "Well, I just thought it was the best thing to do. No one told me. Well, me wife." "If you had nothing to do with it why didn't you come forward to the police, because you'd read the newspapers surely, where I had been asking for witnesses?" "As I said in my first statement, I had swung a kick at the fellow, and had shouted out, 'You're a troublemaker,' and I feared that I might be put away for that." "If you'd had nothing to do with it you'd have nothing to fear." "There's no answer to that. I was frightened." When the detective asked why he had moved house immediately after the murder, Dalton replied, "I refuse to answer that."

When the detective asked why he had gone to that particular club, Dalton replied, "I haven't been up The Nightclub for at least three or four months. But some time during that time I've been told there's a group of people that have caused trouble from time to time and when the trouble started, I assumed it was them." "So if you are aware that this group frequent The Nightclub and they are trouble, why go there?" "I didn't think at the time that there would be people there to cause trouble, I don't consider Thursday a night where you get any place packed." "If you're a man who attempts to avoid trouble, why stay when the trouble started?" "As I've already said in my statement, it was only a scuffle in the first instance and as soon as it started again Summers left and I followed." When told he might be charged with murder, he exclaimed, "I don't fucking believe this, I can't believe it."

"THEY ATTACKED US": A "SCAB" PROVOKES UNION MEN

Stranger homicides are not always chance encounters between uncontrolled toughs in a pub: sometimes the men are drawn together through other, perhaps economic, ties. For example, the question of which union man will relent first during a strike and return to work is often a matter of mere personal circumstance, as is the response of his fellows. No matter: police found the "scab's" younger brother, eighteen-year-old David Carstairs, lying unconscious on the "floor," northern dialect for the pavement, in this smoky colliery town. The police constable later wrote that the victim was lying on his back and obviously in "need of urgent medical attention." Carstairs' face was bleeding profusely, and blood had congealed around his eyes, nose and mouth. He was crying and screaming in pain, and could only repeat, "I'm hurting, let me get up." The constable persuaded him to remain on the pavement until the ambulance arrived, and asked Carstairs, "Who has done this?" Carstairs, seriously injured and soon to lose consciousness forever, only intoned, "I want to get up" till the ambulance service rushed him to the hospital.

Brain-damaged, Carstairs would linger in hospital for four months before he died. When the forensic pathologist later examined his corpse, he saw a slim young white male, six feet tall, weighing eleven stone, with a 36-inch chest. What was most striking about the body stretched out before him was that it was heavily tattooed: the pathologist counted a "Dragon motif on left upper arm, 'Dave' with heart and skull motif on right upper arm, 'Four skins' on lower abdomen, 'I love sex' on the right thigh, 'Bimo' alongside penis, male and female logo on the right side of chest, small tattoos on left knuckles, left wrist, and left ankle." The pathologist's report continued:

> I understand that this young man, together with his brother, became involved in a fracas with striking miners outside the brother's house. Carstairs was apparently struck over the head with a wooden object having the same general dimensions as a baseball bat. He was not apparently knocked unconscious at the time – he was able to speak after a fashion whilst being taken in an ambulance to the local hospital. Shortly after his admission to the casualty department, his condition deteriorated in the space of a few minutes. He became unconscious with a fixed, dilated right pupil, whilst he developed reflexes indicative of brain damage. Had he survived, the indications are that he would have been hugely disabled and quite unable to look after himself or to enjoy any quality of life. In my view, his death resulted directly from the head injury he received.

The Police Report

The surviving Carstairs brother, Grant, was thirty-one years old. Married with one young son, he lived in a terraced house at number 18, Bentley Road. A member of the National Union of Mineworkers, Grant was employed at the town's major colliery. Police noted that he had "supported the union in the spring when a strike was called, but at the end of September he had decided to go back to work; and as a result he was subject to numerous attacks and abuse, his house was stoned and windows broken." That Friday, Grant's wife knew that as the weekend approached, it was likely that striking miners might drink heavily and become abusive towards them. Fearing for the baby's safety, she left the family home with her child to stay with a friend. Grant was at home alone till his younger brother, David, decided to make a gesture of solidarity and spend the weekend with him. Unfortunately, as a "manly" and threatening response to the many attacks on his home, Grant had made a club that police described "as a very nasty and dangerous weapon" – he had driven nails through one end of a stout piece of wood three feet long and two inches thick. His younger brother, David, also armed himself, keeping near him a wooden sledge-hammer shaft some three feet in length.

Just before midnight, the Carstairs brothers heard the sound to which they had grown accustomed since the strike – that of stones hitting their windows. Each carrying his weapon, they leapt out into the street and saw the group across the road shouting and jeering at them. David drew first blood: he approached one of the miners, Harrington, and struck him across the chest with the sledgehammer shaft. Harrington, police noted, "quite rightly defended himself and grabbed hold of David and pulled the shaft away from him," then hit him back with it. That was the end of sufficient provocation, but the fight continued. A second miner, Morton, joined Harrington in the attack on David. With that, the elder Carstairs began striking the other miners with his nailed club: the two suffering the blows, Penrose and Cordon, "quite rightly defended themselves" and retaliated. To confirm this version of events, police later noted that Penrose had marks across his back, and Cordon had slashes on both his legs, that were consistent with being hit by the nailed club.

Neighbours had called the ambulance and police, all of whom arrived soon after the miners had left the area. David Carstairs was taken to the Royal Infirmary, suffering from severe head injuries, while his elder brother was treated for an abrasion above the left eye. An hour later, police saw the group of miners not far from the house: Harrington, Morton, Cordon and

Penrose were arrested on suspicion of assault and taken to the police station. A few hours later, Grant Carstairs was also arrested.

During the initial interview, Harrington told police that he and his wife had been drinking at the Thistle public house, where they had shared a drink with the rest of their group. At closing time they left the pub and walked home along Bentley Road. As they approached Carstairs' home, "the conversation turned towards the scab's house," and Harrington picked up a stone and threw it at a partially boarded-up window. The stone hit the board and bounced off. Harrington said it was at this point that the Carstairs brothers had come out of the house wielding their clubs, and that David Carstairs had hit him across the chest with it. He had grabbed hold of David by the scruff of the neck and had pulled the shaft away from him. He then hit David Carstairs on the right-hand side of the rib cage with the shaft, and as he did so the shaft bounced out of his hand and fell on to the pavement. Harrington then left him and walked back towards his wife and claimed not to have seen anything else.

One neighbour who witnessed the fight told police that she had seen the fracas: "I saw Grant and his brother both come out of number 18 and run across the road towards these youths. I could see that there was some sort of scuffle taking place: my attention went to two youths who were attacking a man laid in the road. One of these youths had hold of a stick and I saw him lift his arm and strike the youth laid on the floor with the stick. I couldn't say where the blows were landing. I saw him hit this youth with the stick, I would say more than twice but I can't honestly say how many times. This youth on the floor was just laying there and wasn't doing anything to defend himself. The other youth was stood over him and by the way his body was moving – I took it that he was kicking the lad on the ground but I couldn't see his legs so I don't know. He certainly wasn't punching him."

A second neighbour, so upset by what she had witnessed that she sobbed throughout her interview with the police, confirmed and enriched this account: "About midnight I heard such a scream coming from outside. I saw on the road outside my home a group of about six youths gathered around and attacking a lad that was laid in the road. There seemed to me feet and legs swinging out at the lad and it wasn't very clear what was happening. I shouted at them to stop but they were making that much noise themselves that I don't think they heard me. I saw one of the youths, who had a long club in his hand, lift the club up and land a blow to the front part of his head. He was laid face upwards at this time. I then saw the club come up again and I managed to scream and as soon as I had screamed they all looked up at me and started running."

Two striking miners who were present at the assault were not charged, but treated as witnesses. Penrose, twenty, told police: "I am aware that a man named Grant Carstairs lives on Bentley Road, and that he has returned to work. As we got near to his house, Harrington who was in front of us picked a stone up from the driveway and threw it across the road and it hit one of the windows. A short while later Grant Carstairs came out of the front door of his home. There was a younger youth with him. Grant was carrying a long stick with nails sticking out of it and the other youth was carrying what looked like a pickaxe handle. Grant came across the road and hit me across the back with the stick. I fell down with the pain, he then hit me on my right shin with the stick. I grabbed hold of his legs and pulled him to the floor and started thumping him to defend myself. We got up and I threw Grant on to a car bonnet and punched him again, he still had the stick in his hand. I then saw Harrington walk from where he was towards the young lad with the pickaxe handle. He grabbed hold of the handle, pulled it away from the youth, and then Harrington hit the youth with the pickaxe handle. I'm not certain which part of the body he hit the youth on. I did not see if the youth fell down or not because we left and we didn't want any trouble. I only saw Harrington hit the young lad once – I don't know if he hit him again or not. As far as I am aware I am the only person who hit Grant, the other lads may have hit him but I don't know."

As in all battles, each participant saw only his immediate environment. Twenty-one-year-old Cordon confirmed the outline of the story and told police that after the Carstairs brothers ran at them, "Grant Carstairs went towards Penrose and hit him about the body with the club. Penrose went down on to his knees then grabbed Carstairs' legs but Carstairs broke loose and came at me swinging the club. He hit me several times on both my legs causing several small puncture marks and scratches to my left knee. He then swung at my head but I held my right arm up to fend off the blow which caused two small scratches on my forearm. He also caused one small puncture mark to the upper left side of my chest. I did not strike Carstairs at all and could only manage to try and fend off the blows: while all this was happening I was not aware at all as to what the others were doing. I did not see what the other man with Carstairs was doing, he did not strike me with his club nor I him. I then took the opportunity to get away."

Interrogations

When the police informed Harrington that David Carstairs was in hospital and in a "very serious condition – so you must realize that this is a very serious matter," Harrington was astonished, and expostulated, "Christ! I didn't know that. Is he bad?" "He is very poorly," the police replied. "What can you tell us about what happened? Do you want to start from when you threw the stone at the window?" "All right, yes, I threw it," Harrington admitted: "We were walking down Bentley Road and they got on about where that scab lived and I just picked a brick up and slung it. I carried on walking and our lass said, 'Look out' and then I saw them two: one of them hit Morton across the back and the other one hit me just there [indicating the front of his chest]. I just got hold of him by scruff of neck and pulled that stick off him. I just cracked him with it. I had hold of his collar and he had his other arm up and I just hit him there [indicating left side of his rib cage]. When I hit him the stick bounced out of my hand and I just pulled him across road and he fell backwards. I just walked away then. I didn't look, I just kept on walking." "Was there anyone else near him?" "I don't know, I didn't see anybody, but our lass told me later that when he was down Morton kicked his head – but that's only what our lass told me." "As far as I understand it, you also hit him when he was down?" "No, just like I said, I pulled it off him, hit him at the side and then pulled him over road." "Did you hit anybody else?" "No, just him."

"We appreciate that you were attacked by these two but that wouldn't have happened if you hadn't thrown the stone, would it?" "No." "Don't get me wrong. They shouldn't have been carrying those sticks and they will have to answer for that; but at the moment we have a lad seriously ill in hospital, apparently because of the injuries you inflicted on him. I want to be sure, did you only hit him the once?" "Yes. I just threw him down and he fell over backwards and then I just walked off with Elaine, and the others were still fighting. As soon as the lad hit the floor I turned round and went, so I don't know what happened to him after that. On the way home my wife says, 'There was no need for Morton to kick him in the head.' I didn't see that, it's just what she told me."

The second miner to be charged with murder, Morton, eighteen, signed his own statement. "I drank four pints of bitter. We all walked along Bentley Road, and Harrington just said, 'Where's that scabby bastard live?' He then picked up what looked like a large stone, said, 'That's it, isn't it, with boards over the windows?' He then ran to the middle of the road and threw a brick at the window and broke it. We just carried on walking, and Colin started to walk behind us. As we went by the house where the window had been broken two men suddenly ran out towards us and one of them pointed to us and said, 'Them over there.' I knew one of them was called Carstairs who is a working miner. He had a long stick in his hand with large nails through the end. I don't know the other man's name: he was carrying something that looked like a baseball bat or large stick. I started to run away because I was frightened but I only got about ten yards and stopped to look back. On doing so I saw the man Carstairs go for Penrose with his stick but Penrose grabbed him around the waist. Penrose then slid down his body until he was on the floor with his arms round Carstairs' feet. Carstairs then brought the stick down in a blow to Penrose's back. I then looked over to my right and saw Harrington fighting with the other man. They were wrestling over the stick, each man would keep at least one hand on the stick all the time and then try to strike the other a blow with his fist. The man managed to hit Penrose in the face with his fist, but Penrose pushed him to the ground, causing him to let go of the stick. Harrington then kicked the man whilst he was on the floor, twice in the ribs. He then hit the man twice with the stick to the upper part of his body. The man on the floor didn't move after that and didn't get up from the road. I then ran back to help Penrose who was still fighting Carstairs – who still had his stick with the nails in. I grabbed hold of him round the arms in a kind of bear hug. Harrington had also come to help as well but I'm not too sure what he was doing. Carstairs then bent over a car bonnet and I grabbed his hair with my right hand and made as if to hit him with my left but he brought the stick up and caught me under my left arm, causing a considerable amount of deep scratches. I then just pushed him away and ran off."

When police told Morton he was seriously implicated in the affair, he shouted, "They attacked us!" The detective continued, "We have read the statement that you made earlier and I would say that most of what you said in that statement is true, isn't it?" "It all is!" "But I think you left the part out about you kicking that lad, didn't you?" "Yes. I know." "Well, shall we go into that?" "I just kicked him when he was down on the floor. It was stupid. I kicked him on top of his head. I don't know why. Then I went over to my girlfriend." "So this lad's on the ground, and you go and kick him?" "Yes. Temper, I think." "Do you want to make a written statement about that?" "I might as well get it over with," Morton concluded, before writing:

> I want to say now that after Harrington had hit the young lad with the pickaxe handle after he fell down, I went across and just kicked the lad once on the top of his head and then I went to help with the other kid. It wasn't a really hard kick, I think I did it in temper. When I got over to the other lad he hit me with the stick and that's when I got my injuries on my arm and shoulder.

The Victim's Brother

The detective moved to establish responsibility and intent: "Right, Grant, since I saw you at the hospital we have now found out that you and your brother came out of the house with two lumps of wood. One of the lumps of wood had nails knocked through it and I would like to know which one of you was carrying that?" "I was. Our David had the sledgehammer handle." "Did you knock the nails through the wood?" "Yes. I made it about a fortnight ago because of all the trouble. I only wanted to scare people away with it. I didn't intend hitting anybody with it." "That's a very nasty weapon you've made. You do realize that there can't be any excuse for carrying something like that?"

"I know; but I just wanted to scare people off, not hurt anybody. You must know about all the trouble since I went back to work; but last night our Dave came round to stay with me and we were just sat in room when 'bang, bang, bang' on window and I knew somebody was throwing [stones] again. So our David got the sledgehammer handle, and I got that other thing with the nails, and we went outside to see who it was. When we got outside that lot started shouting 'Scab' and that, so we went across to sort them out. I thought they would go when they saw the sticks. I knew I was swinging the stick about, but they seemed to be going all over me. I didn't have enough arms: I might have hit somebody, I don't know. I remember I got it caught on somebody's pullover, it might have been then, but they were all over me. I was thrown over a car bonnet, and when I looked round I saw our David laid in the road. I don't know who hit him, he followed me out of house and he was behind me, that's all I know. I never even see him get hit. All I remember was swinging the stick. It all happened that fast, everybody was at it." "You must realize that if you go and bray² somebody across the back with that thing, they are entitled to defend themselves?" "Yes, I know that. I never thought this would happen. I just wanted to scare them off."

Following the interview, Carstairs prepared his formal statement: "I work at Nether Pit and I came out on strike in March. I was on days regular because my baby son was ill and my wife couldn't get any sleep. About a month ago I decided that I would have to go back to work because I hadn't paid my mortgage, and I had a big electric bill and they were threatening to cut me off. My gas bill was due, I'd got no money apart from the twenty pound a week from the social security. I started back at work and the first week I had no problems but on that Sunday I went to the pub in Bentley and a gang of blokes were ready to have a go then, but they didn't. The following Sunday night there was some bricks thrown at house: they didn't break any windows and I don't know who it was. They were shouting 'Scab' and somebody paint 'Scab' on the pavement. During that week there was a group of women started walking past the house shouting 'Scab' and other names. I think it was the Saturday before last some men came to the house banging on the door saying they wanted to talk to me. I went out but the police on guard told me to go back inside and the police spoke to them. A week last Monday I stopped going to work because my wife was frightened to death and afraid for the baby. Some more women came that day shouting and bawling, but the police moved them on. Last Friday there was about twenty blokes came to the house shouting and the police had to move them on. We didn't have any problems then until Wednesday this week when there was an almighty barny and two big pebbles came through the window and one of them landed on my wife's lap. This frightened her to death again: it weighed about a pound and a half.

"My brother David came to stay with me Friday night. We were sat in the front room when there were several bangs on the windows and I heard glass breaking. I think it was a window that was already broken. Me and my brother decided to go out to see who it was. My brother had a sledgehammer handle and I had a length of wood what I made a couple of weeks ago. I knocked some nails through it and put some tape round the handle. We only carried these to scare people off and I'd heard there was a gang out to get me. We went outside and I saw a gang of lads and lasses and they started shouting 'scab bastard' and then a couple of them started coming towards us. I shouted at 'em, 'It's you who's put my windows through, is it?' I can't remember what they said, the next thing I remember is they were all on top of me and I was swinging that wood about. I don't know if I hit anybody with it or not. Next thing I remember is somebody on my back and I was thrown on to the bonnet of this car and they were all punching me. Somebody grabbed hold of my hair and pulled me on to floor and they all started kicking me then. When I was on floor I managed to roll over and get up. I swung stick again and they all decided to go. As they were going two more came towards me and I thought they were going to have a go, and I went to hit them with the stick until I realized it was two lasses. Then I stopped and told them to get off with rest of them. I looked round and saw that my brother was laid in road, I don't know what happened with him, I didn't see that happen."

Resolution

Before Carstairs died, Harrington and Morton had been charged with grievous bodily harm with intent: after his death, the charge was altered to murder, but the court found them guilty only of manslaughter. Harrington was jailed for four years, and Morton given three years in youth custody. Grant Carstairs was found guilty of possessing an offensive weapon and given a suspended twelve-month prison sentence. Both the police and the court concluded that while Carstairs had acted inappropriately and aggressively in running out of his house to confront the strikers, Harrington and Morton had acted with equally inappropriate violence; moreover, Harrington had triggered the incident by throwing the first stone.

---

1   For a provocative discussion of the international data on this matter, see Martin
    Daly and Margo Wilson, 1988, *Homicide*, New York: Aldine de Gruyter.
2   Strike.

"THE CIVILIZING PROCESS"

TO CONTROL THE awesome murderous potential of human beings, the modern democratic nation-state must bring together government, law and culture in a civilized form of conspiracy, the aim of which is to create a social milieu in which the very idea of extreme violence becomes intolerable to the citizen. Thus an ethical atmosphere, a sensibility, must be created in which government and people are parsimonious in the use of violence (as it has increasingly been in England since the Civil War); in which a just law closely monitors its citizens' behaviour (some 30 per cent of British young men have been before the courts) and provides no legal occasion for killing; and in which the culture intensifies the "propaganda" inhibiting persons from violent action. This retailing of compassion and control ensures that common personality traits are consistent with a need for order. Police states require no such personalities, since they govern by fear and enforced deference: democratic states must ensure such gentility is inculcated in the nursery.

THE LAW ON HOMICIDE

The English monetary economy and the mercantile system thrived on the maintenance of order, since the merchant class required that their interests be protected. Yet the gentry distrusted the oppressive Continental methods – an intrusive and brutal police, the "spies and informers" used, for example, by the French monarchy to control its subjects. "In place of police," Douglas Hay says of the eighteenth century, English men of property strengthened the courts to adjudicate disputes, and developed "a fat and swelling sheaf of laws." England was to be governed by a rapidly developing common law accessible to an increasing proportion of the population. Hay notes that such a judicial system was

> essential for the protection of the gentry from royal greed and royal tyranny and for the regulation, in the civil side of the courts, of the details of conveyancing, entailing, contracting, devising, suing and releasing. Since the same judges administered the criminal law at its highest levels, on the same principles, even the poorest man was guaranteed justice in the high courts.

Often, the court costs of the poor were paid by their employers, landlords and local associations – their motives a "tangle of self-interest and paternalism." A balanced social order was in place, in which many could aspire to the estate, the beliefs and the behaviour of their betters. The feudal system's ideology of personal honour and vengeance had no place in such an evolving commercial state.[1]

If the initial thrust of this law had been primarily to protect *property* (attempted murder, after all, was only a misdemeanour till 1814), homicide in England has been the preserve of the central government for the better part of a millennium. For the most part the government has not abused that responsibility. Even the harsh "bloody code" of the eighteenth century often seemed more threat than substance since it was muted in practice by "a uniquely liberal criminal procedure, which mitigated the violence of the law." Bound together in a commercial society with a mounting ideological consensus that rejected personal vengeance, the English – "masters of the art of being ruled" – became ever more constrained in their violence to one another. They had begun the construction of an unaggressive personality structure.[2]

Among the more useful clues to a civilization's sensibilities are the judicial circumstances in which it is considered lawful to kill another human being. English culture has for long been one in which a killing is perceived as a failure, a declaration of the offender's moral and personal bankruptcy; and this mentality is reflected in the law. Twentieth-century English law makes virtually no provisions whatever for legal homicide, and specifically rules out violence to protect property. A homicide is

"permitted" only in the rare instance when it is "reasonable" and necessary
to defend oneself or another from murderous or grievous assault, and
"where killing the attacker is the *only* practicable means of preventing the
harm." Moreover, "a person's opportunity to retreat with safety" and "his
willingness to temporize or disengage himself before resorting to force"
are all taken into consideration.[3]

Compare this with American culture, in which a killing can still be
perceived as a triumph, an achievement, a success. For more than a
century, violent men and violent acts have been tolerated, even glorified, as
when the *Kansas City Times* in the latter part of the nineteenth century
wrote of a cowboy bank robbery in which a little girl had been shot in the
leg. The newspaper compared the robbers to the knights of "storied
Odenwald, with the halo of medieval chivalry upon their garments, and
[they have] shown us how the things were done that poets sing of":
indeed, the journalist thought the cowboys were "so diabolically daring
and so utterly in contempt of fear that we are bound to admire it and
revere [them]." Thus American culture dedicated itself to the proselytiza-
tion of aggressivity and a contempt for emotional repression, and it has
paid a heavy price for doing so. "Americans don't understand about inhibitions," accurately observes a character in the film, *Shadowlands*. This is
so tangible and far-reaching that it prompted Christopher Lasch to write
scathingly of this U.S. "culture of competitive individualism," which
carries "the logic of individualism to the extreme of a war of all against all,
the pursuit of happiness to the dead end of a narcissistic preoccupation
with the self." Such a culture may sentimentalize compassion, but it sys-
tematically roots it out of the social system.[4]

This set of attitudes is reflected in, and reinforced by, American laws.
Compare the English prohibitions on violence with, say, the penal code of
the state of Texas, which officially declared homicide as a valid response to
a wide range of provocations, and made it legal to kill a human being under
any of eleven vague circumstances: "Killing a public enemy; executing a
convict; acting in response to a lawful order or directive by a police officer;
aiding a police officer; preventing the escape of a person legally apprehended or captured; suppressing a riot; preventing the successful comple-
tion of a criminal or felonious act; responding by a husband to provocation

by an act of adultery; defending a person or property; defending oneself against an unlawful attack; and defending or upholding property rights." The basic thrust of the law is clear – that a person may kill in defence of *any* threat to his person or property, or on behalf of the authorities. The effect upon the society in thus trivializing homicide and desensitizing the population to violence is incalculable.[5]

THE "ADVANCE OF THE SHAME FRONTIER"

What is the process that moves a nation in a peaceable direction? The capacity of human beings for almost limitless violence – for torture, rapine and murder – is extraordinary, as any psychiatrist will testify. It has only been a short time since that capacity was firmly controlled in much of western Europe, allegedly among the most civilized of regions. In the Middle Ages, such capacities were utterly unconstrained, even revelled in, by those with the power to indulge them.

> Neither eating, drinking, nor sleep has as much savour for me as to hear the cry "Forwards!" from both sides, and horses without riders shying and whinnying, and the cry "Help! Help!," and to see the small and the great fall to the grass at the ditches and the dead pierced by the wood of the lances decked with banners. (War hymn, attributed to the medieval minstrel Bertran de Born)

How can this ecstasy in violence be diminished, these militant values be transformed? How are aggressive impulses restrained and humanistic values transmitted?

In his two brilliant volumes on the subject, Norbert Elias showed how people in every civilization are not just taught arbitrary rules of behaviour, but are required to *internalize* these rules, wrapping them in emotionally charged feelings of revulsion, shame and disgust. He begins his treatise with an explication of the evolution of table manners, describing the customary method of eating in the Middle Ages. People ate together, "taking meat with their fingers from the same dish" and drinking "wine from the same goblet," with none of the modern disgust for such mixing of personal filth, none of the "invisible wall of affects which seem now to rise between one human body and another, repelling and separating."

But what Elias calls "the embarrassment threshold" is raised when the ruling élites, for their own reasons, "decide" to encode a new inhibition in the population. The feelings of disgust for such matters "are first transformed in the upper class," then the infinite hierarchy of social gradations allows the downward slide of this delicacy – aspiring individuals emulating their social superiors. New sensibilities are transmitted in this manner. What was once the feeling of joy medieval folk felt at seeing half a pig or calf upon the table, or knifing into a pheasant "still adorned with its feathers," is transformed into a sickening thought:

> From a standard of feeling by which the sight and carving of a dead animal on the table are actually pleasurable . . . the development leads to [the modern] standard by which reminders that the meat dish has [anything] to do with the killing of an animal are avoided to the utmost.

This new standard is reinforced by anxiety-arousing social taboos, which are internalized in socially nurtured "feelings of displeasure, distaste, disgust, fear, or shame." In this manner a behaviour that once inspired gusto now provokes an equally profound, culturally mandated, stomach-churning revulsion.

A similar process underwrites the transformation of aggression. Elias noted that in the medieval period, "the pleasure in killing and torturing others was great"; and such a pleasure was entirely acceptable for warlords with private armies. To change the medieval order of personal revenge into a modern nation-state, it was necessary to radically alter the *mentality*. First, "cruelty and joy in the destruction and torment of others" had to be "placed under an increasingly strong social control anchored in the state organization." This is impossible without a stable state in control of its population: only in such societies can individuals become "attuned, from infancy, to a highly regulated and differentiated pattern of self-restraint," to the point where this self-control – even compassion for others – acquires "a higher degree of automaticity," becomes, as it were, second nature. Thus the social structure begins to demand from its citizens an *emotional* structure, a personality, that is consistent with its newly defined requirements. Now it insists that emotional expression be "more subdued, moderate and calculated," and that "the reserve and mutual consideration of people increase." Put in another way, "the embarrassment threshold" is raised for all extravagant moods of rage, piety or delight, as people learn to mute the theatricality of their emotional display.

People were thus increasingly socialized to control and displace anger, and to seek alternative means of protest for their frustrations and disputes. As Ted Gurr emphasizes, this is quintessentially a *cultural* process, and with it came an abandonment of more than just personal retaliation – for a new sensibility made the entire violent lexicon equally distasteful, including execution, torture and physical punishment. The cultural "apparatus which shapes the individual" was harnessed to produce a structure of fears, "experienced as shame and delicacy," which increasingly invalidated all forms of interpersonal aggression. Through "the advance of the shame frontier," the upper reaches of society began to repress once-pleasurable violent emotions and smother them with anxiety. In a relatively fluid and integrated structure such as England's, where social aspirants were allowed to glimpse the path to improving their estate, they too had to adopt the new sensibilities – or face ridicule, disenfranchisement and punishment.[6]

By the eighteenth century, ritualized politeness and civility among the English upper and middle classes were firmly entrenched, as they substantially remain today. Maria Sifianou's international comparison emphasizes that in contemporary England still, "verbalizations of thanks and apologies are imperative even for minor relevant situations." Tact and politeness remain *the* middle-class cultural imperatives; and these qualities are defined in terms of

> consideration of other people's feelings by conforming to social norms and expectations [which] include the use of standard forms such as *please* and *sorry* in appropriate situations, requests rather than demands for people to do things for you, and the display of "good manners."[7]

Such controls minimize the number of social situations in which trivial provocation can occur, or lead to more serious confrontations.

SELF-CONTROL

Thus a wise central government seizes the monopoly of force and begins the construction of a controlled personality, steeped in revulsion for, and avoidance of, violence. What happens in the absence of this process? In his study of the "moral and sensual attractions in doing evil" in contemporary American working-class culture – still locked in many ways in pre-modern sensibilities – Jack Katz shows how homicide is commonly conceived as "righteous (i.e., moral) slaughter," how remorse and regret are largely removed from the equation. Permitting an armed street culture in which "dissing" another – showing disrespect in matters as trivial as maintaining eye contact for too long – is considered legitimate provocation for homicide is reminiscent of nothing so much as medieval Europe.

Perhaps half the American homicides are provoked by such "trivial altercation." Moreover, the culture allows the "impassioned killers" to see themselves as fundamentally moral, "defending both the morality of the social system and a personal claim of moral worth," as "upholding the respected social status of husband, mother, wife, father, property owner, virile male, deserving poor/self-improving welfare mother, and responsible debtor." It is precisely here – in creating a street atmosphere tolerant of confrontation – that American culture unknowingly encourages those at the bottom to cross the line to homicidal assault. It is precisely here that the dominant ethos desensitizes its population to murder. The mayor of Washington, D.C., was merely reflecting this mentality when he defended his city's reputation for violence with the infamous remark: "Outside of the killings, [Washington] has one of the lowest crime rates in the country."[8]

Why should trivial altercations provoke so many homicidal assaults? Michael Gottfredson and Travis Hirschi conclude that the undersocialized members of *any* civilization "will tend to be impulsive, insensitive, physical, risk-taking, short-sighted, and nonverbal," and therefore most likely to risk criminal acts. In such under-controlled people, outbursts of violence can be sparked by mere "momentary irritation," because "people with low self-control tend to have minimal tolerance for frustration and little ability to respond to conflict through verbal rather than physical means." Thus the noisome "irritation caused by a crying child is often the stimulus for physical abuse," and the disrespect from "a taunting stranger in a bar is often the stimulus for aggravated assault." Most commonly, those who lack self-control appear to be found at the bottom of the social hierarchy, those whom élite propaganda finds it the most difficult to reach – the least educated, with the least prestige to lose (and the most to gain) from violent display. The English achievement, then, has been to extend that self-control to large sections of the working classes.[9]

CULTURALLY GENERATED REMORSE

One of the key questions then becomes, how can we know that many more have learned a minimal self-control in England? How can we even be sure that such internalized mechanisms exist? What manner of proof, what form of confirmation, would be necessary to demonstrate our assertion that English civilization has socialized proportionately more of its members into a deep shame and remorse about homicide? One stratagem would be simply to *deduce* it from the low homicide rate; but that is insufficient, for there could well be other forces shaping the avoidance of aggression.

A second useful test would be the prevalence of killers' authentic expressions of remorse: the testimony by killers, dubious and self-serving as it may sometimes be, can be illuminating. American killers tend more consistently to speak of their acts in satisfied and *justifying* terms, as if they were the central success, not the fundamental failure, in their lives. Take, for example, the Texan who had just shot his wife and, leaning over her bloody corpse, shouted with a form of pride to the neighbours, "I told her I was going to do it. Call somebody to come and get her or I will shoot her again." This heroic and "manly" mystique is largely absent in English cases, our own and others. Tony Parker quotes one murderer – an extreme expression, it is true, but one that crystallizes the norm – still consumed with remorse twenty years after he had beaten and burned to death his infant son.

> There's been too much that happened for there ever to be forgiveness [for me]. An innocent child died at my hands, it's not something can ever be wiped away. If there ever was to be forgiveness for me, given by a god or by

Lorna [ex-wife] as I think she has done, or my daughters, it'll still never be given me by myself. If every single person in the world, in this one and the next, if they all said, "Phil, we forgive you," I'd still never say it to myself. The world is lacking a person because of me. That thought's always there in my mind at the back, and sometimes it comes sweeping forward to the front and blots out everything else. Sometimes I've thought that [hanging] could never have been as bad as sentencing me to go on living with all this remorse.[10]

The position of the remorseless professional killer is also clearly established in America in a way it is not in England. In the often-brutal urban culture, killing for gain is reduced to an unimportant matter. One "hit man" in the drug business reflected a widely shared belief when he told Mary Dietz that in Detroit, "A person don't think nothin' about killin' somebody here in this city." If the killing is considered significant, it is commonly presented as the *victim's fault*. American serial killer Eileen Wuornos reached for more than mere judicial exoneration when she insisted that her seven murders were misunderstood, her crimes were small, her motives innocent:

I'm not a man-hating lesbian who only killed to rob, robbed to kill. This is a downright fabrication, and very far from the truth. I am not a murderer. By definition, murder is wilful killing. I'm not a serial killer. I've killed a series of men but it was in self-defense. It wasn't premeditated design: my only premeditation was to go out and make another dollar. It wasn't in my mind to go out and kill a guy. I was a nice person, I've been treated like dirt.[11]

Mercifully, there seem to be few English equivalents of this cultural form, in which the murder is *entirely justified* in the mind of the killer. In one well-known U.S. case, Louella Feary describes her murder of her brutal husband: she shot him, then he staggered around the room in a complete circle, returned to Louella, and said, "You've done it now, Lou. You've really done it."

And with that he fell down straight out on the floor. Flat on his face. I took the gun and fired at him once more. Don't know what made me do it the second time. I guess I was just so mad at him for all the trouble he'd caused me. He deserved it.[12]

Again and again, cultural differences intervene to regulate the manner in which killers legitimize their depredations. This is not to say that English killers do not similarly minimize the evil of their crimes, as when one rapist insisted he "was kind" to his victim. Yet a much lower proportion of the English population is able to rationalize its behaviour in these terms; and English culture has been infinitely more successful in socializing its underclass to hold negative associations for aggressivity.

In American underclass culture, however, the civilization is unwittingly rich in exoneration. As an illustration of this process, FBI scholars Robert Ressler, Ann Burgess and John Douglas describe the justificatory mechanisms proffered by a serial rapist/murderer. The killer raped first when he was fourteen years old, and after many months of intensive psychiatric therapy he began to kill his victims. Ultimately, he was able both to glorify and excuse his crimes by painting himself, like so many American killers, as a victim of circumstance and a rebel against injustice. Each murder had its own unique rationalization: in one, the victim's attempt to escape enraged him – "I was thinking, why did she run? It made me mad. I was angry and frustrated." In another, he claimed to have murdered because his victim was a racist.

I put my hand over her mouth and stick the gun to her head and tell her if she screams I'm going to blow her head off. She asks what I want and I tell her I want money and to rape her. She balked on that and said, "No white man fucking me no time." I'm thinking she's one of these prejudices types. I said, "I'm gonna do what I want" and I backhanded her [and] I cocked the trigger. And this time I'm feeling good because I'm domineering over her and forcing her to do something and I'm thinking this prejudice bitch is going to do what I want when I want her to do it.

Yet another killing was justified because the victim's remarks merely irri-
tated him: "She asked all kinds of questions: why I wanted to do this?; why
did I pick her?; didn't I have a girlfriend?; what was my problem? I am
resenting this all the time, telling her to shut up. I just start stabbing her."[13]

Often they fully absorb the ideology masquerading as science that is
passed on to them by enthusiastic goalhouse bio-psychiatrists. Perhaps the
prime, if unintended, function of this pseudo-science is to provide further
exoneration for the killer. In this manner, one American serial killer cancels
any potential remorse with *both* biological and psychological "explanations" of his behaviour:

> I am labeled as a serial killer. If so – so be it! I have been told I have what is
> called a biochemical disorder. I have what is called *elevated kryptopyrroles*.
> This is a chemical that shows up in the urine when I am angry. I am differant
> than the average human. No one else in my so called family has any disorder
> whatsoever, so why me!? All these years I did not know what controled me.
> Now we all understand so think about the man or woman, may be even a
> child who gets so mad that they loose control. Can it be they have what I am
> lead to believe?! We all get a mad on but we all do not control it in the same
> way. Built up stress is another cause of this because it is hidden anger. Watch
> out dear people; any of you can become a serial killer such as I.

English killers are less likely to dispense such self-serving rubbish.
Moreover, fewer men attempt to legitimize their behaviour through spe-
cious claims of provocation, or to excuse their acts with this convenient
pseudo-biology – utterly dubious because it can provide neither any known
biological mechanism nor any explanation why such homicidal psychology
and/or biology should be so much more common in America.

This same killer complains of "partial disorientation, abnormal EEGS,
nervousness, depression, dizziness, chest pains, stomach pains, loss of
ambition, decreased sexual potency, irritability, rages, no stress control, no
anger control, mood swings, poor memory, prone to violence, anti-social
behaviour," but who does not have some of these "symptoms" some of the
time, and *why* does he have no anger control, and *why* is he prone to violence? English civilization has a lower toleration for violence and teaches

alternative means of dealing with frustration – by "learning to take it" or by displacing aggression onto inanimate objects (in one English killer's words, "to throw something at something else.") It should therefore be unsurprising that, given so few culturally provided excuses, fewer men allow themselves to respond to homicidal urges, and the few who do are often unable to resolve or forgive their actions.[14]

Such a sensibility is quite different from so much of American "street" culture, where the underclass has been socialized to violence. This historical veneration for aggressive display is traditionally explained in terms of the frontier mentality of the "wild West," but Butterfield notes that "bloodshed that erupted on the Western frontier may [in fact] have been Southern violence brought in via Texas." This Southern working-class violence grew out of the Scotch–Irish settlers' "warrior ethic that demanded vengeance." Such a mentality was a continuation of the medieval blood feud and a notion that "a man's worth resided in the opinion of others." Honour also meant a reputation for valour: "a man had to be prepared to fight to defend his honour if challenged or insulted." The Southern slaveholding gentry "had developed a similar code" and "for the Southern upper class, just as for the lower class, honour became a compelling passion . . . [and] violence could quickly erupt." That code of honour changed its name over time: what began as "reputation" in the South evolved in the next generation into a demand for "respect."

> Now on the streets of Harlem, the term was undergoing another metamorphosis – it was being referred to as disrespect. Whatever word was used, it was still a lethal credo.[15]

SUICIDE

Still, the ultimate "proof" for the existence of a lowered shame threshold cannot be simply loud protestations from the offender. It is when the killer, far from exulting in his triumph, or expressing grief (feigned or genuine), *proves* he is experiencing deep remorse by committing suicide. No single action can be a more convincing demonstration of genuine shame than suicide: in ending their own lives, the killers show they have fully internalized the culture's abhorrence of murder. Thus no quality of low-homicide nations is as revealing as the likelihood that their killers will take their own lives after a homicide. English killers are *much* more likely to take this drastic step: D. J. West's figures for England and Wales are that half of all killers attempted suicide (and 33 per cent were successful) after the killing. This is in dramatic contrast with American killers, of whom only 3 to 4 per cent committed suicide (the figure rises to 10 per cent for Canada, and as high as 42 per cent for Denmark). The English statistics are even more extreme in certain types of homicide: West found that 85 per cent of the women (and 58 per cent of the men) who killed their children committed suicide.

This is the closest we can hope to get to proof that, quite unlike their American counterparts, English killers have decisively crossed the shame frontier, much more fully internalized society's abhorrence of their act. Nowhere is this phenomenon more concisely illustrated than in the suicide note from a thirty-two-year-old South Yorkshire drifter, whose body was found hanging from a tree in Cambridgeshire. He had previously served six years in prison in the 1980s for raping a sixteen-year-old girl, and then attacked and murdered twenty-two-year-old Sandra Parkinson, a waitress at a holiday resort, as she went for a walk. The note was addressed to Parkinson's family: "I can't do anything to help you through your grief. All I can do is kill myself. I hope it helps, even if it's just a bit."[16] Such a troubled, violent and impulsive drifter on the edge of English society can no more make amends for his act than anyone who kills – since murder is perhaps the only crime for which there can be no proper restitution – but his note and his self-destruction suggest clearly that he felt belated shame for his monstrous act.

Thus English murderers are still commonly overwhelmed with repugnance for what they have done; and this is long before they have had the opportunity in jailhouse psychology sessions to memorize the parole-earning techniques of remorse-simulation. Research on this matter remains in a stunted infancy, but it seems impossible to contest Marvin Wolfgang's suggestion that the suicide of killers is a clear reflection of a deep internalization of social taboos. In any case, West's collection of British cases makes it clear that following a killing, the offender is often so overwhelmed with guilt and remorse that he can find no alternative to taking his own life; as with one young tough, already twice convicted for assault causing bodily harm, who attacked and robbed an elderly book-maker. After the victim died in hospital, the young man was convicted for manslaughter, and hanged himself in his prison cell as, years later, did Frederick West.[17]

WHY THE WORKING CLASS?

The most terrifying human being I have ever seen was not in the slums of Detroit, Belfast or Washington, but in a fast food restaurant in central London. A bodybuilder with enormously overdeveloped musculature, he was well over six feet tall and clad only in a black leather waistcoat and trousers, with high-topped boots: an intense look of rage and hatred habitually twisted his face. But there was only one chance in a hundred thousand that he would seriously harm anyone that year, and his appear-ance was a pose. It was reminiscent of nothing so much as the rural English gentry Maddern described for the fifteenth century, who surrounded themselves with a cloud of threatening gestures and appearances while perpetrating little violence at all. Now such a posture would be ridiculed in the middle and upper classes, and it has devolved to the margins of the working class: even there, the urban riots and soccer hooligans claim astonishingly few lives.

We will probably never resolve what is ultimately a political debate regarding whether the impoverished are so because they have limited abil-ities, or whether those who are impoverished are oppressed and discour-aged from developing their abilities. Perhaps both views share a measure of the truth. In any case, for our purposes it is enough to emphasize that violence in general and homicide in particular are overwhelmingly the pre-serve of the bottom of the working class. Undoubtedly this is, as Ted Gurr says, primarily "because the lower classes did not assimilate and still have not wholly assimilated the aggression-inhibiting values of the middle and upper classes." In D. P. Farrington and D. J. West's definitive long-term study of London males, "the worst offenders were drawn from the poorest

families in the worst housing." Possessing alternative means of status en-
hancement, the middle classes appear to have absorbed quite a different
message for dealing with confrontation, humiliation and frustration. A
middle-class English schoolgirl explained it best to me: "You're brought up to
take it – you don't want to make a scene – you don't want to step out of line."[18]

How does the working-class mentality differ from this? Eric Dunning,
Patrick Murphy and John Williams see "aggressive masculinity as a dominant characteristic" of the bottom of the working class; a class culture that
tolerates what is by English standards "a high level of open aggressiveness in
social relations." Such young men spend much of their early lives on the
streets, and "tend to interact aggressively" and "develop dominance hierar-
chies" that are based largely on the "ability to 'handle oneself.'" Parents in
this class "exert less pressure on their growing children to exercise strict and
continuous self-control over aggressive behaviour," often even encouraging
violence as a sign of manliness. Moreover, because these parents resort
more often to physical punishment in their own homes, their children are
exposed to violent and aggressive adult role models; they mature with fewer
inhibitions – and more positive associations – towards aggressivity.

The conferring of prestige upon men with a "proven ability to fight"
permits a congruent "tendency for such males to enjoy" violence; and
fighting becomes "an important source of meaning, status and pleasurable
emotional arousal." This positive emotional charge to aggressivity makes
them less likely to "back down" during disputes, even "actively to seek out
fights and confrontations." In fact, Dunning and his colleagues remark,
among the *defining characteristics* of this lowest class are the "great number
of contexts in which the open expression of violence is tolerated or even
positively sanctioned," and associated with pleasure, not guilt.

One reason aggressivity remains so valued in this class is that its
members "are typically denied status, meaning and gratification" in the
middle-class professional world – "the major sources of identity, meaning
and status available to men higher up the social scale." Unable to find these
gratifications in the larger society, such men are more likely to turn to
behaviour such as "fighting, physical intimidation, heavy drinking and
exploitative sexual relations" for the validation of their "masculine street
credentials." Still, that violence has its own rules, even in this class: it is

confined to specific settings such as "gang fights, football and weekend evenings with male peers 'downtown.'" More importantly, however, men whose aggression is utterly uncontrolled – who will fight without let or regard for the consequences – risk being "labelled as 'nutters' by their peers."[19]

Precisely, for even in street-tough violence, there are in England clear cultural "rules of disorder." In their study of football fans, Peter Marsh, Elisabeth Rosser and Ron Harre perceive the "symbolic" and ritualistic nature of much of the fighting, and note "the general consensus that *there are limits* beyond which one should not go." These cultural limits include a widespread agreement "concerning when an opponent has had enough." Typically, only a few blows "are required to settle even the most venomous face-to-face conflict," and those who transcend these boundaries, who go "beyond the point where honour is seen to be satisfied do so at the risk of censure." As important, the fighter who can no longer bear the assault can disengage simply by emitting "submissive or appeasement signals":

> In backing down, the loser has to do very little more than cease any actions which might be construed as hostile or threatening – he has to keep quiet or "button his lip." He should also look down at the floor – never at his opponent. Once he has done this he is unlikely to be attacked further.[20]

Such delicate constraints have no currency in the slums of Washington, Chicago or Los Angeles.

In America, homicide is also overwhelmingly committed by men of low socio-economic status, but at a much greater rate. Jack Katz notes that homicide is rare among the American middle and upper classes, and "that these rare events are qualitatively different from" the trivial provocation of the working classes, their "righteous slaughter" of provocateurs. Indeed, in the fullest U.S. study of the phenomenon, Edward Green and Russell Wakefield found that

> only 2.5 per cent of the upper-class homicides, as compared to between one-third and one-half (in other studies) of the lower-class homicides, were the result of a trivial altercation, [and 26.9 per cent of upper-class

spouse killings] were linked to pecuniary motives such as insurance benefits or property inheritance.

Indeed, one-fifth of these middle-class killers were so "fastidious" they had to hire someone else to do the killing. One of the key questions for future investigation then becomes why the American middle and upper classes have so signally failed to send inhibiting messages to the bottom of the social order.[21]

AN ENGLISH "MACHISMO" REMNANT

Nevertheless, feudal notions of manly vengeance still survive in remnant form in England in the confrontational norms which govern certain segments of the working class. In these terms, the murderous fight that is described below between two rivals in the grime of an industrial city is a curious anachronism that violates the dominant culture's assumptions of appropriate violence. In England, an average of 136 friends or acquaintances are murdered each year, most commonly as a result of a quarrel. In this particular illustration, two acquaintances fought to the death in a pub toilet, to determine who was "Cock of the Market," the toughest man in the market.

The setting was a racially mixed, high-unemployment northern town, once the seat of a large woollen industry. In a pub in the town's market, a savagely beaten, heavily tattooed white body lay on the floor of the "gentlemen's" toilet. An ambulance crew called to the scene tried to revive the victim, but the police surgeon concluded that "there was no sign of life" and certified that the man had died. The pathologist's initial comments on the victim observed "severe head injuries to the left side of the face," "a pool of blood around the head, twenty-four inches by nine inches" and "directional blood splashes on the toilet walls and toilet door, consistent with the deceased having been kicked or struck while he lay on the ground."

Peas in a Pod: Killer and Victim

The dead man was Geoffrey Carter, a forty-two-year-old demolition contractor, six foot one, twelve and a half stone, married with three children.

Carter himself was no innocent: he had a long history of violence and theft, and a three-page conviction sheet that opened in 1959 – including four counts of assault occasioning actual bodily harm; one conviction for common assault; five convictions for burglary; one for unlawful possession of a firearm; three convictions for larceny; one for excess alcohol; three for theft; three for drunk and disorderly; one for fighting in the street; and one for carrying an offensive weapon. His body was decorated with tattoos – "Who Cares" at the base of the left thumb, "Kimmy" on the left wrist and "Baby Face" on the outside of the right calf.

The killer, who might just as well have been the victim, was John Sackville, a nineteen-year-old steel erector, six foot one and eleven and a half stone: unmarried, he lived with his father and stepmother. Sackville had received a form of education at a comprehensive school; after leaving school at sixteen, he had trained in the martial art of kick-boxing. In the few months prior to the killing, he had begun to deploy his aggressive repertoire, being convicted for assault occasioning actual bodily harm (for which he was given a verbal caution) and for threatening behaviour (for which he was ordered to pay costs of £25).

Witnesses Reconstruct

That September Sunday, Carter and a friend were enjoying their customary pastime – heavy drinking. Carter began playing pool with his killer, John Sackville. The games, which continued for several hours, were ultimately won by Sackville, seven games to six, a form of threat in both their eyes. After winning, Sackville began to make derogatory remarks about Carter's age: young men like himself were superior in games playing, sex and fighting strength. At least one witness saw this as a direct challenge: Carter and his friends would no longer be the market's "Big Men." None would back down from the impending confrontation.

Christopher, a thirty-year-old pylon painter who witnessed the fight, recalled: "We were discussing various things. In the main it was just 'barroom' talk. Myself and Sackville began arguing over our ages. He was inferring that because he was young, he was better than myself, Walt and Geoff Carter, who were older men. Geoff and Walt weren't really bothered by what he was saying, but to me he had a bad attitude. He seemed very cocky in his attitude. I said to him, 'If you're that good, let's go into the toilet and sort it out.' He replied, 'Come on then. Let's have a go.' He wasn't backing down. He gave the impression that he was quite prepared to have a fight with me in the toilets. I wouldn't back down either. As far as I was concerned, he started the trouble and I was going to stop it. We both stood up. Geoff said, 'There's no need for this crack this afternoon. We're here for drink and not this hassle.' Geoff had stood up by this time and had a private word in the lad's ear. I couldn't hear what he was saying to him. In view of this, I sat down. As far as I was concerned, that was the end of the matter. Geoff spoke with him for a while. They were not arguing. There were no raised voices or fighting between them. After a short while both Geoff and this lad walked into the toilets. They both walked in quietly. There was no contact between them or any indication shown of any trouble or aggression between the two whilst on their way into the toilet."

Shortly after the two men entered the toilet, Christopher told police he "heard noises coming from the toilet, banging, like dull thuds. I also heard sounds like someone banging up against something metal. I thought it was someone banging up against the Durex machine. The sounds continued for a couple of minutes. My thoughts were that these noises were as a result of a tussle taking place in the toilet between Geoff and Sackville." A second witness continued, "Shortly after this, Sackville walked out of the toilet area. As he came out of the toilet, he was looking about. He appeared frightened. He looked as if he wanted to run, but was containing himself. Sackville had a reddening to the right cheekbone near the eye: it looked to me as though he'd been smacked – as opposed to being punched. He walked straight through the pool room and went out the door." The witness then entered the toilet and saw Geoff: "He was laid on his back in front of the urinals at an angle with his head towards the door. He was making gurgling noises and his face was covered in blood."

A woman who witnessed the events confirmed this account, and remembered seeing Carter on the floor. "Blood was coming from his nose and mouth. He was having difficulty with his breathing. I could hear gurgling sounds. I continued to support this man's head to try and ease his breathing, which deteriorated until it finally stopped."

Arrest and Interrogation

Immediately after leaving the pub, Sackville bumped into his brother, David, an unemployed plumber and himself a renowned street-fighter, who later told police that his brother "looked strange, I could tell he'd had quite a bit to drink. He said, 'I've had a fight with Geoff Carter. He's dragged me in toilet and cracked me twice. I've cracked him and laid him out.' Carter is a man I know well: at Christmas 1988, he assaulted me outside the Fighting Cock pub. I said, 'Go to our house, I'll be ten minutes.' I returned home at 7:15 to find John there, along with Yvonne and my two children. I went into kitchen and heard John shout, 'Lock door, Yvonne, he's going to come down with a baseball bat, I know he is.'

"At about 7:30 P.M. our Gail rang our house. She said, 'Dave, there's been some trouble at pub.' I put our John on to her. He said, 'It's me what's had a fight with Geoff Carter.' I could hear our Gail screaming, 'Oh John, he's dead!' Our John started crying, he broke down and said to her, 'It's not me, I've just had a fight with him.' I took him in kitchen with our Neil, who had arrived at my house by this time, we tried to calm him down. Our Neil went to phone and asked our Gail to find out exactly what had happened. Neil came back in and looked at John and said, 'It's right. He's dead.' He started crying and told me to ring the police."

Sackville was arrested at once. He made no attempt to deny his fight with Carter, and told police, "I were int' Sparrow on my own. I was sitting near that Geoff Carter and his mates – we were drinking. I know Carter's reputation, he's supposed to be 'Cock of the Market.' I were talking to his mate Jimmy, he's a biker. He told me Geoff Carter were best fighter round here. I just said, 'Well, there might be somebody who can do him, you never know,' and Jimmy said to me, 'Why, does tha' think tha' good enough?' I said, 'No, not me, somebody might.' Jimmy said he wanted to take me into toilet. I told him I didn't want to fight him. Then that Geoff Carter said, 'If anybody's going to take thee into toilet, it's me.' Then Carter dragged me by my arm into toilet and said, 'Come on, have a go at me then.' So he hit me and I went down. I got up and he hit me again. I went down again and got up and then I hit him. He went down and must have banged his head. He started to get up and I knew that if he had have got up, he'd have killed me, so I kicked him and I just fucked off." Sackville was charged with murder.

In a second and tape-recorded police interview the following afternoon, in the presence of his solicitor, Sackville fleshed out his previous account. "I only know Geoff Carter by sight and by reputation – that he's an animal really like. He's sort of person that if you get on wrong side of him, he'll break your arms and legs, 'Cock of the Market.' We just played pool. Apart from like everytime he wa' taking a shot, he's saying things like, 'I'm the best,' and making his mouth like, 'I'm the number one at pool' and things like that. He wa' beating me at pool. We ended up playing thirteen games, and I won overall, seven, seven-six. He never seemed narked. He kept saying that I hadn't won him. He said he'd let me win.

"So then they wa' just talking about how hard and big Geoff wa' and I said, 'Well he is. I agree he is hardest man in market, but one day somebody's gonna beat him. I don't know who,' I says. 'Well, I do know who, but I wouldn't like to say because I wouldn't like to put any trouble to 'em.' No, I weren't meaning myself. And then they were pestering me to tell 'em who. But I wouldn't let on who it were, because I thought if I'd have let on who it were, Geoff would have gone straight home, got his bat out and gone up and broke their arms and legs, which he has been known to do before. And then we just ended up arguing, me and Jimmy. And Jimmy says, 'Well, does tha' fancy thee chances against him?' I says, 'No, I don't.' We got arguing and he says, 'If tha' wants to sort it out, come on sort it out in toilet.'

"Well, I assumed he wanted to go in toilet so we could have a good argument like, out o' way o' everybody. So I got up and he started walking towards toilet and oh, at this time Walt had whispered som'at to Geoff Carter, and Geoff had got up and while Julie and what have you had been playing pool, he started tipping pool table up. Three or four times, like, and making all balls go into pockets, and spoiling the game. And then they reracked and he did it again. And then Julie came up and said, 'Look, Geoff, calm down, gi'e o'er, you've had too much to drink,' or som'at like that, and he pushed her away and slapped her.

"And then I got up wi' Jimmy to walk to the toilet and Geoff stopped us and he says, 'What you doing?' like, and I says, 'Well, Jimmy's taking me into toilet to sort this out.' He says, 'Jimmy, what tha' taking him in toilet for?' and Jimmy said, 'I'm going to rip his head off and shove it up his arse.' And he turned to me and said, 'Well, he's gonna rip thee head off.' I says, 'Well, I've only come to argue, I'm not really bothered.' I thought he wa' going to argue wi' me."

Only here did the detective interrupt Sackville's caricature of macho posturing: "But you say he was going to rip your head off, to stick it up your arse?" Sackville replied, "I weren't bothered about letting him do that to me. Which he probably would have done. So he told Jimmy to sit down and Geoff turned to me and says, 'If anybody's going to take thee into toilet, I'm taking thee into toilet.' And I says, 'Well, Geoff, I'm not really bothered' like, and before I'd chance to say owt else, he'd grabbed me by arm. We wa' a matter of a foot away from toilet door. In a matter o' a couple o' seconds I wa' in, I found myself in toilet wi' Geoff, and he was stood blocking my entry out o' toilet. And then he said to me, 'Come on, hit me.' And I said, 'No, Geoff,' I says, 'I wouldn't dare, if I hit you, you'll probably bray me all over.' He says, 'No, I waint bray you all over, I'll fucking kill you.' And I says, 'Well, you'll probably kill me.' I says, 'I'm not really bothered.' He says, 'Oh tha' not bothered are tha'?' I says, 'No,' so he hit me. I wa' that shocked at him hitting me. I thought he was just gonna gi'e me a bollocking and he punched me in face. So I fell back and he then said to me, 'Does that bother thee?' And I says, 'No, it doesn't bother me,' so then he hit me on chin. I mean I weren't bothered what he did, 'cos I would have tried to get him into trouble for hitting me. I would have tried getting him into trouble wi' police. I would have reported . . .

"So then he hit me again on chin. This time he knocked me to floor and I got up this time and he said to me, 'Does it bother you now?' I thought if I say 'Yeah' again, or if I say 'No' again, he's just gonna hit me. I says he's gonna kill me here if I'm not careful, so I just swung one punch at him, and I connected it full on his face, [on his] nose and mouth. He then went down, backwards, banging his head on the wall as he went down. I then noticed that he weren't trying to get back up. He just went down and his arms wa' down, and then he rolled to the side as though he wa' going to get back up.

By this time I wa' frightened to death o' him. I thought he wa' going to get up. I thought he wa' going to kill me. So I thought my only chance here is to – kick him and run. And so as he rolled over I just run and I kicked him in his face, full on like, and I jumped over him and then run out o' door. But I didn't make it look as though there wa' any trouble. I just casually walked across the room, unbolted door and closed it behind. Oh, Jimmy shouted me at that time and he says, 'Eh up, cunt, I want thee,' and I just telled him to fuck off and run. I just run, 'cos only thing that wa' in my mind then, I couldn't stop crying all way down home. 'Cos I thought that's it now, he's going to wait for me, wherever he can get me and he's going to break my arms and legs.

"I even told him that I wa' scared to death o' him. So I assumed with him being size that he is and so hard as he is I expected him to just gi'e it, 'Look, get thee sent off home. Don't let me see thee round here again.' Som'at like that, but he didn't. What he came in there wa' intent to gi'e me a good hiding. I've had a lot o' people coming up and giving me hassle. Like 'Oh young Sacky here. If you beat him, you're one o' top lads.' I've always managed to look after myself. Carter normally fights wi' a bat, and if you ever do owt wrong to him or his family. . . . He never gets you on the day normally, if you do have a fight wi' him on day and he loses or any o' his family loses, he goes down and he puts his cappers on and he gets his bat, and then he goes to house and waits for you and then when he see you he breaks your arms and legs. And I do recall that he has done it to two people in Chapeltown for they did bray his son."[22]

The court accepted Sackville's claims: he was found guilty of manslaughter, and sentenced to serve three and a half years in a youth detention centre. Fortunately, such confrontational norms – and a willingness to pursue them to any end – are as yet confined to a very small proportion of the English working class: how long that will remain the case is a matter for speculation.

THE PRESENT

Crime is the modern obsession, and we are bombarded with dubious but alarming criminal statistics by political, ideological and professional groups. Their self-serving aim is to make us see rising crime as the central problem, and "law and order" as the singular solution. Nevertheless, the English homicide rate remains among the very lowest in the industrial world. What Terence Morris and Louis Blom-Cooper said a generation ago is still true today: murder is still regarded as the gravest offence, and it remains "a comparative rarity," by world standards, not "a serious social problem."[23]

These statements must, however, be qualified: while the 1940s and 1950s marked what Ted Gurr called "the low ebb of crimes against persons in virtually every English-speaking country," afterwards the "trends were consistently upwards" almost everywhere in the western world. As elsewhere the English homicide rate increased dramatically during the 1960s and 1970s. In Stockholm, for example, after 1950, murder and attempted murder increased by 600 per cent. Alone among European nations, Switzerland's crimes against persons remained steady; while Japan has experienced "a steady *decline* in serious offences against persons and property since the mid-1950s." Gurr emphasizes that the recent increase "appears to be a minor perturbation, proportionately no greater than upward swings in homicide rates in Elizabethan times and during the Napoleonic wars – swings which proved to be temporary." Historically, each major "upsurge of violent crime" has been a consequence of "fundamental social dislocation," which has separated whole strata "from the civilizing institutions which instil and reinforce the basic Western injunctions against interpersonal violence." These forces for chaos "may be migrants, demobilized veterans, a growing population of disillusioned young people for whom there is no social or economic niche, or badly educated young black men locked in the decaying ghettoes of an affluent society." But Gurr hastens to emphasize that the "most devastating episodes of public disorder" appear to coincide with the breakdown of the civilizing process, short-term "changes in values which legitimate violence," often transmitted through mass culture. In this sense, the instability of the working-class family and income and the destruction of the institutionalized compassion of the post-war welfare state may have long-term repercussions.[24]

But how can society reverse these tendencies? The *mechanisms* for the inculcation of desired qualities remain unchanged – the family, the

TABLE 7 Offences currently recorded by the police as homicide, per 100,000 population, 1967–1989, England and Wales.

Year	Number	Rate	Year	Number	Rate
1967	354	.73	1979	546	1.1
1968	360	.74	1980	549	1.1
1969	332	.68	1981	499	1.0
1970	339	.70	1982	557	1.1
1971	407	.83	1983	482	.97
1972	409	.83	1984	537	1.1
1973	391	.80	1985	537	1.1
1974	526	1.1	1986	568	1.1
1975	443	.90	1987	602	1.1
1976	488	.99	1988	560	1.2
1977	418	.95	1989	576	1.1
1978	471	.96			

Source: Home Office.

institutions for day care, the schools, organs of mass culture and the church. But a cynical culture has rendered repugnant to the modern ear the essential aims of "character-building" (espoused most notably by the Friendly Societies which insisted upon behaviour they "unashamedly named 'wisdom,' 'prudence,' 'merit,' 'dignity,' 'self-respect')."

Now both extended and nuclear families fall into disarray, and many adults have neither the energy nor ability to teach their children. Moreover, a malevolent and inchoate press chronicles the misdeeds of the fundamental stabilizing cultural institutions – gleefully retailing perceptions of alleged corruption in school, family, royalty, police, government and church. No modern text or institution any longer unselfconsciously proclaims what the elementary textbook for schools in England and Wales could take for granted in 1904, that teachers should "endeavour, by example and influence, aided by a sense of discipline, which should pervade the School, to implant in the children habits of industry, self-control, and courageous perseverance in the face of difficulties," to teach children "to reverence what is noble, to be ready for self-sacrifice, and to strive their utmost after purity and truth," as well as to "foster a strong respect for duty, and that consideration and respect for others" which is "the true basis for all good manners." Such notions must be re-evaluated and broadcast once more if modern societies are to restore the non-violent community.

Why should Switzerland, virtually alone among modernized western nations, have remained aloof from this change? Crime is not a major problem in Switzerland and homicide rates are very low – despite the fact that the Swiss citizen army requires its members to store military weapons and ammunition in their homes, in case of emergency. Moreover, firearms are rarely used in crimes of violence (only three out of the total of ten homicides in a two-year period in Zurich involved firearms). Like England, Switzerland broke away from the feudal state early in its history: indeed, it arguably has the oldest continuous democratic form of government in the world, establishing its own confederation in 1291. The impact of seven centuries of consensual rule, Marshall Clinard comments, left the Swiss with "a broad interest in politics and in political decisions at all levels." As a consequence, Swiss political culture encourages its citizens not only to "feel they are their own masters," but also to develop that special combination of powerful inhibitions at the prospect of violence, accompanied by an hostility to authority and a craving for social order, that seems a part of most low-homicide democracies.[25]

THE FUTURE

A society that does not transmit a stable central core of values from generation to generation places its entire structure in jeopardy. If the civilizing process is to continue, then it must be repeated within each generation. But how can this be sustained when the major institutions charged with disseminating values appear to be in retreat? The organs of mass culture are flooded by amoral international representations; the extended family with its mild alternative authority, the grandparents, is dispersed; and the much-maligned traditional nuclear family appears "damaged beyond repair." Cambridge University's long-term delinquent study concluded that "a constellation of adverse family background features (including poverty, large family size, marital disharmony, harsh and erratic child-rearing techniques and parental criminality)" were fundamentally linked to all forms of violence. Regrettably, there is no sign of attempts to ameliorate these social factors – quite the opposite.[26]

Michael Gottfredson and Travis Hirschi have underlined the problems in the inculcation of self-control by troubled families: those with criminal histories themselves tend to be inadequate parents, punishment "tends to be easy, short-term and insensitive – that is, yelling and screaming, slapping and hitting"; moreover, such parents often fail even to *recognize* deviant behaviour, let alone deal with it. Indeed, there is a widespread concern that even in non-criminal families, the single parent – usually the mother – must disperse her energies in attempting to earn a living, an activity usually "at least to some extent shared in the two-parent family." Thus, they argue, the single parent is "less able to devote time to monitoring and punishment," and statistically "more likely to be involved in negative, abusive contacts" with the children. In 1991, 31.2 per cent of all births in England and Wales were to unmarried women and the proportion of people raising their children on their own is even higher: in such a milieu, the value of professional daycare facilities is beyond calculation. If Gottfredson and Hirschi are right, then the values underpinning stable and compassionate relationships must be reinforced by society, not denigrated.[27]

For its part, the educational system would be well advised to spend less energy on the hypotenuse and more on humanity, since it has unrivalled access to the child's attention, and unparalleled opportunities to inculcate the basic notions of compassion for other persons and repugnance for violent display. However, the schools appear largely to have relinquished that portion of their responsibility. Nonetheless, any process of renewal must begin in modern nursery education, the Cambridge studies testify. Farrington and West urge the establishment of "free high-quality pre-school intellectual enrichment programs to children at risk," and the training of parents in the use of "appropriate child-rearing techniques." Such simple but vital suggestions include teaching parents "to notice what children are doing, to state house rules clearly, to make rewards and punishments contingent upon behaviour, and to negotiate disagreements so that conflicts do not escalate."[28]

Gurr is probably right to suggest that the post-1970 increase in homicide is a "minor" and probably "temporary" perturbation. Nevertheless, several hundred lives might be saved each year if the homicide rate were returned to its extremely low pre-war levels. This cannot be done by "law and order" campaigns from the conservative right, which everywhere in the world are meaningless stratagems by which politicians seize and maintain power – for there is little relationship between the severity of the law and the control of aggression. Neither can it be done by campaigns for universal affluence from the radical left, for there is no solid evidence anywhere directly connecting economic deprivation with violence, or affluence with peace. How could it be otherwise, when such civilizing inhibitions are *cultural* processes, not judicial or economic; they are about compassion and control, not punishment or material goods? Any serious attempt to deal with this matter will move instead to reinforce the civilizing process, using the major cultural forces of our time – the mass media, highly qualified daycare personnel, the schools, and a reinforced or redesigned family – to reimplant in youth a genuine compassion for others and a repugnance for violence.[29]

THE COST

There is a price to be paid for every human achievement. The costs to which we allude in instilling inhibition include a potential loss of intimacy, a compromising of personal feelings of authenticity and perceptions of smothering under the weight of the social contract.

The middle and upper classes began this process of internalizing inhibitions, and its impact upon them naturally remains the most intense. The bizarre behaviour that occasionally emerges from these classes is not just a corollary of the arrogance that comes with too heady a share of power, prestige and wealth – or the astonishing ignorance of life that comes with being so isolated from the ordinary human experience. It is also a consequence of socialization that insists that *all* emotions be excised from the personal repertoire; demands that the human passions of anger, love or frustration must remain not only unexpressed, but also unfelt. Alice Miller has written about this as a form of soul murder: a child may lose all sense of emotional authenticity by being so denied.

During an extended interview, one mature daughter of the gentry spoke bitterly of the constraints placed upon her natural responses. Among her class, not only was the expression of anger "bad form," but so was the expression of *any* emotion. Ultimately, that denial of expression came to be experienced as a taboo on her humanity. Such smothering expectations left many of her class and generation unsure of who they were as human beings, unaware of their true feelings, wrapped in a feeling of emotional death. Nothing expresses this middle-class conundrum better than John Cleese's soliloquy in a recent film:

> Do you have any idea what it's like being English? Being so correct all the time, being so stifled by this dread of doing the wrong thing . . . we're all terrified of embarrassment – that's why we're so dead.[30]

Another social cost of this may be an apparent loss of intimacy, at least in public: on the streets of Paris, socio-linguists observed an average of 100 "touches per hour." In London, there were none at all. A truly civilized "civilizing process" will go beyond mere repression and inhibition to develop a social philosophy based upon compassion for others while revelling in the exploration of the positive self.[31]

1   Douglas Hay, 1977, "Property, Authority and the Criminal Law," in Hay *et al.*, *Albion's Fatal Tree: Crime and Society in Eighteenth-Century England*, Harmondsworth: Penguin, pp. 18, 32, 37.

2   Ian Gilmour, 1991, p. 148; Linda Colley, 1992, op. cit., p. 16; Ferdinand Mount, 1993, *Times Literary Supplement*, 4711, p. 14.

3   Lord Hailsham (ed), 1990, *Halsbury's Laws of England*, 4th edition, London: Butterworth, pp. 349–351.

4   Quoted in H. D. Graham and T. R. Gurr (eds), 1969, *The History of Violence in America: Historical and Comparative Perspectives*, New York: Praeger; Christopher Lasch, 1979, *The Culture of Narcissism: American Life in an Age of Diminishing Expectations*, New York: Warner, p. 21.

5   As of the early 1970s: the provision allowing the husband to kill his spouse and her lover when caught *in flagrante delicto* has recently been dropped. Henry P. Lundsgaarde, 1977, *Murder in Space City: A Cultural Analysis of Houston Homicide Patterns*, New York: Oxford U.P., p. 161. In the 1980s, many states attempted to implement similar "make my day" legislation.

6   Norbert Elias, 1982, *State Formation and Civilization*, Oxford: Blackwell, p. 235; Quoted in Norbert Elias, 1978 (1st German edition, 1938), *The Civilizing Process: The Development of Manners*, New York: Urizen Books, pp. 193, xvi, 69–70, 115–116, 120,

127, 142, 192, 194, 200–202. Gurr, op. cit., p. 342. Both books are now published by Blackwell in a single volume. For the beginning of a discussion of how individuals use cultural materials to "write" their own personal narratives, cf., for e.g., George S. Howard, 1989, *A Tale of Two Stories*, Notre Dame: Academic Publications.

7   Maria Sifianou, 1992, *Politeness Phenomena in England and Greece: A Cross-Cultural Perspective*, Oxford: Clarendon Press, pp. 42, 94, 88, 75.

8   Jack Katz, 1988, *Seductions of Crime: Moral and Sensual Attractions in Doing Evil*, New York: Basic Books, pp. 44, 19, 22, 31, 39; Mayor Marion Barry, quoted in Ross Petras and Kathryn Petras, 1993, *The 776 Stupidest Things Ever Said*, New York: Doubleday, p. 35.

9   Michael R. Gottfredson and Travis Hirschi, 1990, *A General Theory of Crime*, Stanford: Stanford U.P., p. 90.

10   Lundsgaarde, 1977, op. cit., p. 57; Tony Parker, 1990, *Life After Life: Interviews With Twelve Murderers*, London: Pan, p. 163, slightly edited. Barry Mitchell's cases, and my own, consistently display this remorse, if in muted form. Parker's most recent work, *The Violence of Our Lives: Interviews With Life-Sentence Problems in America* (1995, London: HarperCollins), describes American killers who seem genuinely remorseful: firm conclusions must await much more extensive research.

11   Mary Lorenz Dietz, 1983, *Killing For Profit: The Social Organization of Felony Homicide*, Chicago: Nelson-Hall, p. 93; Michael Reynolds, 1992, *Dead Ends*, New York: Warner, pp. 2–3, edited.

12   From "Family Members as Murder Victims" by Stuart Palmer, in Suzanne K. Steinmetz and Murray A. Straus (eds), 1974, *Violence in the Family*, New York: Dodd Mead & Co., pp. 94–97, edited.

13   Robert K. Ressler, Ann Wolbert Burgess and John E. Douglas, "Rape and Rape-Murder: One Offender and Twelve Victims," in Burgess (ed), 1985, *Rape and Sexual Assault: A Research Handbook*, New York: Garland, pp. 217–218.

14   The American killer's rationalizations are from the personal files of Christopher Berry-Dee, 1994, with permission. For contrasting British murderers' recollections see, for example, Barry Mitchell, 1990, *Murder and Penal Policy*.

15   Fox Butterfield, 1995, *All God's Children: The Bosket Family and the American Tradition of Violence*, New York: Alfred A. Knopf, pp. 9-11, 207.

16   Quoted in *Guardian Weekly*, Aug. 28, 1994.

17   West's figures are now unfortunately outdated, but they have not been replaced by better international surveys. My own Home Office statistics for the 1980s show a much reduced figure; but this is misleading partly because these statistics only represent suicides that take place before the police intervene, partly by what are now more intensive suicide watches in prison. See Nancy H. Allen, 1983, "Homicide Followed By Suicide: Los Angeles, 1970–1979," in *Suicide and Life-Threatening Behavior*, vol. 13, no. 3, pp. 155–165; D. J. West, 1965, *Murder Followed By Suicide*, London: Heinemann, p. 16; Marvin Wolfgang, 1957, "An Analysis of Homicide-Suicide," *Journal of Clinical and Experimental Psychopathology*, vol. 18–19, pp. 208–217; Valerie Hearn, 1993, "Homicide/Suicide: A Test of Status Integration Theory," unpublished MA thesis, University of Alberta; Edward Green and Russell

P. Wakefield, 1979, "Patterns of Middle and Upper Class Homicide," *Journal of Criminal Law and Criminology* 70: 177–78.

18   Gurr, op. cit., p. 343; D. P. Farrington and D. J. West, 1990, "The Cambridge Study in Delinquent Development: A Long-Term Follow-Up of 411 London Males," in J.-J. Kerner and G. Kaiser (eds), *Kriminalitat: Personlichkeit, Lebensgeschichte und Verhalten*, Berlin: Springer-Verlag, p. 132.

19   Eric Dunning, Patrick Murphy and John Williams, 1988, *The Roots of Football Hooliganism: An Historical and Sociological Study*. London: Routledge & Kegan Paul, pp. 208–212.

20   Peter Marsh, Elisabeth Rosser and Ron Harre, 1978, *The Rules of Disorder*, London: Routledge and Kegan Paul, pp. 107–108, 116. In their study of the 1974 and 1975 football seasons at Oxford United, the authors note that only 0.1 per cent of the fans were injured each game; that more than half of these injuries were simple accidents such as falling; and that even in "those involving deliberate violence it was impossible to find any cases of 'innocent bystanders' being hurt and most of the injuries consisted of small cuts and bruises."

21   Katz, 1988, op. cit., p. 44; Edward Green and Russell P. Wakefield, 1979, "Patterns of Middle and Upper Class Homicide," *Journal of Criminal Law and Criminology* 70: 177–178.

22   "Cappers" – steel-toed boots.

23   Terence Morris and Louis Blom-Cooper, 1967, "Homicide in England," in M. E. Wolfgang, *Studies in Homicide*, New York: Harper & Row, pp. 29–35.

24   Gurr, 1981, op. cit., pp. 338–340, 343, 346.

25   Quoted in Norman Dennis and George Erdos, 1992, *Families without Fatherhood*, London: IEA Health and Welfare Unit, p. 97. Marshall B. Clinard, 1978, *Cities with Little Crime: The Case of Switzerland*, Cambridge: Cambridge U.P., pp. 1, 37, 110–111, 114.

26   Linda Colley, 1992, op. cit., p. 16; Gurr, 1981, op. cit., p. 343; Philip Jenkins, 1992, *Intimate Enemies: Moral Panics in Contemporary Great Britain*, New York: Aldine de Gruyter, p. 231. See Tom Pitt-Aikens and Alice Thomas Ellis, 1989, *Loss of the Good Authority: The Cause of Delinquency*, London: Viking.

27   HMSO, "Population Trends," no. 68; David Farrington, 1991, "Antisocial Personality from Childhood to Adulthood," *The Psychologist: Bulletin of the British Psychological Society* 4: 389–394; Michael R. Gottfredson and Travis Hirschi, 1990, op. cit., pp. 97, 100–101, 104, 106.

28   D. P. Farrington and D. J. West, 1990, op. cit., p. 132.

29   Gurr, 1981, op. cit., p. 340.

30   Monologue in the 1988 film, *A Fish Called Wanda*.

31   See Alice Miller, 1981, *The Drama of the Gifted Child: The Search for the True Self*, New York: Basic Books; Sifianou, 1992, op. cit., p. 75.

Appendix

TABLE 8 Principal suspects by age and gender, England.

Age	1982 Male	Fem	1984 Male	Fem	1986 Male	Fem	1988 Male	Fem	1990 Male	Fem	Total
0–5	0	0	0	0	0	1	0	0	0	0	1
6–12	1	0	0	0	0	0	0	0	2	0	3
13–20	92	14	78	10	85	6	83	10	80	5	463
21–34	195	28	192	31	224	17	203	37	228	27	1182
35–64	124	10	134	21	141	19	116	23	144	20	752
65+	11	1	14	0	14	1	8	2	9	2	62
Total	423	53	418	62	464	44	410	72	463	54	2463*
	89%	11%	87%	13%	91%	9%	85%	15%	89%	11%	

Source: Home Office.
*Total is slightly different due to minor variations in official recording techniques.

TABLE 9 Victims by age and gender, England.

Age	1982 Male	Fem	1984 Male	Fem	1986 Male	Fem	1988 Male	Fem	1990 Male	Fem	Total
0–5	27	29	26	24	18	20	40	33	36	25	278
6–12	9	10	12	9	6	4	9	5	8	5	77
13–20	44	35	34	17	46	29	31	17	34	17	304
21–34	82	59	84	65	98	76	99	50	114	61	788
35–64	98	74	113	75	112	72	117	68	143	67	939
65+	26	28	17	42	20	45	19	28	28	41	294
Total	286	235	286	232	300	246	315	201	363	216	2680
	55%	45%	55%	45%	55%	45%	61%	39%	63%	37%	

Source: Home Office.

TABLE 10 Victims: circumstances of killing, where known, England.

	Quarrel	Theft	Other Circs.	Mental	Suicide	Gang War	Terrorist	Misc. Other	Total
1982	258	39	50	40	43	3	11	77	521
1984	278	51	40	38	39	2	8	62	518
1986	277	37	50	39	44	5	2	92	546
1988	258	44	50	19	40	6	1	98	516
1990	312	37	49	33	29	8	3	108	579
Total	1383	208	139	169	195	24	25	437	2680
	(52%)	(8%)	(5%)	(6%)	(7%)	(1%)	(1%)	(16%)	(96%)

Source: Home Office. "Quarrel" includes disputes, jealousy and revenge. "Gang war" refers to various forms of hooliganism, including fights between bands of men after a night of drinking.

TABLE 11 Victims: methods of killing, England.

	Sharp or Blunt Instrument	Hitting, Kicking, Strangling	Shooting	Other	Total
1982	234	159	42	86	521
1984	255	146	56	62	518
1986	276	160	47	63	546
1988	229	161	37	88	516
1990	251	179	55	94	579
Total	1245	804	237	393	2680
	(46%)	(30%)	(9%)	(15%)	(100%)

Source: Home Office.

Elliot Leyton was born in Saskatchewan and educated at the universities of British Columbia and Toronto. A professor of anthropology at the Memorial University of Newfoundland, he is a past president of the Canadian Sociology and Anthropology Association, and has held teaching appointments and delivered lectures in Europe, the United States and Canada. Because of his recognized expertise in the psychology of the multiple killer he has established close links with police forces around the world including the RCMP, the FBI, New Scotland Yard and Dutch Interpol. His previous books include *Dying Hard*, *The Myth of Delinquency*, *Hunting Humans* and *Sole Survivor*.